The Changing Welfare State in Europe

The Changing Welfare State in Europe

The Implications for Democracy

Edited by

David G. Mayes

Professor of Banking and Financial Institutions, Director, Europe Institute and Director, NZ Governance Centre, University of Auckland, New Zealand

Anna Michalski

Associate Professor, Uppsala University, Sweden and Research Fellow, Europe Institute, University of Auckland, New Zealand

Edward Elgar

Cheltenham, UK • Northampton, MA, USA

Published by
Edward Elgar Publishing Limited
The Lypiatts
15 Lansdown Road
Cheltenham
Glos GL50 2JA
UK

Edward Elgar Publishing, Inc.
William Pratt House
9 Dewey Court
Northampton
Massachusetts 01060
USA

A catalogue record for this book
is available from the British Library

Library of Congress Control Number: 2013946814

This book is available electronically in the ElgarOnline.com Social and Political Science Subject Collection, E-ISBN 978 1 78254 657 3

ISBN 978 1 78254 656 6

Typeset by Columns Design XML Ltd, Reading
Printed and bound in Great Britain by T.J. International Ltd, Padstow

Contents

Figures

Tables

Contributors

Tess Altman is a Sessional Academic at the University of Canberra, Research Officer at Volunteering ACT, and will shortly commence as a Policy Officer with the Australian Multicultural Council Secretariat.

Christine Cheyne is Associate Professor of Resource and Environmental Planning, Massey University.

Katherine Lyons is a Research Assistant in the School of People, Environment and Planning, and Tutor in Academic Writing at Massey University.

David G. Mayes is Professor of Banking and Financial Institutions, Director of the Europe Institute, and Director of the NZ Governance Centre at the University of Auckland.

Anna Michalski is Associate Professor at the Department of Government at Uppsala University, Sweden, and Research Fellow at the Europe Institute at the University of Auckland.

Zaidah Mustaffa is Lecturer in Management and International Business at the University of Auckland.

Cris Shore is Professor of Social Anthropology at the University of Auckland.

Mark Thomson is Honorary Research Fellow at the Europe Institute at the University of Auckland.

Preface

The Changing Welfare State in Europe: The Implications for Democracy is a collaborative effort centred on the University of Auckland Europe Institute. It was made possible through the inclusion of the institute in the RECON (Reconstituting Democracy) project funded by the European Union's sixth framework programme.

The work on this book took place over a period of years when national economies and welfare systems were put under severe strain caused by the impact of the financial and economic crisis. Before the crisis welfare systems were set to undergo profound change due to a number of identifiable challenges that were, however, not always fully understood. The process of change advanced in a slow and path-dependent manner influenced by national specificities deciding the extent and sequence of reform. On the whole, despite distinct national trajectories, these trans-formations appeared to proceed according to the same template. Intensified European policy coordination from the late 1990s onwards goes a long way towards explaining this development. The economic and financial crisis made it clear however that even though the prescriptions for welfare reform were similar the underlying economic conditions of individual European states and their ability to compete internationally differed greatly. At the time of writing it is too early to predict the impact of the crisis on individual European states with any certainty but one aspect of the crisis is that it struck with very different outcomes in different EU member states. On a more general level, it is also certain that the devastating effects of the crisis in the countries most beset by sovereign or private debt will result in greater economic and social heterogeneity in the EU with strong implications for its ability to devise, fund and implement common policies.

In a context of a deepening economic interdependence among the member states of the EU coupled with an increasing heterogeneous post-crisis fall-out, it seems all the more important that we gain a more comprehensive understanding of the different dimensions of the changes in the welfare state. The immediate management of the crisis has led to a reappraisal of economic and social governance in the EU that is bound to have implications on democratic governance at both national and European level. This book contributes to the body of research-based knowledge that is necessary to conduct informed debate the implications for democracy in Europe of the system of multi-level governance that has already emerged in the area of social and economic policy.

David G. Mayes and Anna Michalski
Auckland and Uppsala

Acknowledgements

The editors are above all indebted to the book's contributors who worked hard to finalize their chapters on time.

We acknowledge our debt to the EU taxpayer through the funding of the RECON project. The willingness to fund the independent analysis of problems is an essential feature for policy development for the general benefit in a democracy. The European Commission may not agree with our conclusions but we trust that the work is useful.

We take this opportunity to thank our partners in RECON for their comments on the work as it went through, particularly Erik Oddvar Eriksen, John Erik Fossum, Agustin Menendez, Geir Kvaerk, Marit Eldholm and Wautraud Schelkle. Within the Europe Institute in Auckland, Mark Thomson provided invaluable assistance. Sincere thanks are also due to Janet Mayes, who prepared this book for publication.

We wish Zaidah Mustaffa, who continued to contribute despite illness, a speedy recovery.

1. Introduction: the changing welfare state

Anna Michalski and David G. Mayes

The traditional welfare system involves the reallocation of resources from those in society who are doing relatively well to those who are in difficulty, usually so that the standard and quality of their life can be brought up to some level which society feels is the minimum acceptable. Determining such transfers and the taxation required to achieve them lies at the heart of the democratic system. However, as time passed the concept of the welfare system became more sophisticated, more pervasive and much more linked to the development of society as a whole rather than just to alleviating the worst individual circumstances. There is thus a close interaction between social policy and the process of achieving faster economic growth. The idea that welfare and growth were somehow antithetical has now largely disappeared with the shift from an emphasis on the state's role of correcting market failures to a human development perspective which instead recognizes social policy as an investment factor. In that perspective, improved health, education, housing and employment all contribute to factors that underlie sustainable economic growth. However the process of taxing one group in society for the greater good and the benefit of others still remains deeply politically contentious, particularly in view of the argument over incentives. A badly structured system demotivates the richer in society from increasing their efforts as they are seen to be 'losing' too much of the product of that effort to others, while those receiving may feel that there is no great benefit from work and effort as the financial gain is negligible and the loss of time substantial.

These contending aspects of welfare state systems are inherent to the distribution of wealth in society and throughout history the weight accorded to different elements pertaining to management of society's resources has varied between countries. In Europe, different perceptions of an appropriate balance between the market and society are at the origin of the emergence of distinct welfare systems shaped by the interplay between economic, social and political factors, and underlying values, norms and traditions. Modern social models therefore reflect decades of political struggle over scarce resources, sometimes referred to as the 'power-resources mobilization paradigm' (Arts and Gelissen, 2002, p. 154) and are firmly anchored in national norms concerning social justice, equality, and the role of the state. As the 'national state cannot easily escape its historical inheritance' (Arts and Gelissen, 2002, p. 154) institutional inertia and path dependence are mechanisms that explain why welfare states tend to change only slowly and incrementally. Historically grounded societal norms explain the persistence of quite distinct popular attitudes towards taxes, the role of the state in dealing with societal risks and the development of civic and social rights.

The aim of this book is to explore a number of recent themes in the evolution of welfare policy in Europe and its impact on democratic governance at the European and national levels. It addresses the implications of policy reforms in Europe with the wider questions surrounding governance in a multilevel polity and perceptions of legitimacy. It has been written with the ambition of highlighting under-researched aspects of European welfare systems as they emerge after two decades of change in the global economic environment and, more recently, in the wake of the global economic and financial crisis. In this period, national welfare systems have seen major reforms to the structure, content and delivery of social policy provisions on the national level at the same time as European economic and monetary integration has resulted in deeper interdependence and vulnerability of national structures.

The book addresses the crucial question of the wider implications for democratic government brought about by these developments. It offers a wide perspective of changes to European welfare states in covering countries in both Western and Eastern Europe while it provides depth to the analysis through a number of detailed studies in different dimensions of welfare. Moreover, it introduces important points of comparison by analysing and contrasting social and economic developments in Europe with those of the US, New Zealand and Australia. The following chapters build on the classical literature on welfare models to which they bring a deeper and wider perspective by focusing on instances of innovative policy developments in a comparative perspective and discussing issues that arise from the complex mix of integration and coordination among the member states of the European Union (EU).

The individual chapters in this book address questions such as:

- How are different EU member states responding to the challenges of meeting the rising costs of welfare provision? What are the implications of growing inequality between and within countries in Europe?
- What new hybrid forms of welfare system are emerging as a result of increasing public-private initiatives? What is the implication of a rising fragmentation in the social policy mix?
- What are the new ways in which coordination of European welfare policies is conducted? Do they engage authorities and political institutions in the member states or are new European governance models a challenge to established patterns of national policy-making?
- What are the implications of these changing systems of welfare provision for democratic legitimacy and perceptions of accountability of the public actor on local, national and European levels?

BUILDING AND COMPARING WELFARE MODELS IN EUROPE

Analysing national economic and social structures and categorizing them into social models has been recognized in academic literature as a useful avenue for theorizing about differences between welfare states and factors that influence their composition. It has enabled the construction of typologies that make comparative research possible. The comparative approach was suggested in *Three Worlds of Welfare Capitalism* by the Danish sociologist Gøsta Esping-Andersen, who wrote that 'only comparative empirical research will adequately disclose the fundamental properties that unite or divide modern welfare states' (1990, p. 3). In that book, Esping-Andersen makes the now classical distinction between three types of welfare states: a liberal regime encompassing Anglo-Saxon countries, a conservative regime encompassing Continental and Mediterranean countries and a social democratic regime encompassing the Nordic countries. The 'fit' of these typologies with existing welfare regimes was, however, disputed from the start and led to reappraisals and refinements of the initial categorization by both Esping-Andersen himself and others. For instance, the Mediterranean countries were not treated separately in Esping-Andersen's first account of welfare state models but have been considered as constituting a separate category in later works. In works by Liebfried (1992), Ferrera (1996) and Bonoli (1997) the Mediterranean countries are treated separately from the Continental regime, organized in a distinct category which emphasizes these countries' more fragmented welfare state regimes, characterized by a lack of articulated minimum social protection (but with certain rights linked to citizenship), low social expenditure as a percentage of GDP and a high level of familialism. In a similar vein, scholars who focus on the performance of national labour market regimes and competitiveness also emphasize the existence of a Mediterranean model which in this context distinguishes itself by 'employment protection and early retirement provisions which exempt segments of the population from participation in the labour market' (Sapir, 2006, p. 376).

Besides these four standard classifications of western welfare state regimes, other atypical regimes have been identified. One often-cited regime encompasses the antipodean countries (Australia and New Zealand) which, according to Castles (1998), warrant classification in a separate category as their social regimes incorporate distinct solutions to redistribution and social inclusion/protection often by having recourse to regulation in lieu of social transfers. Finally, some countries are referred to as 'hybrid' cases. Such countries, for instance the Netherlands, defy classification in any specific model. The Netherlands has been classified as belonging variously to the Scandinavian, social-democratic regime (Esping-Andersen, 1990) or the Anglo-Saxon, liberal regime (Korpi and Palme, 1998) whereas most scholars put the country in the Continental regime (Arts and Gelissen, 2002, p. 151).

Organizing the countries in Central and Eastern Europe, which in the last 20 years underwent a profound transformation from the authoritarian command economy to the democratic market economy, into a specific welfare regime category is more difficult. Early on in the reform process these countries decided to pursue economic, social and democratic reforms in parallel to preparing for their accession to the EU, thereby conditioning their domestic reforms to the regulatory framework of the EU. As it turns out, some of the more disputed domestic reforms concerned areas of social policy where the EU has not developed any regulatory regime and holds little in terms of regulatory power. Therefore, in some Central and Eastern European countries pre-Communist social regimes were revived while other countries opted for market-based liberal reforms upon independence, in some cases under strong influence of the advice of international financial institutions, such as the World Bank. The picture that emerges is a rather mixed one. The countries in Central and Eastern Europe display important differences in relative wealth and economic development as well as the design and structure of their welfare institutions, and level of spending on social programmes. Despite these differences, some scholars have argued for treating the

Central and Eastern European countries as belonging to a new, fifth, welfare state model. Nonetheless, the similarities displayed in their social models are 'mainly of an institutional character, resulting from their similar past and the similar challenges they face regarding their transformation to democracy and market economy' (Żukowski, 2009, p. 29).

As welfare state models have made empirical comparison possible, scholarly debate has moved on to consider the classification of individual countries, the explanatory value of welfare state typologies and the validity of the theoretical premises of these concepts (Arts and Gelissen 2002, p. 155). Typologies underscore the fact that different types of welfare state exist and that these welfare states have indeed developed different solutions to similar problems. It is hard, however, to disentangle the factors that condition change or inertia in different models as well as those underlying the relative effectiveness of existing welfare systems. Comparative scholars are faced with the task of determining the role played by endogenous versus exogenous factors, such as investigating the influences of international policy coordination processes (Hartlapp, 2009). Welfare models have been instrumental in analysing the impact of the European policy coordination processes on national welfare systems by comparing how different models have reacted to transnational learning and policy diffusion and whether indeed such processes have resulted in convergence of regulatory regimes or not.

In their turn, the policy coordination processes on the European level have further encouraged comparative analysis across types of welfare states which not only clarify 'ideal' types of social models but have also led to evaluation of the performance of specific social policies and the effectiveness of specific welfare state models (Sapir, 2006). As European economies have become increasingly interdependent and EU member states have come under regulatory and statutory obligations to follow rules pertaining to the internal market and the EU's economic and monetary regime, comparisons of the performance of national social regimes have become increasingly pertinent as witnessed in the elaborate systems of monitoring of the Stability and Growth Pact (SGP), the Macro-Economic Imbalances Procedure and the Europe 2020 Strategy brought together in 2011 in the European semester. In view of the increasing economic and social diversity among EU member states in the wake of the economic and financial crisis, the EU is bound to devise increasingly sophisticated approaches to deal with the tensions of an economic, social and political nature.

UNDERLYING CHANGES TO EUROPEAN WELFARE REGIMES AND ORIENTATION OF SOCIAL POLICY REFORM

Economic and demographic conditions, history and tradition along with normative and value-driven aspects have shaped the existing welfare state models. These have come to differ in the type and scale of social provisions offered and in the nature and scope of institutional arrangements. Studies suggest that over time the articulation of social policy goals, their normative justification and contextualization as well as their regulatory content have taken on similar features in mature welfare states. Behind this convergence, however, lurk more profound challenges, as western societies face similar challenges to national welfare state regimes. These challenges stem from the profound changes that globalization has brought to economic, social and political interaction in the world and from changes within societies in terms of rapid ageing of the population and individualization of lifestyles and choice. External and internal challenges drive fundamental transformations to the basic dialectic relationships in social policy: the boundary between public and private spheres; the place of the individual in relation to the collective; and the respective roles of the state and the market. The recognition of common challenges has enabled further comparative research into the actual reforms carried out and opened an opportunity to justify public action on the European level with the purpose of identifying, diagnosing and devising policy reform advice.

Deep-lying challenges have exposed the vulnerability of national welfare states in the state's capacity to devise, organize and administer social welfare provisions as well as ensuring the financing of welfare systems. Even before the financial and economic crisis imposed a regime of fiscal consolidation, the necessity of long-term financial sustainability of welfare systems had changed the orientation of social policy towards a social investment perspective where social services are seen as investments into the productive (social) forces in society. The social investment perspective brought about a reorientation of social policy which in the decade before the financial and economic crisis led to a seemingly contradictory development. Actual policy changes pointed towards path-dependence and maintenance of levels of public spending while steps towards decreasing the generosity of benefits, reinforced regimes of conditionality and recipients' obligations bore witness to retrenchment. In a parallel trend, the private sector was given a greater role, either through private institutions or the voluntary sector. The reduction of the scope and, in certain cases, generosity of welfare thus predates the current era of austerity but was dramatically intensified by the financial and economic crisis of 2008, in particular in countries experiencing sovereign debt problems where retrenchment became an unavoidable means to restore public finance deficits.

The notions of expansion and retrenchment which underlie many studies of welfare policy change have been referred to as belonging to a quantitative approach that concentrates on the transformation of old social policies and consequently fails to detect the complexity of social reforms underway (Bonoli and Natali, 2012). These reforms contain both elements of safeguarding policies of replacement of income through benefits and pensions as well as new social policies which cater for new risks and previously excluded groups (Häusermann, 2012). Active labour market policy is a good example of this mixed approach being built on the activation of job-seekers through re-skilling, stepped-up placement services and conditionality as well as the provision of new services such as child care. Activation of job-seekers, combined with social security into the concept of flexicurity, represents one of the most widely implemented policy reforms in European countries in the last decade, but amounts to neither retrenchment of overall social provisions, nor retention of the protection of established workers; it rather constitutes a reorientation of labour market services to adapt to rapidly changing societies. Active labour policy is often linked to the 'commodification' of workers leading to increasing income differentials as the overall competitiveness of the economic is at stake. In Denmark and Sweden measures to increase the employability of workers through life-long learning, re-skilling and subsidized employment in the public sector are part of the activation policy and demand sizeable public funding which is reflected in these countries' maintenance of high levels of social policy expenditure. But the logic of retrenchment can also be observed when active labour market policies address people with low skills through different kinds of conditionality linked to unemployment benefits with the aim of lowering the cost of labour and employing various measures to 'make work pay' such as tax reductions.

The expansion of choice as a fundamental aspect of welfare service provision whether in education, health or care is generally seen as a flexible response to individualization in terms of lifestyles, tastes and the emergence of new needs arising as a result of changing family patterns. The marketization of these services has enabled private institutions to play an increasingly dominant role in areas such as health care, education, social care and labour market policy. Again, the entry of private players did not necessarily result in reduced costs and increasingly the realization of efficiency gains and recipients' satisfaction are also being questioned (Hartman, 2011). The decentralization and marketization of services assume an active and informed role being played by local and regional authorities and consumers, which in the case of under-resourced or vulnerable consumer groups, such as the old and sickly, they may not be able to play in full. Moreover complex contractual arrangements between public authorities and private operators intended to increase efficiency and off-load costs from the public balance sheet may actually result in a loss of transparency and increased fragmentation of the supply of services.

The marketization of social services is not only prominent in the health, elderly and child care sectors and education but also in the area of pensions where supplementary pensions have become obligatory in most European countries and fuelled the expansion of capital markets through investment in private pensions. Ageing populations constitute one of the greatest challenges to the sustainability of national welfare systems as actual and future pension liabilities weigh heavily on public finances, as well as taking up the bulk of health and care budgets. Pension system reform is one of the main themes of the EU's policy coordination processes and certainly in the case of the countries in the euro area is treated as a matter of common concern.

The governance of welfare state reform has become a prominent theme in social policy literature (Bonoli and Natali, 2012; van Berkel, de Graaf and Siro vàtka, 2011; Graziano, Jacquot and Palier, 2011). The literature deals with the perspective of the European dimension in reforms undertaken on the national level in Western Europe. The European dimension has contributed to an awareness of common challenges but also encouraged convergence, sometimes implicitly, at other times explicitly, towards similar types of reforms. This convergence of governance is visible in the nature and orientation of reforms based on the approach of New Public Management. The European Commission, inspired in the 1990s by the work of international organizations, such as the OECD, the World Bank and the IMF, converged on the New Public Management principles as they correspond more easily to the output legitimacy which underpins transnational public policy than concepts linked to republican notions of democratic government based on public administrations being closely linked to the national state and citizens as bearers of constitutional and political rights. The prominence of the market, the increasing fuzziness of the dividing lines between the public and the private and the individualization of choice underpinned by the notion of individuals as consumers rather than citizens reinforce the perception of governance as a 'management' tool rather than a principle of democratic government.

EUROPEAN SOCIAL POLICY

In recent decades, the existence of a European social model is increasingly contested. Social policy as a counter-balance to the market forces released by the creation of the Internal Market was part of the constituting debates in the 1950s and 1960s when the policies of the European Community (EC) were gradually being forged. The setting-up of a fully-fledged social policy was, however, never seriously considered and the most significant step taken was the drafting of an article explicitly setting down the equality between female and male workers inserted into the Treaty of Rome at the insistence of the French government. The absence of political consensus regarding the social dimension of European integration is noticeable from the perspective of the relative similarity of the welfare systems of the six founding members of the EC. Scharpf (2002) discusses the decisions of the governments at the time not to adopt social policy as a necessary element of the Internal Market as an example of a 'road not taken', as this period with hindsight represents a time when national systems could conceivably have converged towards a single model had the member states so wished. From this point of time (mid 1950s) onwards, the EU has through a series of accessions come to include states with national welfare systems displaying diverse characteristics.

Notwithstanding the impossibility of developing welfare state characteristics, the EU has not been devoid of action in the social field. With the development of the four freedoms of the Internal Market, the freedom of movement of workers was strengthened by a number of rights in the form of EU directives touching primarily on working conditions, including health and safety, equality between men and women (later enlarged to include all forms of discrimination), and the protection of migrant workers and their families. By 2009, the EU's social regulation was composed of approximately 80 binding provisions (Falkner, 2009) and in addition to regulation the EU had set up a number of structural funds, notably the Regional Development Fund, European Social Fund, the Cohesion Fund and the European Agricultural Guidance and Guarantee Fund whose objectives are to fund activities which improve social cohesion in Europe.

Even so, the focus on the cross-border implications of economic integration linked to migrant workers has been the dominant approach to social regulation in the EU as welfare state provisions have remained solidly in the realm of the nation state. Scharpf (2002) pointed to what he defines as a 'constitutional asymmetry' within the EU, in that the Treaties transferred extensive regulatory competence to supranational institutions in the area of the Internal Market while in the area of social policy little regulatory power has been granted. According to Scharpf, the constitutional 'supremacy' of the market is at the origin of the activism of the European Court of Justice (ECJ) in extending free market principles, as seen for instance in the rulings on Vaxholm/Laval and the Viking cases. Another aspect of the asymmetry is the Commission's status as European competition authority which has empowered it to pursue member states' governments for granting state aids and to order the break-up of national monopolies. As state aids, among other things, are part of a government's arsenal to bolster economic activities in depressed areas and sectors deemed important for social cohesion, whereas national monopolies are at times used for retaining or increasing employment for social purposes, national resentment has been great when the Commission or the ECJ have ruled against the conformity of national measures to EU competition rules. Individual member states have increasingly taken exception to the Court's rulings on the primacy of the principle of market integration over national social norms and regulation, be it in the labour market or in the health sector.

The deepening of the constitutional asymmetry is visible in the setting up of EMU with a supranational monetary policy, a common currency and binding rules on budget deficits and national debt in the SGP.[1] At the time when EMU was agreed, a consensus among member states' governments on how the economy operates made it conceivable to centralize monetary policy without simultaneously centralizing economic policy. Price stability was the overriding concern and therefore attention was focused on the fiscal policies of the then-to-be euro countries followed by the development of binding rules on national debt and budget deficits. The issue of coordination of national policy in economic and social areas was addressed by convergence based on soft instruments, such as benchmarking, sharing of experience and naming-and-shaming (Schäfer, 2004). This meant that the constitutional asymmetry was perpetuated in the policy framework surrounding the EMU: full transfer of sovereignty of monetary policy to the ECB rendering national governments' recourse to competitive devaluation of the national currency impossible and binding rules to prevent national indebtedness and budget deficits over certain limits while 'the overall policy-mix was to be achieved by soft coordination of national policies' (Schäfer, 2004, p. 6).

Given the problem in many European economies with high unemployment, including high long-term unemployment, the first policy area where national policy coordination was undertaken was the labour market. Some academics have pointed to the market logic behind the choice of a 'commodification' of workers (Schäfer, 2004; Flear, 2009) and the problem of competitiveness of European economies, due in part to the inflexibility of labour markets. Others have rather emphasized the choice of labour market policy as a consequence of micro-economic logic in the White Book on Growth, Competitiveness and Employment of 1993 and the work in the area of cohesion policy to bolster employment in economically depressed or disadvantaged regions, in particular the local employment pacts. The European Employment Strategy (EES) got off the ground in 1994 and was codified in the Amsterdam Treaty in 1997. Arguably, the negotiations leading up to the Amsterdam Treaty constitute a second 'road not taken' in that the Treaty did not grant competences for a Community social policy, referring only to the possibility of adopting directives that stipulate minimum rules in a few policy areas, predominately related to labour market policy, whereas it explicitly avoids measures with financial, administrative or legal implications (TFEU, art. 153).

Although already practised in the SGP and the EES, coordination of national policies and soft governance was formally introduced as a new mode of governance in the first half of 2000, shepherded by the Portuguese government then holding the presidency of the EU. The declaration of the European Council at the summit of March 2000 launching the Lisbon Strategy with the aim of turning the EU into the world's most competitive knowledge economy with a high level of employment and social cohesion also contained a section designating the Open Method of Coordination (OMC), the method of choice for implementing the goals of the Lisbon Strategy (European Council, 2000).

It is conceivable that national policy coordination under the OMC was designed with the purpose of maintaining the constitutional status quo between the liberal market impetus of the treaties and the limited regulatory power granted to social policy on the European level. For various reasons member states had no interest (or lacked political will) in raising the constitutional status of social policy. The OMC was seen as a governance instrument that would not violate the principle of subsidiarity, i.e. national competence in the area of social policy, as coordination of national social policy would not amount to introducing elements of Keynesian fiscal policy on the European level which was feared since it would imply a fundamental appraisal of the fiscal rules of the SGP. Because the OMC relies on national coordination and voluntary convergence, the EU institutions were not mandated to survey member states' compliance to common rules nor summoned to rule on breaches of EU legislation.

UNRESOLVED ISSUES IN WELFARE STATE GOVERNANCE

One of the major issues in modern government has been how to pursue greater efficiency in the delivery of public services on the one hand, and how to take that delivery beyond the bounds of direct political influence so that the service can meet longer term aims and somehow be above the short term concerns of those who need to seek regular re-election. One of the most obvious areas where this applies is in health care. The decision about how large the health care budget that is publicly financed should be, is clearly political, as is the decision as to how that finance is to be raised – how much from taxation, how much from insurance contributions and how much from user charges. However, how a health centre or a hospital is to be run to achieve the maximum benefit for its customers raises issues of medical decision making and business efficiency over which elected politicians may have little expertise. The tendency therefore is to delegate authority to professional agencies, which have clear terms of reference and operate under actual or effective contracts to provide services, often against quality criteria. However, it is difficult to specify such contracts clearly or set them out in a way which is readily divorced from politics. In cases such as central banks it has been possible to define objectives clearly in a way that the large majority in parliaments can agree and hence run a stabilizing policy over a much longer time period than the life of an individual government. Some welfare services can fall in the same bracket, such as public libraries and national parks, but even with universities ministers can find it difficult to set out a framework that captures what society in general wants. What they can do is set out relatively objective means of determining standards and assessing performance against standards. This normally involves setting up a second agency which acts as a monitor. In recent years European states have realized that it is difficult to put forward fiscal programmes that are sustainable. Thus having an independent agency that investigates governments' plans and expresses an opinion on their validity is a help not just to the domestic democratic process but to the European level one as well, where countries are heavily inter-dependent.

In the same way that members of parliament and local councils typically do not have the qualifications to run a large business, so they do not have the qualifications to assess service quality. What they can do, however, is read the reports from those who can and hence make a decision on the way forward – whether an agency needs improved objectives, whether it should change its approach or indeed whether it should have the task taken away from it for poor performance. The area is fraught with difficulty. One of the best arbiters of quality will be the consumer. However, if they do not have a choice, which is often the case outside cities, it is difficult to observe the consequences. Even with schools and doctors it has proven difficult to administer such regimes and to apply appropriate incentives. One result can be to polarize resources, where good schools attract richer parents, who can contribute resources to the schools, which makes them even better. Hence in many respects, as Vibert (2007) suggests, the rise of independent agencies may actually improve democratic accountability, since their operations have to be much more transparent in order to permit the independent assessment. Issues such as a lack of local involvement can form part of the requirements of the agency. Thus consultation with consumers may be extensive.

Competition Among Areas

One of the problems for public sector provision of services is that it often tends to be a local monopoly. Thus it does not make much sense to have competing water supply systems and sewerage disposal systems, multiple sets of wires to deliver electricity, pipes to deliver gas etc.[2] Hence it becomes more difficult to offer people any realistic choice within an area. If they do not like the social provision in one area then they have to move to another. The drawback about this tendency is that areas may become more polarized. At a local level, parents may be very concerned about the schools their children can go to, but the same problem occurs at the national level. Someone facing services that do not meet their need in one member state may factor that in when thinking about moving elsewhere. To pick the example chosen by Mayes and Thomson (2013), the provision of child care varies considerably across member states. People who are keen for both parents to be able to work might prefer the Nordic countries because they have both greater provision of nurseries, kindergartens and pre-schools than elsewhere and a high level of state support. Those who wish to spend more time with their children might consider the Netherlands, where part-time jobs are much more prevalent and not such an inhibition to returning to a good career once the children can go to school. Clearly child care provision is a second order determinant.

However, the child care example raises another feature of the problem which inhibits mobility, namely that much child care is provided informally, either by family members of by friends and acquaintances through voluntary links or more formal clubs. Money or tokens may exchange

hands but there is no requirement for qualifications. This social infrastructure and the degree to which one is included in society are extremely
important to the quality of life.

A Broader Approach to Insurance

The new member states have in the main had to construct new welfare
systems as the means of financing and supporting the previous ones has
disappeared. On top of that substantial inflation eroded the value of such
benefits that did exist so many became ineffective. They thus faced the
problem of having a substantial proportion of society that was unable to
cope in present circumstances and was unable to obtain work in order to
try to build up their own resources. The retired were particularly
vulnerable. The state industry for which they had worked was no longer
there to provide their pensions. As a result many of the states have
constructed a three tier welfare system. The first and basic tier caters for
those who have no or little capacity to build up a means of payment for
themselves. They have to be financed by the contributions of others,
usually through the general tax system, although it is possible to do
something through family responsibility. The second and main part of the
system is to build up insurance through workers' contributions (some of
which usually come from the employer). Thus an employee slowly builds
up a fund from which they can draw for health care, education,
unemployment and eventually a pension. While such funds will obviously have a strong element of insurance in that they can draw much
more than their contributions in the event of serious difficulty, the
pension element will tend to be much more directly contribution based,
so that those with higher paying jobs will get larger pensions. This
system therefore grows with the contributors and as people have longer
in work so their ability to have better pensions grows. The third tier is
voluntary and enables those on higher incomes to decide whether they
want more than the other tiers offer, say in the form of private health
treatment.

  The advantage of this structure is that ordinary tax rates can remain
quite low and indeed several of the countries have gone for flat rate
systems. It is usually argued that low tax rates provide a very considerable incentive for people to work more or to seek slightly better paying
jobs because they get much of the benefit of the extra income. The lower
level of transfers also means that other tax rates can be relatively low,
such as corporate taxation, which will enable these member states to be
quite attractive to inward investment. The key is that take home pay after
making the insurance contributions will still be as low as in other

countries but because people feel that they are contributing to their own future welfare needs they feel much more comfortable about it even if the financial consequences are relatively similar.

Involvement of the Private and Voluntary Sectors

The limits to resources have led to innovation by the public sector in trying to get involvement by the private sector in the achievement of its welfare goals. The idea of public-private partnerships, used quite extensively in the UK, has inherent appeal. Take the case of hospitals. Only the public sector has sufficient command over resources to create the large scale hospitals that are necessary to be able to provide the full range of modern medical procedures. Many wealthier or busier people would however like to buy extra services and 'jump the queue' for treatment. By charging them appropriately this can give the opportunity to plough back funds for the treatment of the poorer. Similarly, the best staff, who could command high salaries in private facilities, can get that opportunity if they also use the same facilities to help patients through the publicly provided system. Thus there are real as well as financial benefits from such cooperation. This cooperation can become very disadvantageous for the public sector if the participation is largely financial and if the arrangement is not well managed. The private sector is adept at extracting the short-term rents and leaving the public sector with the longer-term liabilities. There is also a prima facie conflict between the objective of the firm, which is to maximize the return to its shareholders, and the duty of the welfare state which is to enhance the well-being of its citizens. This can be mitigated where there is a separate agency that has to address the setting of prices or investigate evidence that the consumer has been exploited. Clearly ombudsmen can also be used to ensure that individuals are fairly treated by such organizations.

One other idea, which has also been used in the United States, is to get local businesses to refurbish the area in which they are situated and to provide a range of local services. However, the key feature which affects the democratic nature of these agreements is that once agreement is reached then all businesses are required to participate – at least financially. If this were not done then there would be ample opportunity for free riding. However, since it is business which is deciding on the form of the regeneration, although of course this needs to be approved by the appropriate local authority, it may turn out to be different from what the local population would like to see. Since businesses will finance 'voluntarily' only what they perceive to be in their own interests, this makes popular objection difficult as the alternative may be no contribution.

Voluntary participation also poses some conundrums. Those who contribute either financially or in time or kind do so not just because of what they feel they wish to support but also because of what they enjoy doing. Thus it may be much easier to get people to plant trees or clear up rubbish from the shoreline in summer than to get them to work at night in a hostel for the homeless in the middle of winter. People do not necessarily volunteer for what society at large thinks is more important. Secondly, voluntary contributions may be made where gaps are perceived in public services, e.g. in fire services in rural areas, life-saving or emergency helicopters. However, where the gaps are can become endogenous. If the authorities find that they can get public support for a service they may reduce their own support. Thus voluntary funds that are raised to improve a service may end up simply keeping it going if taxpayer funding is then reduced. There is no contract between the donors and what the public authority decides to do with its own funding.

Indeed this forms part of a wider problem of both moral hazard and adverse selection. As we have noted, people who think they may be a claim on an insurance system will take out insurance and indeed may move to where the insurance system is the most generous. In so far as insurance is available then there is less pressure on the individual to reduce the risks they take. In part adverse selection can be reduced by making contribution compulsory. In the same way the moral hazard can be reduced by requiring a degree of contribution by the insured whenever there is a claim. This works particularly well where the first loss is borne by the insured and only when it is large enough does it get met by the insurer. Both may be addressed to some extent by having risk-weighted contributions. However, these incentives still do not work if society is not prepared to face the hardship that may come from those who refuse to insure. This applies particularly to areas such as child poverty or care for the aged.

IMPLICATIONS FOR MULTILEVEL GOVERNANCE IN THE EU

Economic systems are inherently asymmetric. Those in difficulty have no choice but to adjust while those who are relatively better off do not have to do so. Thus countries running a balance of payments surplus can build up reserves, whereas those running deficits will eventually find that they cannot borrow further – although this may take a very long time. Of course one might query why countries would want to hold such reserves rather than increasing consumption and allowing themselves to become richer by revaluing. At the individual level, those who lose their jobs have to cut back on their spending as they erode their savings, while those who retain them or indeed get an increase in pay have no need to adjust their pattern of consumption if they do not wish to do so. Nevertheless, in addition to the indebtedness of the more troubled euro area countries there has been a running up of private sector obligations, where claims of the banks in the stronger countries on those in the weaker has also built up.[3]

While the closer association of the European countries allows much more effective policy learning than has been the case earlier or elsewhere, it imposes its own pressures, as countries might feel obliged to change their systems as a result of the pressures of economic competition, not because of any change in domestic social views. Higher social charges may be a component in labour costs and hence as other layers of protection are removed, this may encourage 'social dumping', where employment shifts to low social cost locations. Up until the enlargements of the EU of the last decade this worry had not turned out to be much of a reality (Chassard, 2001). Even then the dominant concern lay with emigration from the new member states to the others. The irony behind these concerns is that the migration of persons and production is itself part of the operation of a successful social policy, contributing to a reduction in inequality in the EU as a whole. The principal difficulty has been that social policy has been largely national and the extent of transfers from richer to poorer countries in the EU has been strictly limited. Without such fiscal transfers, not only is it much more difficult for the less well-off member states to address their social difficulties but any asymmetric shocks within the euro area become hugely difficult to address, especially for a highly indebted country.

The EU is not alone in facing these problems and their democratic consequences. Indeed because of the fundamentally national responsibility for welfare systems this is scarcely surprising. However, what we do notice is that the pressures on the euro area from sovereign debt problems in some member states and the subsequent severe inequalities and unfairness that result are leading to a rethink of where the democratic boundary to national responsibility should lie. With the implementation of the 'six-pack' and 'two-pack' measures in 2012–13, the member states' range of choice is reduced, and albeit reluctantly the degree of cross-border assistance is increasing. Furthermore, despite the process of harmonization and development being voluntary under the OMC, it is clear that policy learning in the field of social welfare has been rapid over the last 15 years or more.

CHANGING WELFARE STATES IN PERSPECTIVE

The continuing integration in Europe, particularly within the EU, has heightened the debate on European welfare models. There is considerable variety in how one can address welfare problems, in part reflecting the relative importance one attaches to improved income, employment or full inclusion in society as captured in the welfare triangle (Chapter 2, Figure 2.1). This variety runs right across Europe from the greater focus on employment among the Nordic countries, through the greater emphasis on market mechanisms and the direct importance of relieving poverty in the 'Anglo-Saxon' countries to the significance of the family and community in the solution which pervades the 'Mediterranean' approach. In this volume, we have chosen to raise a number of challenges and trends that are common to European welfare states and that constitute the backcloth against which the drastic changes in welfare state provisions were brought in in the wake of the financial crisis and the sovereign debt crisis. More specifically we discuss the relevance of conceptualizing the development of social and economic regimes in terms of welfare models given the strong influence of change brought about through a deep-rooted transformation of social values and lifestyles as well as the impact of globalization on terms of trade, production patterns and factor price levels influencing states' international competitiveness. We also address policy coordination on the European level which has become the established mode of governance in the EU in areas with a direct influence on national welfare systems and the practices of democratic government.

Patterns of Welfare States in Central and Eastern Europe

In Chapter 2, David Mayes and Zaidah Mustaffa explore the ways in which the changes that occurred in the last decade have altered the structure of European welfare systems. It takes as its point of departure the classical description of European welfare states in four general categories: the Anglo-Saxon; the Continental; the Scandinavian; and the Southern. The neatness of this categorization is now being disturbed by three developments: the enlargement of the EU to twelve new members drawn primarily from central and eastern Europe; the forces of globalization; and growing heterogeneity among and within welfare states. The authors argue that these factors have complicated categorization of welfare state regimes as there is simply no single model. Dissimilarities appear not only between states but also within states among different policies, and to complicate the picture further, single policies often display different logics, for instance in education or health. Nevertheless, the authors find that the forces of globalization and the process of policy transfer on the European level have resulted in convergence. But this convergence is not directed towards uniformity as European states have adopted aspects of all four general models. The new member states of the EU contribute to a blurring of the four general models through the extreme financial pressure they sustained when reforming their welfare systems, which led them to adopt truly specific solutions that confound the traditional welfare state patterns.

Changing Conditions for Social Insurance in Europe

The changing nature of social insurance in the EU is examined by Katherine Lyons and Christine Cheyne in Chapter 3. The authors argue that, following the sovereign debt crisis in Europe, the EU faces the urgent task of rebuilding economic prosperity for all. The recently adopted fiscal compact and accompanying sanctions represent a significant step in responding to the crisis through stimulating growth, creating jobs (especially for young people), addressing overspending, and restoring confidence in the euro area's common currency. According to Lyons and Cheyne the historical emphasis on social insurance based protection and solidarity (and the more recent associated focus on the social investment welfare state model) must be maintained as part of the project of deepening political integration and democratic governance. In examining the governance of social insurance in the EU, they find support for two models of EU democracy: (con)federal, with decisions being made supranationally, and unitary, with member states making their own decisions, and argue that, in addressing the causes and effects of the sovereign debt crisis, democratic governance and risk-pooling should not be compromised.

Active Labour Market Policies and the Human Development Perspective

The chapter by Mark Thomson takes as its point of departure Amartya Sen's capability approach which looks at inclusion as meaning raising effective freedoms by involving people in decisions through more participatory forms of democracy. In the case studies of three 'active' welfare states (Denmark, the UK and the Netherlands), the author investigates how reforms in both formal activation policies as well as in the governance of activation affect both the quality of democracy as experienced by those being 'activated' and its future form. One example of change is in multilevel governance structures in Denmark which have undergone a shift of responsibility for social provisions away from the regional to the local level accompanied by an increased emphasis on behalf of the state on management-by-objectives. The chapter critically assesses the European Employment Strategy and its concern with creating more and better jobs through the combination of flexibility and security.

Inequality, Decentralization and Voluntarism

The aim of Tess Altman and David Mayes in Chapter 5 is to explore three related trends which contribute to important changes in the way social welfare and democratic decision making interact. These trends are: growing inequality, an increasing devolution of powers to local authorities and institutions, and a rise in voluntary provision and contributions. The overarching concern is with the effects of localization and voluntarism on equitable and democratic welfare provision. Equality of access, opportunity and treatment is held as one of the defining characteristics of a socially inclusive democracy. However, the current global climate is instead one of increasing polarization and growing inequalities as the 'good' sides of globalization tend to benefit only certain localities while disparities occur both between countries and within countries, with the rich tier of society becoming richer at the expense of the poorer tier. These inequalities have been exacerbated by the recent global financial crisis. Overall, the authors question how far competition among areas is realistic in Europe in the way suggested by Tiebout (1956) concerning the US. In that model, polarization is sufficient for electors to reinforce their own position. Thus a richer community that values low density housing and has little need for publicly provided services can manage to operate a low tax regime. Not only are its demands on the public system low but the tax take per head of population is high hence permitting the lower rates. This may also affect the region's competitiveness since post tax incomes can be higher even if pre-tax incomes are lower than elsewhere.

The Growing Role of Social Service Solutions Outside the Public Sector

In Chapter 6, Tess Altman and Cris Shore explore the role of the private and voluntary sectors in filling the gaps in public sector social welfare provision and consider the extent to which this augments or weakens the democratic process. While the public sector has tended to be the major provider in European social welfare systems, since the late 1980s there has been a notable shift towards privately provided support and grey services as governments have sought solutions outside the state system. This trend has been fuelled by an increasing emphasis on measures that encourage efficiency, productivity and competitiveness as well as pressures on the sustainability of welfare systems further exacerbated by the global financial crisis. The chapter's empirical focus is on case studies from Britain, the US and New Zealand on the Private Finance Initiative, Asset-Based Community Development and new contractualism. The findings of the case studies are used to analyse the contradictions between the goals of social protection and regulation that underpin European social policy and the demands for increased flexibilization and privatization promoted by the European Single Market and the rulings of the European Court of Justice.

The Rise of the Unelected

In Chapter 7, David Mayes and Zaidah Mustaffa explore the implications of replacing direct government provision of welfare services by expert technical organizations which provide a multitude of services for government departments under the terms of performance contract. The existence of these organizations breaks the direct link between the citizen *cum* customer as a participant in the democratic system and the state as the provider. These organizations display a huge variety in forms and tasks and operate according to controversial processes where major objections include a lack of accountability and a less-than-expected cost-efficiency. In some countries this has generated considerable mistrust. The authors investigate the case of the health service in the UK where there are some one thousand quangos. It explores their variety, how they operate and the assessments of their performance that have been made. Using this experience, Mayes and Mustaffa draw conclusions for the implications for democratic arrangements in the EU.

European Governance: the Case of Advanced Policy Coordination

In Chapter 8, Anna Michalski traces the significance of the diversity among national welfare states for the search for a common system of governance in Europe. In view of the substantial degree of the hetero-geneity among national economic and social conditions as well as the structures and aims of national welfare models, the EU has opted for soft governance in the area of welfare in the form of the OMC. Over time, however, the OMC has become increasingly criticized for being deficient in terms of democratic policy making. The criticism focuses on the de-politicization of the governance process, the dominance of national executives and the technocratic nature of policy making that the method has resulted in. Despite the method's claim to safeguard national sovereignty, empirical evidence indicates that soft governance has implications for the legitimacy of the EU and the democratic processes and institutions of the member states in a subtle, but still significant, way. As a result of the EU having opted for a decentralized approach to European social welfare coordination, considerable strain has been put on the traditional roles of national and subnational democratic institutions, national parliaments and local and regional authorities.

NOTES

1. The ability of the Commission to enforce the rules of the SGP was doubted from the inception of the EMU as the Maastricht Treaty did not include coercive instruments. The SGP was built on an iterative process of monitoring and assessment of national economies followed by recommendations proposed by the Commission and sanctioned by the Council. As the decision to fine a country breaking the SGP rules had to be unanimous, the targeted state could block the decision. Already the Lisbon Treaty changed this provision and such decisions no longer required consensus (TFEU articles 121–122). The so-called six-pack legislative package further reinforced the governance by applying a reversed majority implying that a majority of the member states has to vote against the recommendation of the Commission to punish a member state in breach of the rules of the SGP.
2. Of course in the case of electricity, gas or even railways, one can distinguish between the provider of the network, which is a monopoly activity, and those who provide services through it. Thus a variety of generators and even retailers can provide electricity through a given grid. Different companies can run trains on the same tracks. This feature is less common for social services, although technically possible through shared use of buildings, for example.
3. The debate on these balances, built up under Target 2, has been particularly strong in Germany: see CESifo (2012).

2. Social models in the enlarged European Union

David G. Mayes and Zaidah Mustaffa

INTRODUCTION

The purpose of this chapter is to explore the way in which the developments of the last decade have altered the nature of the structure of European welfare systems. Up until recently it was accepted that welfare systems in the EU could be characterized under four general headings: 'Anglo-Saxon', 'Continental', 'Scandinavian' and 'Southern' (see Muffels et al., 2002; Sapir, 2006), although the exact titles and countries included varied among studies.[1] The characteristics can readily be summarized under what is described as the 'welfare triangle' (see Figure 2.1, which is adapted from Muffels et al.). However, this neatness is being disturbed by three main factors.

Most obviously there are 12 new member states, drawn primarily from central and eastern Europe. Second, welfare regimes have been subjected to the forces of globalization and integration. Indeed, the EU has been encouraging a process of mutual learning through the Open Method of Coordination (OMC) that applies in this area, which has been a contribution to countries adopting some of the better ideas from their neighbours and hence blurring the boundaries. Last, as pointed out by Schelkle (2008), welfare systems are not homogeneous. Countries do not necessarily approach education and health in the same way that they approach employment, disability or old age. There is variety even within the provision of public services, such as libraries, transport and public open spaces in a single country.

It is therefore necessary to provide a reassessment of the position. It is not the purpose of this chapter to provide a definitive reclassification but to ensure that the range of current approaches is clear. The research behind this chapter was a contribution to the RECON project (as discussed in the preface), which investigated the implications of the

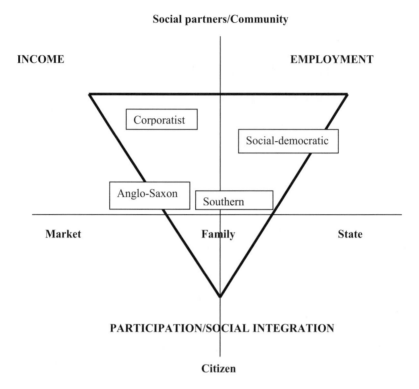

Source: Muffels et al., 2002.

Figure 2.1   Welfare regimes and the welfare triangle

whole range of public policy for the likely forms of democracy that may exist in the EU in the future.[2] Hence it seeks to set out the range of welfare regimes that need to be evaluated.

   The chapter is in three main parts. The first spells out the issues in more detail and the empirical approach that is employed. The second looks at a set of case studies for health care in Estonia, the Czech Republic and Poland, while the third sets out the implications for an assessment of the consequences for democratic processes in the EU.

THE EVOLUTION OF EUROPEAN WELFARE REGIMES

A Categorization of Welfare Regimes

There are many ways of categorizing welfare schemes but a simple and widely used example is the welfare triangle shown in Figure 2.1. The key element of this triangle is to establish what the principal objective of welfare is. The main choice has been over whether the system should seek to assist people to have employment or whether it should try to make sure simply that they have adequate minimum incomes to get by irrespective of whether they can find employment. Of course in practice no regime is at the extreme. Those countries that focus rather more on income support nevertheless are keen to see that people are employed, as this is essential to the viability of the scheme – people have to be earning and paying in. In the same way those schemes that are strongly weighted towards employment nevertheless have to handle those who are unable to work. The dichotomy can thus be readily exaggerated. It is also important to recognize that these classifications reflect the balance of the regime and are not a simple quantification how much effort[3] is going in any dimension nor indeed on the extent of the result – whether or not due to public sector intervention.[4] The role of the state in the economy in terms of taxation and expenditure is greater in the UK than it is in Germany for example. Arts and Gelissen (2002, p. 137) conclude from a thorough survey of the literature 'that real welfare states are hardly ever pure types and are usually hybrid cases'. This does not devalue the usefulness of the classification, if only for heuristic purposes. Indeed Esping-Andersen (1997) argues that creation of these 'idealized' welfare types is more helpful to understanding if the actual states are more hybridized.[5]

The third principal objective set out in the figure is broader, namely the ability to participate and be fully included in society rather than simply to be in work or with sufficient income to avoid poverty. This approach focuses more strongly on 'capabilities', concentrating on the ability of people to perform a full role in society. Thus social welfare is thought of in much wider terms of social inclusion, going beyond having an adequate income and employment. Such inclusion is particularly import-ant for minority groups and immigrants.

The traditional characterization of the four main regimes identified in Europe is also set out in Figure 2.1. The development of these types of regimes is ascribed to Esping-Andersen (1990) although he delineated only three regimes, the fourth, southern, regime being suggested by

Liebfried (1992), Ferrera (1996) and Bonoli (1997). The general membership of the regimes is clear from the names. The northern continental regimes belong to the corporatist/continental group, typified by Germany; the Nordic countries belong to the Nordic/social democratic regimes, the southern European countries to the southern/Mediterranean regime and the UK and Ireland to the Anglo-Saxon regime (i.e. it is not a description of ethnic origin). In so far as there is a clear characterization, the corporatist/continental regimes emphasize income replacement in the event of difficulty, reflecting their insurance base, whereas the Nordic/social democratic regime emphasizes employment.[6] There is thus more emphasis on trying to get people back into jobs in these regimes. A crucial facet here for example is the treatment of child care. In the Nordic regimes it is thought important that both parents should be able to remain in full-time work as far as possible. Therefore there is a strong emphasis on the provision of child care and kindergartens rather than the provision of assistance to enable one parent, or indeed both on a shared basis if we consider the case of the Netherlands, to remain at home to look after the young children.

The social democratic regimes also place more emphasis on the inclusion of the individual/household in society than their corporatist counterpart. The Anglo-Saxon and southern regimes both put more emphasis on a range of objectives, although the Anglo-Saxon regimes have a heavier emphasis on income preservation. However, it must be stressed that this characterization represents the view of Muffels and Tsakloglou (2002) at the start of the 2000s. Others held somewhat different views about the positioning[7] and, as the next section discusses, these positions have clearly changed since then.[8] One caution for example is that the UK system has been much more effective than its continental counterparts in maintaining employment and avoiding long-term unemployment. This must question where the balance of policy actually lies and something nearer the centre might make more sense.

A second problem is that the simple characterization into a triangle does not reflect the nature of the differences fully. The figure shows a second overlay of where the responsibility lies for achieving the outcomes, represented by the horizontal and vertical axes bisecting the figure. On the horizontal dimension the balance between market and state is set out whereas on the vertical the balance is between responsibility of the individual and responsibility at a more aggregate level, represented by the social partners in the extreme or perhaps a wider view of society, which might be the case in a more tribal environment for example.[9] So, if the emphasis is on market solutions it is essential for the state to ensure that markets operate well, hence the emphasis in policy will be on trying to make sure that all participants are well informed and that transaction costs are low, with vibrant competition, so that it is easier to find a new job, that opportunities exist for working different numbers of hours, for a range of skills etc. Where families are important, then more of the solution is expected to be internal. This is particularly important in a regime based on insurance. In an individualistic environment each person has to arrange their own insurance. This inevitably involves a more intrusive system as a larger proportion will be exposed to a particular shock, their resources for handling such shocks will be more limited and external mechanisms will be required. Within an (extended) family arrangement there is already more opportunity for risk sharing.[10] Liebfried (1992) suggests that one of the characterizing features of the southern 'Latin Rim' countries is the lack of any clear concept of acceptable minima or a right to welfare.

The Evolution of Welfare Regimes in Recent Years

There is considerable debate about the degree to which countries belonged to the four types of welfare regime described in the previous section even at the beginning of the 1990s when the concepts were being promulgated. Since then there have been clear changes in regimes. Muffels and Fouarge (2002) argue for example that the Netherlands has moved from being in the corporatist/continental group to adopt many of the characteristics of the social democratic and liberal/Anglo-Saxon groups, with its adoption of active labour market policies and a strong move towards getting people into employment and off welfare. Dependency ratios among people of normal working age in the Netherlands had reached the position by the late 1980s that the system was unsustainable.

This move away from passive regimes and a much stronger requirement on people to seek work and reskill has also characterized the Nordic group and such ideas that would once have been attributed largely to the 'liberal' group are becoming universal. Esping-Andersen himself (1996) is rather reluctant to admit that these changes represent a shift from one category to another as he places a strong weight on history in defining the general approach. Thus adopting some 'liberal' approaches in some areas does not make the Nordic countries any the less 'Nordic'.

Perhaps the concept that typifies the change is 'flexicurity' (Madsen, 2008; Wilthagen, 2008). This concept, promoted particularly in Denmark and the Netherlands, but adopted more generally, seeks to draw a distinction between offering people security in a particular job as opposed to offering them the security of having *a* job, albeit one that may change quite frequently. It thus seeks to encourage flexible labour markets, where firms can adjust rapidly to new opportunities and new firms with innovations can enter and older firms that have become uncompetitive can exit at relatively low cost, thus leading to a faster rate of economic growth. However, at the same time it seeks to ensure that the individual employee can move smoothly from one job to another and not endure extended periods of unemployment between jobs. In practice most job changes occur without unemployment. Indeed people leave before they are fired or made redundant.

Making this happen requires good information in the labour market about opportunities, a cutting of the search costs for new jobs, increasing the ability of families to move to new locations (which also involves a framework for replacing the social capital lost in such moves) and providing ready opportunities for reskilling. It also requires good incentives for people to find new jobs and skills and avoid unemployment. Thus this is a mixture of the market approach favoured by the liberal regimes and the employment focus of the social democratic regimes.[11] However, it does not necessarily imply that all parts of the welfare system have changed in the same way – education and pensions may be treated differently for example. The EU has now explicitly adopted the ideas of flexicurity (Wilthagen, 2008), which became part of the European Employment Strategy (EES) in late 2007. It is thus inevitable that social policy in all of the member states will tend to show more of these characteristics.

Muffels and Fouarge (2002) also argue that it is probably not appropriate to treat Italy as single country. Southern Italy is clearly in the 'southern' cluster but Northern Italy might be better described as being part of the corporatist cluster, much more akin to France for example.

Much of the driving force for these changes has come through the EU itself, although each individual country, whether inside the EU or not, faces similar challenges. Not only has the whole process of opening up markets increased competition but the EU actively encourages policy learning among its members. In the field of social policy, the principal process is through the OMC (Hodson and Maher, 2001).[12] Under the OMC, the member states, with the assistance of the Commission, determine a series of objectives that are desirable in each field and share experience on best practice.[13] The Commission monitors progress, although there is a substantial element of self-assessment. Although initially annual, a longer-term view and review are now taken. While there is no compulsion for uniformity and any given objective can be achieved in a variety of ways, such an arrangement is bound to encourage a measure of convergence. The actual convergence may be exaggerated by the measured degree of convergence as this tends to list measures applied rather than an evaluation of what is achieved by them. Nevertheless because the member states are compared there will inevitably be peer pressure to act and to improve performance.

Social policy also forms part of the Lisbon Agenda and as such is associated with the achievement of a structure that will encourage an increase in productivity. Schelkle (2008) argues that, despite these factors leading to common features, the national systems are likely to retain strong elements of their own simply because of the forces of history and how embedded their particular approaches are. However, she goes on to point out that one should consider the components of welfare systems rather than trying to label the systems as a whole because each of these components is not necessarily dealt with in the same way. She suggests that there are three common features to European social models in that they address encouraging productivity, income maintenance and basic security through some form of Beveridge style generalized insurance. Nevertheless, since these dimensions can pull in different directions, a country has to decide on their balance. It cannot simply try to improve in all three dimensions in the light of the contradictions. In a detailed assessment of the Dutch social security system Bannink and Hoogenboom (2007) show that policies can be assigned to all four welfare models as providing the best description even within narrow categories such as disability or old age. They argue that such different approaches are inherent as the 'risks' involved are different. The provision of libraries or sports halls does not face the same concerns as child care or old age pensions. These characteristics are at the heart of whether universality or selectivity should be applied to a particular service.

As the EU has opened itself up internally and externally, social welfare regimes have come under pressure. Sapir (2006) argues that some regimes are prima facie unsustainable in a competitive environment whereas others are not. He uses a simple two-way classification according to efficiency and equity shown in Table 2.1 that implies that the regimes that are associated with inefficiency will have to change. (The regimes that are currently efficient may also need to keep evolving to maintain that efficiency.) Thus in his view it is the continental and Mediterranean regimes that need to change. The former because the nature of its labour laws make its labour markets inflexible and reduce the sustainable growth rate and in the latter case the inflexibility has a wider cause across the public sector. Thus it is not equity per se that matters, that choice is still available to the European countries, but having an efficient system that can cope with the demands of a competitive market. The Anglo-Saxon regime puts more emphasis on allowing market forces to operate in the welfare field than does the

Nordic regime, where the state has a much stronger role to play. That choice is therefore also open.

Table 2.1   The sustainability of welfare regimes

		Efficiency	
		Low	High
Equity	High	Continental	Nordic
	Low	Mediterranean	Anglo/Saxon

Source: Sapir, 2006.

Whether one agrees with Sapir's particular characterization or not, it is clear that market pressures have led to the evolution of welfare regimes, particularly with regard to labour markets. What is more difficult to argue is the degree to which there is an implication for the size of the public sector. Using the example of 22 OECD countries, Mayes and Virén (2002) suggest that there is some prima facie evidence that, beyond a certain point, an increasing share of the public sector in the economy has a detrimental effect on overall output. Furthermore the evidence suggests that most of the old member states are beyond that point (whereas as most of the new member states are not (yet)).

However, the observance of this relationship does not of itself imply any particular causation and hence third factors could be at work, which contribute to the finding. There is no need for us to enter this controversial debate or form a view of the validity of concepts such as the Laffer curve but the pressures that governments feel from these problems and indeed the disquiet that lenders feel and hence the price they impose on increasing debt beyond a certain point are tangible influences on social policy.

The recent financial crisis has added new problems for social welfare systems from two directions. The first is simply that like any adverse shock to the economy it puts strain on social welfare systems as incomes fall and the demands on the systems rise. This creates the normal dilemma of how far this difficulty should be borne by the present generation and how much by the future. In a properly designed system the answer should be future generations because the system is balanced (normally around a growth path). Adverse shocks today will be offset by favourable shocks tomorrow and a cushion will be available today from previous surpluses. Finland is a case in point. Despite having an adverse shock worse than the 1929 depression in terms of loss of GDP in 1992–95 it had returned to a sustainable position within 10 years and hence can weather a shock which is larger than that in most EU countries. Regrettably this is not true of most member states whose welfare systems have been based on optimistic views of growth rates and an absence of severe shocks.

The more direct impact of the financial crisis for several countries has been that it has placed a major demand on public finances that was not planned for. Someone has to pay. It could be relatively neutral for the welfare system if both the current and future extra revenues are extracted from those who are not and do not become increased beneficiaries from the system. Where the effects have been dramatic, as in the UK, Latvia, Ireland etc., this outcome is unlikely. While pensions and other insurance systems including health and unemployment can be self-financing, a substantial proportion of public services will be financed through taxation rather than through direct revenues in the form of user charges. Hence the problem cannot be avoided, although its incidence will vary considerably according to the structure of the regime.

The problem of sustainability in welfare systems is thus accentuated and brought forward in many countries but not changed in its fundamental nature. Hence the impact of recent events is likely to increase the pace of evolution of welfare systems and existing characterizations of systems within the welfare triangle will become increasingly outdated. There is no obvious way this representation can be turned into a dynamic framework but the present concerns are clearly dynamic in character and the question is how well they can cope with shocks.

In her study of the changes in social welfare systems in the UK, Germany, Sweden and Greece in recent years, Schelkle (2008) suggests that while there has been increasing communality in trying to focus on structures that will benefit the productivity and hence the standard of living of society, the member states have gone about it in clearly different ways. Thus we can avoid getting into discussions about what constitutes the European social model. Such classifications as do exist tend to describe a very broad model and are primarily concerned to set out what features distinguish European models from that in the US.[14] Classifying the UK and the US as both being 'liberal' regimes as in Esping-Andersen (1990) puts two very different approaches in the same basket – one only has to think about US complaints about 'socialized medicine' in the UK to realize the extent of the difference.

THE NEW MEMBER STATES

The welfare regimes for the 'old' member states were mainly long-standing. However, the collapse of the Soviet Union and along with it the political and economic structures in the rest of the Council for Mutual Economic Assistance (CMEA) meant that new social welfare systems had to be built. By and large the physical infrastructure and skills for the operation of such systems still existed, and in some cases were more pervasive than in some OECD countries, but the financing framework did not. Hence those based entirely on current financing, such as pensions, got into serious difficulty immediately as the source of funding dried up and inflation eroded the value of what could be paid. In areas such as health care the infrastructure in the form of hospitals and their staff remained in place but deteriorated rapidly as it became difficult to keep them in good condition, pay the staff, provide the necessary materials, medicines etc. and cope with the exit of those whose skills were much more valuable abroad. Education faced similar challenges. The basic systems were good, especially in encouraging the talented, but they faced attrition.

At the same time it was necessary to refocus the systems to a market economy. Many of the state enterprises in which people had been employed disappeared, and the way the labour market operated changed. Thus the route of financing many operations changed as they could not be financed by the sale of goods and services but through taxation. Setting up such a system was not easy and yields were initially low. The position in Poland was particularly difficult: by the end of the 1990s only half of the population of working age were in employment (Golinowska, 2009) and by 2002, 20 per cent were unemployed – all this despite the significant emigration of the workforce. The consequence was that although new well structured systems might be designed their scale could only be modest initially. However, it was also thought that the transition process would be less demanding initially and hence many schemes were over ambitious. The new schemes were therefore subject to revision, especially after the Russian crisis and default which provided a major adverse shock to what was a relatively fragile recovery. It was thus not until the turn of the century that more enduring schemes were seen. The loss of a decade meant that in effect many systems were being operated as if there were little history.

As a result, many of the new welfare systems in the new member states have characteristics that are rather different from those in the group they joined. A simple example is the nature of the tax system. Flat income taxes at relatively low rates have proved relatively popular as these tend to get both good compliance and provide strong incentives to work, work longer and seek better jobs as much of the benefits of higher pay are retained by the earner. At the same time this results in a strong element of contributions to social insurance also being income related. Not surprisingly therefore education is seen by many as a corner stone in the system, providing both human capital and social justice (Hengstenberg, 2009).

The new member states thus have welfare systems that are in many respects different from those of the older member states. It is not obvious that they should be classified together as a single group as, just as in the old member states, there is considerable variety. Simply because of the lack of income and newness the systems will provide more limited benefits than their old member state counterparts except where the infrastructure continues to operate, as it has in areas of education.

The older member states have gone through two main phases. State-provided welfare systems were introduced because existing privately provided systems, whether on a user pays or a charitable basis, were thought inadequate. In some areas, such as education and health care, they largely supplanted the private sector system. As time has gone on, both the demand for these services and the ability to pay for them has increased to the extent that private provision has grown again. In the transition countries the problem has been different. There has been an urgent need for the services in a period when the state was unable to provide properly. Thus shadow systems have grown up. Where there are skilled personnel eager to work and be paid they are happy to provide some level of service outside the official system. In the older member states the problem is that the best (and more entrepreneurial) can be bid away from the state sector.

The market is becoming increasingly international, in part because of the deliberate efforts of the EU to make freedom of movement of labour and services a reality. Thus skilled people move from the lower income countries. While some of the movement, especially of the less skilled, is clearly temporary – moving without families and remitting as much of their income home as possible before returning when they can afford the lifestyle they want – movement of the skilled may often be more permanent as they can afford to bring their families with them.

It is thus important to differentiate the provision of services through the public sector from the provision of income support, whether in the form of benefits for the young, disabled, sick and unemployed or in pensions for those who are beyond what is regarded as normal working age. Transfers whether among individuals or across time can be more directly financed. However, the transition economies faced exactly the same problem as the older member states in that at the time they introduced the schemes it was not possible for many of those in need to build up their own resources. This pushes countries towards a pay as you go system, where the current contributions go towards the financing of others' current expenditures rather than the building up of funds that can be used to support the individual's own future needs. The latter such schemes are essentially compulsory saving.[15] However, the system will nevertheless be described as insurance as the expectation is that future incomes will meet future claims.

Several countries have introduced 'two pillar' systems. The first pillar is PAYG (pay-as-you-go) with a strong element of state funding to provide minimum levels of benefit to those who are unable to make contributions themselves, such as the disabled and those who are already retired. The second pillar is funded and will increase in importance until all the working population are full members, which in many cases will not be for another 30 years.[16] The evolution of the system in Poland is of particular interest (Erdmann, 1998), as it is paid for by employer contributions. Initially the old system continued, with a rise in social benefits as a proportion of GDP. This was then replaced by a new and less generous universal system to which employees also contributed, which sought to provide such benefits on an affordable basis,[17] before the second, funded pillar could be added as incomes rose far enough to make it plausible.

It thus appears that there are two characteristics to the social welfare regimes in the new member states that are of particular relevance to the present analysis. First, that while the regimes in these states have many similar features as a result of the common problems that they faced, they also have many differences. Second, these regimes run across the existing four-group classification of the old member states. While some may be near enough to one or other model many cannot well be classified as belonging to any specific group. The case of Poland, as described by Golinowska (2009), see Table 2.2, has elements of three of the four regimes. According to Golinowska, Ksiezopolski (2004) labels this a 'paternalistic-market hybrid'.

The point is not that the new member states form a coherent fifth model that should be added to the existing four, but that the changes among the older member states and the variety of the new member states mean that the neatness of classification is breaking down. While there has been some convergence, it is not at present reasonable to suggest that the four models can be replaced by a generic European model of which the 27 member states have various varieties. The position is simply more complex with a degree of cross fertilization. One irony noted by

*Table 2.2   The position of Poland according to the features of the
Esping-Andersen welfare state regimes*

Welfare state regimes	Decom- modification	Defamiliali- zation	Private- public mix	Social ties and social capital	Inequalities
Liberal	X				X
Conservative		X			
Social democratic					
Southern European			X	X	

Sources: Golinowska, 2009; Ksiezopolski, 2004.

Golinowska et al. (2009) is that non-governmental institutions are usually not very well developed in the new member states and hence collective action has to be more state based than in the older member states.

Some Examples from Health Care Systems

Health care systems in the new member states have had to undergo major changes in structure – 'Big R' reforms in the terminology of Berman and Bossert (2000). We illustrate what this implies by taking the cases of Poland, the Czech Republic and Estonia, which between them cover large, medium and small-sized countries. However, our choice of countries is in part driven by the availability of the data. While these countries have clearly different systems, they faced a common problem and their solutions to it have many common features. This helps to illustrate how the new member states have welfare characteristics which mean that they do not obviously belong to one or other of the pre-existing groups in the welfare triangle.

Poland

In the Communist era, Poland's state system was highly centralized with a welfare system that provided a uniform framework. There was little scope for tailoring the system at the local level for individuals' needs and priorities. Following the collapse of that regime, Poland underwent massive reforms of the state that covered public administration, the judicial system, education, social insurance and security, and the welfare system. The Polish pension system is primarily based on defined contributions, where both employees and employers contribute 16.26 per cent of salary, divided 9.76 per cent and 6.5 per cent respectively between a pension scheme and a social insurance scheme for disability and survivor benefits. This is subject to minimum pensions, where any shortfall (based on contributions) is paid by the state. The schemes are not funded and work on a PAYG basis. However, this has been subject to the introduction of an additional new, funded pension scheme in 1999, voluntary for those between 30 and 50 years old and compulsory for those workers aged 30 and under at the date of its introduction. The resulting system with its two components is similar to that which was introduced in Sweden in the 1990s (somewhat contradicting the precepts of the traditional Scandinavian model). The contributions are invested in some 15 different private funds (originally 21 when the scheme was introduced) but the three largest have 55 per cent of the total between them (Wiktorow, 2007).

In general terms, the current Polish public health care system follows the model of universal provision but is attempting to produce an element of choice for the individual and competition among providers. The system in many respects resembles those in the UK and New Zealand for example.

Poland initiated its health care reforms effectively on 1 January, 1999. The previous health care system suffered from lack of financing, bureaucracy and centralized administration, and low rewards for medical personnel (Regulski, 1999). Poland also suffered from a growing 'grey market', reflecting the expanding distance between the need for medical services and the actual possibility of getting the service through the public system (Regulski, 1999). The initial development of the new regime reflected clear differences of view among the political parties. Health care reforms in 1990, immediately after the collapse of the Communist regime, were mostly crafted by the minority social democratic wing of the Liberal party – the Freedom Union (UW). The Liberals' 1992–93 reform proposal included establishing regional health care bodies responsible for financing and planning, contracting with regional health care providers, restricting privatization of health care providers, and combining hospital and ambulance care. Solidarity, on the other hand, proposed greater roles for small independent insurance institutions, privatization of health care providers and decision-making empowerment of physicians and a clear separation between hospital services and the ambulance service (Bossert and Wlodarczyk, 2000). Solidarity's proposals were supported by the post-Communist and peasant parties. However, when the post-Communist and peasant parties won the election in 1993, they implemented the Liberals' proposals but introduced market competition and de-emphasized the integration of hospital and ambulance care provision. The Solidarity-Liberals coalition, which won the 1997 election, rejected the acts passed by the previous government and adopted health care reform plans much closer to the ones they suggested in 1992–93. The health care system after the 1997 election still reflected the Liberals' proposals because of the intervention of the then Liberal finance minister, Leszek Balcerowicz. Solidarity's proposed fully independent health care funds were predicted to lead to state debts and the government resorted to establishing large regional health care institutions, instead of small independent ones. The regional institutions have no powers over funds and premium collections. Funds were transferred to these regional health care funds through the state's social insurance system. Doctors and physicians did not possess bargaining mechanisms with the funds and fee-for-service. The boards of the funds were assigned by regional assemblies rather than general election, which was what was initially proposed. In summary, the Solidarity government deviated from the initial reform initiatives. The 1999 reform resulted in 16 regional insurance funds and one supervisory body to ensure uniform services. The 2004 reform exercise in the country established the National Health Fund, with 16 regional departments.

Increasing role of private health care providers

Poland's health care system before the 1990 reforms was defined by highly centralized and hierarchical administrative bureaucracy (McMenamin and Timonen, 2002). Market mechanisms were introduced into the health care system in the 1990 reform plan to try to ensure increased quality and efficiency in the national health care services. The increasing role of private sector health care providers was intended to create market competition between health care providers and, in turn, improve the quality of health care services. Some private hospitals were set up in combination with public and black market practices (McMenamin and Timonen, 2002). Rising direct payments in health care, primarily to private health care providers in Poland after the fall of the Berlin Wall, were linked to the health care reforms in the country (Maarse, 2006). The private health care providers are thought to be more able to provide rapid and better health care services, compared to public ones.

The number of private health care providers increased rapidly over the reform period. Tyszko et al. (2007) report that no private outpatient health care institutions existed prior to 1999 in either urban or rural Poland. In 1999, 2248 non-public outpatient clinics emerged (2047 in urban areas and only 201 in rural areas). By 2005, the number of non-public outpatient clinics increased to 9015 (7151 in urban areas and

1864 in rural areas), a 75 per cent increase over 1999 to 2005. A similar
trend was observed for non-public medical practices in the urban and
rural areas. A trend within the health care provision has been to combine
private practices with part-time public sector employment (Maarse, 2006)
so that both institutions and individuals provide a combination of
privately and publicly funded services. Privatization of hospitals, on the
other hand, was not as rapid as for outpatient clinics. In 1995, there were
only nine private hospitals, 0.07 per cent of the total number of hospitals
in the country. The number increased to 72 in 2003, and 147 in 2004
(Tyszko et al., 2007). However, the emergence of private health care
providers in Poland should more accurately be defined as the
re-introduction/reconstruction of the practice, rather than a novel incident. Private health care providers existed during the pre-Communist
period in the country until such practices were banned when the
Semashko-type of health care system[18] was introduced. Nonetheless, the
re-emergence of private health care providers in Poland can be considered as demand-led privatization.[19]

Financing/funding
The first aspect of the health care system to be reformed was the
financing methods. State ownership of hospitals and other medical
institutions was also abolished, except for teaching medical institutions.
Under the first insurance bill, employees paid a contribution rate of 10 to
11 per cent. In 1998, the contribution rate was reduced to 7.5 per cent as
part of personal income tax (hypothecated tax). In 2000, the contribution
rate was raised to 7.75 per cent due to intensive pressure from several
groups, especially medical representatives, who had envisaged the 1999
health care reform as bringing increases in the sources of public health
care finances. The contribution rate increased again to 8 per cent in 2003
and to 9 per cent in 2007. Premium fees are collected by the Social
Insurance Institutions (ZUS) Kasy Chorych (or Patients' Funds) and then
distributed to 16 regional Patients' Funds, each covering an administrative region. The fund was set up to be managed by a board chosen by
each regional council. The fees that people pay do not reflect the level of
their health risks, just their income.

Each working person in Poland selects a Patients' Fund to which he or
she will contribute, normally following the area of residence. However,
everyone is allowed to move their contributions to another fund, as they
see fit, especially when the other fund delivers better medical service
than the one they were subscribed to. Each person has a signed contract
with his/her selected fund, and is allowed to choose a family doctor and
a preferred medical institution. Only certain medical services are fully

covered for the insured and any excess has to be covered out of his/her own pocket or private health insurance. There were disruptions to the health care funding reforms. Distribution of funds was delayed, and the government resorted to giving loans to the health funds just to keep the new system going; funds were insufficient to cover health care expenditures (McMenamin and Timonen, 2002).

Health care premiums for those on low incomes and specialized medical treatments are to be borne by the state, thus the national health insurance system covers all citizens and their dependents. Hospitals and other medical health care institutions receive payments for their services according to the contracts, and those that deliver better medical services should be able to attract more clients. This should in theory create healthy competition among health care providers and help improve health care service quality in the country. However, as other countries have found, reality is more challenging.

Three main competition-enhancing mechanisms exist within the health care system.

1. Competition between purchasers. People residing in a particular region are automatically subscribed to the regional patients' fund, but they are allowed to change funds even to those outside their region, according to the level of services. Because premiums paid by workers are not paid according to their health risks, this competition creates equity problems because those with low health risks pay for others with serious medical conditions.
2. Competition between health care providers (for contracts). The reform efforts allowed private and public health care providers – hospitals, clinics, and laboratories – to bid for contracts to service the funds.
3. Competition between health care providers (for patients).

In practice patients do not have a real choice of health care providers. Patients may be allowed to choose their own GPs, but only GPs who have signed contracts with their health funds. Only those who are prepared to pay extra out of their own pockets have the real choice of their own preferred GPs. Those who are willing to pay extra, in effect jump the queue for free medical services and unreferred treatment.

The state also contributes to the financing of the health care system through allocating funds for public health programmes, training and developing medical care personnel and medical research, setting standards and quality for the medical services, funding the national health care investments and generally overseeing the entire performance and services of the medical institutions. Medical education in Poland was not up to EU standards, especially in family medicine (GPs). Efforts were made to re-energize GP practices in Poland by retraining medical professionals and building a dedicated family medicine department at the Jagiellonian University, Krakow.

With the introduction of market mechanisms within the health care industry in Poland, the remuneration and wages of medical personnel and practitioners remained low (McMenamin and Timonen, 2002). However, the practice of informal payments to medical practitioners increased their average income to above that of the population average (Chawla et al., 1998). This bypassing of the system results in unequal medical services and access to health care services (Scully, 2007; McMenamin and Timonen, 2002). Those who are willing to pay for unreferred medical services out of their own pockets are institutionalizing the informal payment practices within the health care system. However, by permitting the low wages it does mean that the basic system can be more affordable.

The increase in health care spending in Poland after the reforms and the fall of the Berlin Wall came mainly from the increase in direct private payments to health care providers (Maarse, 2006), with the result that the burden for the average Polish household increased rapidly after the reforms.

The role of family doctors (GPs) was initially to act as gatekeepers to specialized treatment, and the overall primary health care services. The outpatient treatment and hospital admission rate in Poland was considerably higher than those in countries with similar levels of wealth (Berman, 1998), reflecting their greater emphasis in preference to GP facilities.

In summary
The Polish Health Ministry has been criticized for placing greater emphasis on developing and refining the grand reform efforts of the health care system, while doing very little to implement the proposed changes (McMenamin and Timonen, 2002). A study of citizens' perception of the health care reform in 2000 revealed that 77 per cent of the respondents thought the current system was worse than that prior to reform (*Warsaw Business Journal*, 7–13 February, 2000). Patients were uncertain regarding which hospitals they can go to, and how payments for the health care services are made. This dissatisfaction with the health care reforms was worse than that with the government. Furthermore, the introduction of market mechanisms into the health care system was insufficient without the fundamental changes to support market forces (Berman, 1998). The separation between the authorities that fund/finance health care and those that provide health care created an 'illusory'

bargaining system, because in effect local government representatives are those who sit on health funds and own the public health care providers (McMenamin and Timonen, 2002). The health funds were not adhering to the constrained health care budgets, as the reforms intended. The introduction of private health care practices in the system was not successful in improving health care services, according to McMenamin and Timonen (2002). Moral hazard also arose when public hospitals felt obliged to accept more patients just to secure more state funding (McMenamin and Timonen, 2002). There remain disparities in the level of health care delivery services between areas, with big cities like Warsaw having far bigger capacity for health care services than smaller, less densely populated cities. The current health care system suffers from systemic inefficiencies and inadequate resources, while the demand for health care rises with the ageing population. The current reform efforts also did not closely scrutinize issues of medical personnel's remuneration and incentive system.

Political problems attached to health care reform are said to pose even greater challenges. Low salaries of health care practitioners and professionals threatened the health care system. Protests by health care professionals increased, with demands for a pay rise of over 30 per cent in 2006 and a rise of over 100 per cent in 2007 (Komorovsky, 2006). Doctors in Poland worked more than 100 hours a week, while earning only 1400 to 1550 zloty monthly (350 to 390 euro). The government's delayed response to the demands of the health care professionals added to the low regard in which medical professionals were held in the country.

The EU enlargement has also contributed challenges to the Polish health care system. Free movement of health care professionals could contribute to an even more acute shortage in a system already in crisis. On the other hand, the potential increased flows of health care professionals from other EU states into Poland might bring competition into the provision of health care services and in effect increase the quality of health care services (Zajac, 2004). Those who choose to leave Poland to seek opportunities in the larger EU states are most likely to be the young and best qualified, further depriving Poland of good medical practitioners.

The monopoly of the National Health Fund is also a cause for concern. The National Health Fund has already been heavily criticized for its inefficiency in addressing the fundamental problems of the Polish health care system (Krajewski-Siuda and Romaniuk, 2008).

The lack of political consensus in Poland has been argued to be the single most important contributor to the delayed implementation and execution of health care reforms in the country. The direction of Poland's health care reforms and other social structures is dictated by the principles of the ruling government (Krajewski-Siuda and Romaniuk, 2008). The frequent changes of Poland's Health Ministers (six ministers from 2001 to 2005) further added to the complications of the reform process (Kozierkiewicz et al., 2005).

Health funds are linked to the local government authorities and have been posing problems for the efficiency of the entire system. Health care reforms in Poland were executed much later and are less market-oriented than those of other transition economies such as the Czech Republic and Hungary (Bossert and Wlodarczyk, 2000). Nevertheless it is possible to be overcritical. Health care outcomes such as life expectancy improved during the 1990s (Golinowska, 2009). However, this could be attributable to an improved diet and access to better medicines on the opening up to the west and later to the growth in incomes.

Estonia

Health system reform efforts in Estonia started in 1991, when the government introduced a social health insurance system (Habicht and Kunst, 2005). The system was fundamentally based on the solidarity principle. The intended outcome of the health system reform in Estonia was to provide health care services to citizens, regardless of their income or financial situation. People are covered through health insurance funds collected as an earmarked payroll tax. The previous health care system was funded by the state, and the reform efforts shifted to a compulsory health insurance system with an employers' contribution of a flat 13 per cent rate on monthly income. (There is also a 20 per cent contribution towards pensions, making a total 'social tax' of 33 per cent.) Among adults, only students, pensioners and some part-time employees are exempt although there is a cap on the contribution of sole traders. Unemployment insurance is separate, funded by a combination of employer and employee contributions.[20] The state provides for those who are not able to participate in employment, through old age or disability as such people have had no ability to build up insurance before the new regime started. At present the emphasis is still very much on this state provision, given the number of pre-existing pensioners and the lack of time for new pensioners to build up much funding.

Prior to the reforms, the health care system in Estonia was described as 'inefficient' and was mainly focused on institutional care (Koppel et al., 2003). Primary health care was almost non-existent because family medical care was provided by different specialists in different policlinics.

The main aims of primary health care reforms in Estonia were twofold: to introduce family medicine in the Estonian health care system and to reform remuneration packages for primary care doctors and practitioners.

In the first half of the 1990s, there was a second wave of health care reforms along with a decentralized system of health care planning and delivery (Habicht and Kunst, 2005). The Estonian Health Project (1995–99) was launched with financial support from the World Bank. The national and local health promotion projects are financed by the Estonian Health Insurance Fund. Estonia's Ministry of Social Affairs was established in 1993, merging several previous ministries – Health, Social Welfare and Labour. The ministry is responsible for developing health care policies and health care development plans.

In 1997, a third wave of health care reforms was launched. Estonia was ready to launch a more efficient public health system. The primary health care reform was introduced, with general practitioners to function as gatekeepers for increased quality of primary health care services (Habicht and Kunst, 2005). The incentive system of primary care doctors was also reformed. Changes to the family doctors' incentive system were introduced in 1997, and implemented in 1998.

The reform efforts of the primary health care system were intended to achieve the desired results in 2003. All residential areas in the country would receive continuous primary health care from well-trained family doctors. Family doctors would function as gatekeepers to more serious health care services and treatments. People are required to register with a primary care doctor – an independent doctor contracted by the state/Health Insurance Fund. Prior to these reforms, family doctors earned monthly salaries, but post reform in 1998, family doctors were paid on capitation payments, with additional minor payments and fees-for-service. The state allocated funds for primary health care to counties based on the population, with capitation fees of 15 Estonian kroons (EEK) per person per month in 1998 (about one euro). The weights were readjusted in 1999 to be 20 EEK for children under 2, 16 EEK for persons aged 2–69, and 18 EEK for people over 70.

The most recent wave of health care reforms in Estonia was in 2001, when a centralized system for acute in-patient care and high technology medicine was introduced to improve the quality of hospital services. A modern and all-inclusive long-term nursing care system was also introduced as part of the final wave of reforms in the country. The Health Care Board was established in 2002 to ensure health care quality and improvements. This is a governing authority responsible for issuing licenses and registering and administering private health care practices, governing patients' complaints and appraisals of the quality of health care services, and coordinating the roles and responsibilities of the board of health care professionals.

The Estonian Health Insurance Fund provides funding for disease prevention and health promotion activities in 2005. In line with the aim of the Estonian health care reform to introduce family medicine in the system, family medicine courses and retraining programmes were introduced in 1991. Later, in 1993, the family medicine postgraduate training programme was upgraded to a medical specialism (Koppel et al., 2003).

Estonians on higher incomes now face a choice of publicly or privately provided health care (Aidukaite, 2009).[21]

Achievements (of health reforms)

Since the health system reforms of 1993–95, several improvements to the health of the population are evident. Life expectancy increased for men (from 65 in 1990 to 67 in 2005) and for women (from 75 in 1990 to 78 in 2005), infant mortality per 1000 live births decreased from 11.9 in 1992 to 3.3–5.6 in 2005 (Polluste et al., 2005) and this was attributed to the improvement of, and better access to, health care services in Estonia (O'Connor and Bankauskaite, 2008). However, inequalities of health care service utilization can still be observed (Habicht and Kunst, 2005). Differences in health care utilization in Estonia were by far the largest in socio-economic dimensions (income, education level and employment) (Habicht and Kunst, 2005). Estonians with higher socio-economic status were more likely to use health care services compared to those of lower socio-economic status (Habicht and Kunst, 2005). Differences in terms of the use of GPs were also found among rural and urban residents, with the rural residents being more likely to use telephone consultation and GP visits. Urban residents were more likely to use outpatient medical services.

Czech Republic

Historically, the Czech Republic had a Bismarckian system of social and health insurance, inherited from the health care system of the Czechoslovak Republic, which included the modern day Czech Republic before the division of the Czech and Slovak lands.[22] These health policies derived from the Austro-Hungarian Empire of which Czechoslovakia was part before independence after the First World War and the onset of the Communist regime in 1948. Universal coverage, tax financing, and state-owned and controlled health care facilities defined the old health care system in the Republic (Výborna, 1995; Oswald, 2000) but the Bismarckian approach has appeared rather more strongly in the Czech

Republic than in the other Visegrad countries (Hungary, Poland and Slovakia) (Potůček, 2004).

The Czech pension scheme is largely defined benefit in nature, with employees contributing 6.5 per cent of earnings and employers 28 per cent. The payments take the form of a flat rate sum plus an earnings related element based on 1.5 per cent of the earnings base for each year worked (Aspalter et al., 2009). The social insurance scheme, which has separate cash sickness and maternity benefits, and medical benefits elements, is financed by employees contributing 5.6 per cent of earnings and employers 12.3 per cent of earnings. It is administered by the state through the Ministry of Labour and Social Affairs (Aspalter et al., 2009).

The Czech Republic's health care system underwent dramatic reforms and liberalization beginning in 1990 (Vepřek et al., 1995; Výborna, 1995; Oswald, 2000). Democratization of the state was in place and the principle of free choice of health care facility commenced. The process saw the end of the large regional and health authorities. The General Health Insurance Fund Act and the Act on the General Health Insurance Fund (GHIF) were approved in 1991. With the introduction of the Acts, the health care system in the Czech Republic moved to a compulsory health insurance model, with contractual health care provision by a number of insurers (Rokosová and Havá, 2005). In summary, the new system is characterized by compulsory universal coverage.

The 1990s saw more changes and improvements being implemented into the Czech Republic's health care system. The health care facilities and authorities experienced a major overhaul and a new system of home care was set up. Privatization of primary health care, the pharmaceutical industry, pharmacies and health support firms were also well under way.

As in most of the new member states, the first step in the health care sector involved the decentralization of previously state-owned health care institutions. The legal basis in the Czech Republic was the introduction of the Health Care in Nongovernmental Health Care Facilities Act in April 1992. The state-owned District Institutes of National Health were dismantled. Under the old health care system, the country had several regional authorities, and these regional authorities were further split into district authorities (Oswald, 2000). Citizens were assigned a primary physician, who acted as the gatekeeper to specialized care. Doctors and medical personnel also received minimum wages (Oswald, 2000; Lawson and Nemec, 2003).

Under the new system, health care is available to all permanent residents of the Czech Republic and non-residents of the country who work in companies, firms and organizations which are legally registered in the Republic. All health insurance funds are legally bound to accept any persons who meet the criteria for belonging to the health care system. Any person is allowed to change health insurance fund only once in a 12 month period. Those who do not meet the criteria for participating in the statutory health insurance fund can sign up with a contractual health insurance fund. Those who do not fulfill the terms and conditions of the statutory health insurance may take up voluntary insurance with the GHIF.

Hospital administration and operations and specialized tertiary-care medical institutions in the Republic are under the Ministry of Health. Interestingly, however, the central government has not been able to secure legal authority over all hospital care; there are some hospitals that are owned by limited liability firms.

While the early period may have had a rather more market based element to it than in some of the other new member states, during the period 1998–2006 the various Czech governments were dominated by the Social Democratic Party. Nevertheless, simple market pressures led to both privatization of health and social care facilities and the launching of voluntary social and health insurance schemes (Potůček, 2009).

Health care financing
Financing for the Czech Republic's health care systems after the reforms came from five different sources:

1. Payments to health insurance
2. Contributions from the state government
3. Contributions from the local government
4. Direct payments to health care providers, and
5. Others (such as donations).

Figure 2.2 illustrates the health care financing structure in the Czech Republic. The state contributes for those citizens without taxable income. These groups of people include pensioners, children, women on maternity leave, registered unemployed, disabled citizens and those who are eligible to receive social allowance, soldiers and prisoners. The working population pays 4.5 per cent of their taxable income, while self-employed citizens contribute 13.5 per cent of 35 per cent of their taxable income. Employers' contributions to employees' health insurance make up 9 per cent of taxable income.[23]

All citizens must be registered with an insurance institution. The General Health Insurance Fund (GHIF) and branch health insurance funds were set up in 1992 when the health insurance system was

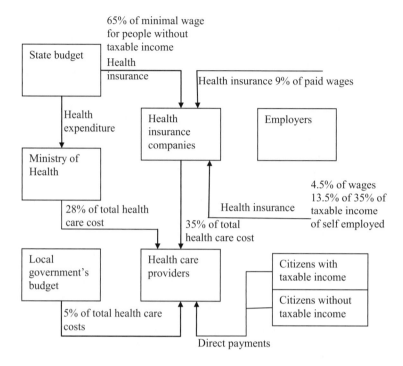

Source: Adapted from Vyborna, 1995.

Figure 2.2 Health care financing in the Czech Republic

implemented (Rokosová and Havá, 2005). The state is the major share-holder of the GHIF (Vyborna, 1995). The GHIF accepts all people who are not registered with any regional or national health insurance institution.

In theory, the new health system was designed to ensure that all citizens of the Czech Republic received health care regardless of their incomes.

Health care providers, on the other hand, received a fee-for-service payment from the state government for health care services rendered. Under the old health care system, health care providers received state grants and budgets according to the number of staff employed, their service capacity and the type of health care institution.

In addition to the GHIF, the state introduced market competition into the health care system, and at one point, the Czech Republic had 19 health insurance companies (Vyborna, 1995). Competition between the health insurance companies prompted some of them to target only those people with high incomes and low health risks. Private health insurance companies also used advertising campaigns that were criticized by the GHIF as wasting money that could have been spent on more efficient health care services. Another tactic by the private health insurance companies to maximize their profits was to encourage the insured to take out extra cover for drugs and services not otherwise listed under the Fee-for-Services and Drugs and Other Medications Price List. (Each medical service and operation was listed and valued according to a points system, and an amount of direct material costs associated with the service. The price (or points and costs) for each medical service was determined by GHIF. The points and costs for each service serve as the basis for fee-for-services rendered by health care institutions.) While this expanded the cover for people it enabled the companies to move into areas where the GHIF could not compete.

This fee-for-service system of health care service payments motivated health care providers to increase their quantity of medical services to clients without much regard to the level of quality of the medical services (Vepřek et al., 1995). The price list was also initially established without comprehensive tests of its feasibility, and was published in a rather rushed manner according to Vepřek et al. (1995). In the second stage of health care reform in the Republic in 1997, more reforms were introduced in the Czech Republic. The fee-for-service and the price list were replaced by a weighted capitation system with increased health care regulations and policies in place (Lian, 2008).

The state introduced a redistribution system for collected health insurance contributions. Health insurance companies were required to surrender 60 per cent of collected contributions and allocations from the state to a special account administered by the GHIF. These sums were then redistributed to health insurance companies according to the normalized health contributions (average contribution for those from over 60 years of age had a weight of three) times the number of insured clients (again with those over 60 years old having a weight of three) (Vyborna, 1995).

Health care reforms in the Czech Republic were criticized by Vyborna (1995) for increased administrative costs (and hence health care costs) due to the setting up of new health care insurance companies, the weakness of the reimbursement system (for private health care providers), and the Fee-for-Service Price List, which inflated the prices of health care services (Vyborna, 1995). Technicalities with the calculation of the newly introduced Fee-for-Service Price List and the reimbursement systems were blamed for hindering the reform exercise. The set up of the

GHIF was also controversial. The institution's largely ambiguous dual roles, as health care provider *and* regulator blurred the transparency of the entire health care system (Výborna, 1995). In theory the increased competition should have stimulated innovation and efficiency, offsetting any increase in costs from the more complex system.

However, currently only nine health insurance companies have survived in the Republic, collectively holding only a 25 per cent market share (Oswald, 2000; Lawson and Nemec, 2003). The demise of the private health insurance companies in the Czech Republic was attributed to their lack of experience in the health sector, leading to an inefficient reimbursement system (Oswald, 2000). The introduction of privately held insurance companies and subsequently competition into the health care system brought negative impacts. Private health insurance companies targeted the young, healthy and rich populations, leaving the unemployed, the elderly, children, the poor, and those with the highest health risks insured under the GHIF. The situation has led the heavily subsidized government agency to be responsible for the sickest and riskiest population in the country. The GHIF now operates almost as a monopoly, controlling more than half of the insured population in the Czech Republic.

Overall analysis
Výborna (1995) suggests that the health care reforms were directed towards a market-based health care system, and to facilitating citizens' personal responsibility for their state of health. The health care system was dramatically reorganized only once (in 1990). However, even when the health care system was targeted for further reform (in light of other parts of the social system, such as pensions and education), the reforms and national health policies were inconsistent. This is attributed to the turbulent political system in the Republic, changing the Minister of Health 13 times from 1990 to 2010. The frequent shift of the topmost position in the ministry led to inconsistencies and ambiguities in health care policies.

The current health care system of the Czech Republic is a step back towards some of the practices of the old Communist regime. For example, patients were excluded from the Republic's policy design and implementation throughout the reforms, which was largely the practice in the old regime (Lawson and Nemec, 2003), and now the health care insurance system is a near monopoly by the GHIF (Oswald, 2000).

The GP sector still operates on the list system, with a weighted capitation payment system. Informal payments are still practised (Lian, 2008). Local managerial influence on the GP system remained unchanged and low, while systems for administering quality of GP services are weak (Lian, 2008).

In summary, the Czech Republic has undergone massive reforms to its health care system, and experienced one of the highest increases in health care spending among the new EU countries. Provision of health care has succeeded in meeting the needs of the wider population (Rokosová and Havá, 2005). The accession to the EU also saw the adoption of new legal acts to keep abreast of other EU members.

The benefit system is of particular interest in that the changes of 1995 introduced an element of means testing which managed to make the system much more closely focused on benefits to children and to reduce its cost (Coulter et al., 1997). To try to make the various schemes more affordable, the retirement age has been increased incrementally and the average pension has fallen as a percentage of average income (although it has not fallen in absolute terms) (Potůček, 2009).

IMPLICATIONS

The analysis in this chapter is only illustrative, as a comprehensive study would be prohibitively expensive. Nevertheless it is possible to draw on other partial studies, such as that by Schelkle (2008), and some common features emerge.

The most important implication from the findings of this chapter is that there is no single model that applies to welfare regimes. In many cases this applies not just among the EU countries but within each country because they do not treat each aspect of the welfare system in the same manner. Thus for example pensions may be based largely on the ability of the individual concerned to fund the pension during their lifetime, whereas schooling may be something that is fully funded irrespective of the means, current or past, of the parents. Even within education, treatment may not be uniform, with people expected to pay in full for their own vocational training and at least in part for the costs of university. To some extent this may reflect the relative balance between public and private benefits. This entails that the size of community relevant for the decision-making over the system will itself vary from the individual to the whole of the EU where transfers are required across borders.

However, there has been a degree of convergence among the member states assisted by the forces of globalization and the process of open coordination in the EU. This convergence has not been towards a single one of the four pre-existing regimes in the 'old' member states but it has moved them towards features that encourage efficiency and productivity. Thus there has been an increasing focus on active labour market measures and a move towards permitting increasing flexibility in the operation of labour markets. At the same time the focus of social policy has become wider, with an enhanced focus on trying to ensure inclusion in society and not simply income (poverty avoidance) and employment.

Economic pressures from the inability to increase debt much further – emphasized by the recent financial crisis – and pressures from ageing have meant that the overall budget has had to be revised.

The new member states have also contributed to a change away from a relatively straightforward characterization into four general regimes: Anglo-Saxon, continental/corporatist, Nordic/social democratic and Mediterranean/southern. They have faced extreme pressures because of the collapse of the funding mechanism for much of existing social welfare and the need to progress rapidly to an adequate new system that is financially viable. This has inevitably resulted in a greater weight on privately provided support and grey services outside official regimes as people have sought solutions, particularly in health care. These pressures have also affected mobility and labour markets, as skilled providers of public services and those who want them have sought employment opportunities and higher incomes elsewhere.[24] The focus in many of these new systems has been on incentives. Thus there has been a strong insurance element in pension and health care systems to encourage contributions from those who expect to be beneficiaries in the future. At the same time income tax systems have tended to have low and, in several cases, flat rates in order both to encourage people to work and increase their skills as they will retain much of their earnings, and to encourage them to declare their incomes.

There is some disagreement over the characterization of the regimes in the new member states. Aspalter et al. (2009), for example, argue that the Czech Republic, Hungary, Poland and Slovenia can be classified as continental/corporatist regimes as they have a 'Bismarkian' approach to social insurance. Deacon (2000) on the other hand suggests that the social welfare systems of the European transition countries are a cross between the Continental and Scandinavian models. The Nordic dual earner model certainly seems apparent in Estonia, possibly reflecting the extent of help received from Finnish experts in getting the system operating (Aidukaite, 2009).[25] Given the extent of means testing in some cases this would also introduce elements of the Anglo-Saxon system, suggesting that these regimes are something of a hybrid. The label of 'post socialist regime' has been applied by some (Aidukaite, 2009), in particular to the Baltic States, where the low levels of income have meant that benefits have had to be vey modest. It is, however, worthy of note that in general they have not followed the advice of the World Bank to create funded systems and have bowed to the economic pressures by using a PAYG approach (Casey, 2004). However, all such generalizations are subject to exception. Latvia for example has implemented a substantial funded pension scheme, which makes it far more like the Anglo-Saxon model, although there the terms are much less controlled.

Although the advent of the new member states has in some respects increased the competitive pressures, as incomes rise so the new member states have been able to expand their systems and convergence has been a clearly bi-directional process. Many of the pressures have come from outside the EU, either literally in the sense of competition, from China in particular, or because the forces are general, such as ageing, and not dependent on the process of closer integration. In so far as there has been increased mobility then this increases the complexity to which democratic processes have to respond. (Some of the mobility has been decidedly temporary as people have moved without their families and look to return when they can be assured of adequate income. Migrants have not been a drain on the social welfare systems in the host countries as the point of their migration is to work and if the job disappears then they tend to return home rather than be unemployed and away from home.)

There thus seem to be two forces at work, which are resulting in a more complex picture than the clear classification set out by Esping-Andersen (1990). Member states have adopted some of the best features of other regimes, encouraged by the deliberate policy learning mechanisms such as OMC in the EU. Moreover they have not necessarily applied them uniformly within the social welfare system, but have rather produced hybrid systems. Second, while all member states have been stressed by the forces of globalization that drive them to address sustainability, the new member states have had to develop systems that work in the short run but nevertheless take account of the lack of funding and lower income levels. While there is a temptation to label at least some of the new members as constituting a distinct fifth regime, perhaps a better characterization is simply to suggest that the boundaries are no longer so distinct and there are now more overlaps, without an overarching structure that would enable them to be labelled as being part of an identifiable and distinctive European social model in anything but a very general sense.

NOTES

1. Arts and Gelissen (2002) provide a very helpful survey of the different studies that have been made since the original Esping-Andersen (1990) book on the issue and tabulate the various suggestions. Most opt for four regimes, with some remaining with three including Esping-Andersen himself and one suggesting five. However, the nature of the fourth regime differs quite a lot and in several cases is not equivalent in any sense to the southern or Mediterranean regime, so five remains a possible set.

2. Social welfare is an inherently interesting topic in this regard as many of the main pressures on it come from the process of integration in the EU, yet the policy area remains a national responsibility (Scharpf, 2002).

3. Interestingly the Anglo-Saxon literature on the subject tends to concentrate on 'how much' while the continental literature tends to focus on 'how' (Arts and Gelissen, 2002).

4. Indeed it is important to recognize that where norms are widely shared in society there is little need for state intervention to ensure that they are followed.

5. It is important to recall that Esping-Andersen (1990) does not cover all aspects of what are these days considered to be policies related to social welfare and hence some of the excluded areas do not fit well into his classification (Gough, 2000).

6. Arts and Gelissen (2002) suggest that the Esping-Andersen analysis uses a simple two dimensional classification according to 'commodification' (the degree to which a service is provided as a right) and 'social stratification' (the degree to which equalization is promoted. If one divides each of these dimensions into 'high' and 'low' then this will give four and not three categories and hence leads to a discussion of what might fill the missing box. Castles and Mitchell (1993) suggest that the Antipodean countries might form this fourth case as they combine a liberal regime with a culture of equality.

7. European Commission (2000) has as one of its main conclusions 'the standard (Esping-Andersen) paradigm for comparative analysis of social models needs review if it is to retain its usefulness for guiding policy development in contemporary Europe' (p. 6).

8. In 1997 the structure of the system in the UK reflected more than 17 years of rule by the Conservative party, whereas by late 2009 it reflected more than 12 consecutive years of Labour party rule.

9. In the New Zealand case for example one might distinguish between the traditional responsibility of the individual whanau or extended families compared with the larger concept of iwi, which has achieved more political importance in recent years as governments have sought to get agreement on a broader scale across Maori.

10. It is surprising (to the authors at any rate) how much countries differ in their willingness to share family risks. In the US for example the family is a common source of finance for small scale enterprise, whereas this is less common in some European countries where banks will normally be the prime lender. It is not clear that this difference stems from experience in risk exposure or clear differences in risk appetite.

11. The generosity of the unemployment benefit and its terms might be the only distinguishing feature between a social democratic and an Anglo-Saxon regime following this approach.

12. Social policy was taken into the open method as a result of the agreement in the Lisbon Council of 2000 – it covers, in particular, actions to eradicate poverty and to tackle social exclusion.

13. Within the social area the OMC has focused on four areas: full employment, social inclusion, pensions, health and long-term care (Hengstenberg, 2009).

14. Golinowska et al. (2009) offer a typical description of the characteristics of such a European model (pp. 15–16):

    - simultaneous and proportional economic and social development
    - emphasis on innovation and a knowledge based economy
    - active employment policy
    - decent and equalized living standards
    - common values: equality, solidarity, subsidiarity
    - social dialogue and social participation
    - social inclusion
    - the significant role of state social policy.

    Some countries clearly match this better than others and in many respects it is an aspiration rather than a description.

15. There are limits even within these systems to the degree to which the future income can be assured, as the beneficiary can always borrow against that future income stream if they can find a willing lender.

16. There is a third pillar comprising contributions to private voluntary schemes, which is available in any country.

17. The contribution rate to cover this was approximately 50 per cent, a much higher burden than in most other countries.

18. Nikolai Aleksandrovich Semashko (1874–1949) was a medical doctor and a politician. The Semashko-type of health care system was introduced in the CEE/CIS countries after WW2, and was defined by state-financed, publicly owned health care services (Saltman et al., 1998).

19. It is interesting that the previous arrangement should be so quickly reinstated, despite the fact that most practitioners had spent all their working lives in the Communist system.

20. Estonia has a flat income tax system, at a rate of 24% in 2005, with a substantial exemption for those on low incomes and a larger exemption for those receiving state pensions. With a VAT rate of 18% the tax take was divided in 2005 into 34.1% social tax and unemployment insurance, 18.3% income tax and 28.1% VAT, that is over 80% of central tax revenues (Staehr, 2009). Estonia developed a second pension scheme, whereby those who were new to the labour force had to join, those who were already in work but less than 50 could join, and those 50 and over could not, in order to create an element of a funded scheme (Casey, 2004). Similar but rather more extensive plans have been implemented in the other Baltic States. It is difficult to ascribe such schemes as being 'European' rather than of any other origin. In recent years New Zealand has also introduced a new voluntary pension scheme called KiwiSaver to which people may commit 2, 4 or 8% of their income. (It is actually rather more than a simple pension scheme as withdrawals can be made for purchase of a first home or in the event of illness or hardship: see http://www.kiwisaver.govt.nz/already/get-money/early/)

21. This also applies to an extent in education.

22. Czech social policy has three main components of which the Bismarckian approach to insurance is only one. It also pursues an active labour market policy and a safety net for those in need who cannot insure themselves, for example because they are not able to enter the workforce (Potůček, 2009).

23. It is helpful to see the financing of health care in the context of the financing of the whole of compulsory social insurance in the Czech Republic. Over a third of the employee's contribution goes to health care (4.5% out of a total of 12.5%) whereas only a quarter of the employer's total contribution of 35% of wages goes on health care. The difference is largely accounted for by pension contributions which take up over 60% of the employer contribution but only half the employee one.

24. The Polish workforce has been particularly mobile, although it has not been concentrated on the more skilled and covered all categories of workers. To some extent those on low incomes have been replaced by immigration to Poland from Ukraine, where conditions have been much worse.
25. This is reflected in extensive child care arrangements and encouragement for single parents to return to work.

3. The economic crisis and prospects for European social insurance and democratic governance

Katherine Lyons and Christine Cheyne

INTRODUCTION

In the wake of the sovereign debt crisis, the need for protection against social risks such as unemployment and destitution has increased. The 2007 banking crisis has led to loss of personal and household savings and assets, wage reductions and increased unemployment. New vulnerabilities have been exposed, particularly in high-unemployment economies and economies that espouse a Protestant work ethic and rhetoric of undeserving poor. Particularly adverse are the consequences for the retired and those soon to retire. It has been estimated that the financial crisis reduced the value of assets accumulated to finance retirement by around 20–25 per cent on average (Antolín and Stewart, 2009) although there has been some recovery since. Effects are sometimes cumulative and hence more concentrated: where workers experience unemployment, pension savings are reduced which in turn has an impact on future retirement income.

The ensuing economic realities demonstrate the fragility of the globalized economy, where a US-generated crisis can reverberate around the world. The broadening sovereign debt crisis and associated austerity measures in Portugal, Ireland, Italy, Greece, Spain and Cyprus threaten to launch a new wave of economic hardship on the EU just as its members had started to recover from the initial shock of the economic crisis. Irwin (2010) describes the spreading debt and fiscal crisis as having a 'contagion effect'.

Protection against risk thus seems critical. Lyons and Cheyne (2011) describe how social insurance allows a risk-pooling that enables lower-risk groups in society to contribute to the protection of higher-risk groups. Sharing the burden this way can help protect society as a whole from economic and other crises, and it can allow redistribution from richer to poorer groups, an idea that may become more popular as publicity grows about the widespread effects of the economic crisis on poorer socioeconomic groups. Such risk-sharing is also consistent with democratic distributive justice and an egalitarian distribution of national income (see Zucker 2001).

The economic crisis has also underscored the risks of under-regulating private sector financial institutions and the need for greater transparency and accountability for public officials and institutions. Democratic government, and institutions and systems of governance designed to protect people from adverse life events, are crucial for ensuring that decisions will benefit society overall. Therefore, this chapter examines current practice in social insurance in the EU and considers the prospects for insurance-based welfare in the wake of the current economic crisis.

We begin with a brief discussion of social insurance and its value in the current social and economic climate. Recognizing the connection between social insurance and democratic governance in the EU, we then study the governance of social insurance in the EU. The specific practice of social insurance governance is outlined, as well as the indirect social insurance the EU provides its citizens through the structural funds, and its more direct influence in ensuring its newer member states have 'European' style social welfare frameworks. The shared governance that the EU and its member states have in this arena provides evidence for two differing models of democracy in the EU – supranational governance, with decisions being made by the EU on behalf of its member states, and national (and regional) governance, with member states deciding their own policies. We therefore also examine the member states' role in their citizens' social insurance. We find that democratic governance is more prevalent in state-run insurance schemes than in the growing number of private insurance schemes. This is troubling, since a lack of transparency in financial decisions by private sector banking and other financial institutions is widely implicated in the economic crisis (see, for example, De Grauwe, 2011).

DEFINING SOCIAL INSURANCE

Before discussing social insurance, it is worth explaining what we mean by this term. Social insurance protects individuals from the effects of social risks, such as unemployment, sickness, old age, and workplace accidents through state-initiated insurance accounts. Contributions come from some combination of individual, employer and state; adverse social circumstances such as unemployment, sickness, old age, and workplace accidents trigger payments.[1] The accounts may be actual, with funds belonging to a specific individual and withdrawals limited to the amount invested, or nominal, with high state subsidies, unlimited withdrawals, and facilities for redistributing funds from lower-risk to higher-risk individuals. The common aim of the various social insurance schemes supported by these options is to protect all individuals within a particular group (such as an occupational class or income band), rather than only those with risk profiles safe enough for an insurance company to survive on premiums alone. This goal, which distinguishes social and private insurance, may be achieved either through direct state subsidy for insuring high-risk individuals, or through compulsory scheme member-ship, forcing low-risk individuals to support high-risk individuals.

Social insurance may also be viewed more broadly. The schemes discussed above provide benefits that help people cope with the effects of social risks. But social investment may alleviate the effects of these events less directly, or simply prevent them. For example, social infra-structure such as hospitals and schools alleviates the effects of sickness and poor education; and investment in a community's economic infra-structure can strengthen the economy and reduce the risk of unemploy-ment (Midgley, 1999). Similarly, investment in human capital, for example by funding training programmes, can help unemployed people become employable, or can serve as skill-set insurance, helping those already in work to stay there. Increasing the capacity of society and individuals to cope with social risks in this way can be seen as indirect social insurance, since people are protected not through cash payments or benefits but through increased opportunities to help themselves. The 'social investment welfare state', focused on education and training, and investment in children, became incorporated into European social policy (see, for example, Cerami, 2011; Morel et al., 2012).

Social insurance's ability to pool risks, either between different indi-viduals or within individuals' lifetimes, allows it to help spread risk more evenly throughout society and lessen the impact of crises on particularly vulnerable groups. The recent crises in Europe provide a clear example of the kind of situation for which social protection is needed. As Vis et al. (2011, p. 350) argue, with deficit spending generally agreed to be 'rapidly approaching its limits', and a 'swift return to a balanced budget' being argued for, the issue of 'who will have to carry the heavy burden of financial and economic recovery' is a pressing one. Social insurance's ability to help society share this burden transparently makes it a particularly useful protection mechanism. This seems to be widely recognized, unlike in the 1970s and 1980s, when economic troubles were partly blamed on 'the "big" (welfare) state'. Vis et al.'s (2011, p. 342) research on public opinion finds that across Europe the welfare state is now viewed as an important part of the solution to the recent economic crises. This translates to policy, as indeed there has not been a 'major onslaught' on the welfare state; while 'more drastic spending cuts are envisaged ... for a variety of political and institutional reasons there will probably be a considerable gap between intentions and achievements' (Vis et al., 2011, p. 350).

The changes that do happen to social insurance will need to be made with public support. The main body of the chapter therefore examines the degree to which decisions about social insurance are made transparently and democratically. These decisions are made at a number of levels in the EU, providing an interesting case study of its governance. The next section therefore discusses the levels of democracy in governance at the EU level, and within its member states, before we look at the governance of social insurance more specifically.

RECONSTITUTING DEMOCRATIC GOVERNANCE IN THE EU: THE ROLE OF SOCIAL INSURANCE

Democratic Governance in the EU

The term 'governance' refers to arrangements for decision-making about issues such as resource allocation (at the state level) and state behaviour (at the EU or international level). These decision-making arrangements increasingly include a range of state and non-state actors. Governance is thus broader than government, which refers to state decision-making.

The World Bank and the OECD have promoted the concept of 'good governance' as a strategy for emerging democracies, particularly in developing countries. *Good* governance has generally been used to imply *effective* governance (Santiso, 2001; Weiss, 2000; World Bank, 1989). The World Bank's (1994) definition of 'governance', like the state-level part of the broader definition given above, focuses on the way power is exercised in the management of economic and social resources, including the political regime, the resource-management process and the governors' capacity to develop and implement policies. However, it argues that countries' internal politics fall outside its mandate, and so concentrates on the economic dimensions of good governance, ignoring the political aspect. Yet, as Santiso (2001, p. 1) argues, good governance (effectiveness) and democracy (legitimacy) are difficult to separate; 'neither good governance nor democracy is sustainable without the other'. By

1999, World Bank researchers had delineated six main dimensions of governance: voice and accountability (including civil liberties and political rights), political stability, governance effectiveness (including the freedom of the bureaucracy from political pressure), regulatory quality (including banking supervision), rule of law, and control of corruption (Kaufmann et al., 1999). Similarly, Heinelt et al. (2006) argue that political and managerial governance complements public participation, and the OECD's Development Assistance Committee (1995) links good governance with participatory development, human rights, and democratization (World Bank, 1994). Democratic governance therefore includes both participatory and representative components, supported by effectiveness elements such as control of corruption and political stability.

As the above discussion implies, perfectly democratic governance is elusive, so there are likely to be flaws in the democratic governance of social insurance institutions. It is true that without democratic representation, social insurance schemes tend not to exist at all (Cutright, 1965; Orenstein, 2008).[2] Yet, while some adherence to democratic principles seems required for a state to develop social insurance, and social protection generally, its internal dynamics and public expectations are more important to how extensive and how generous such schemes become. In order to illustrate our argument we highlight the importance of EU-level governance of social insurance systems in the following section, and then outline four different models of social insurance found in the EU at the member state level. In the final section of the chapter we discuss possible implications of pressures on and changes to insurance arrangements for democracy and welfare in Europe. We begin with the role of the EU's structural funds in funding and governing social insurance, before moving onto social insurance as governed within the member states.

EU-Level Governance of Social Insurance

The EU and its predecessors have traditionally focused more on market integration than on social policy, leaving this largely to the member states' internal discretion. Although their purpose was primarily economic, initiatives such as the Common Agricultural Policy (CAP) had the side-effect of supporting large percentages of some member states' populations. Similarly, the EU's involvement in social security regulation was generally a consequence of the EU's market-creating role (Carmel and Papadopoulos, 2009). Yet, more recently the EU's policies in areas outside the economic and trade spheres have flourished. Although the EU budget is not intended per se to provide European social insurance, or fiscal transfers (Carmel and Papadopoulos, 2009), in practice it does this to quite some extent – particularly as agricultural support has decreased in importance. The EU's structural funds, which aim to bring greater social cohesion through improved social welfare practices, have played an important part here. In particular, their indirect role in insuring EU citizens against social risks, by allowing them to invest in social infrastructure and build human capital, amounts to involvement in social insurance, although indirect and concrete. As the membership has soared from 15 to 27, the EU has developed a narrower, but more direct, influence on national social policies which in its turn has generated an interesting challenge for the assessment of EU governance – how member states and the European Commission handle their shared competency for social policy.

The EU's structural funds

The EU's predecessors, the European Coal and Steel Community (ECSC), the European Economic Community (EEC), and the European Atomic Energy Community (Euratom), were founded on common economic and security ties. Yet, as bonds between European countries have strengthened, and the community has expanded, social policy has grown in importance. Concerns about economic and social disparities began before the EU was formed (Begg and Mayes, 1991; European Commission, n.d.-b),[3] and the mid-2000s accession of Central and Eastern European countries only widened the gaps between the wealthiest and poorest, and least and most generous, member states (Orenstein, 2008). The goal of reducing inequality within the EU is encompassed by the principle of solidarity, which 'can be found in relevant EC/EU instruments from the beginning' (Neuhold, 2010, p. 212), and which has been particularly emphasized since the 1992 Maastricht Treaty (Goetschy, 2009). Meeting this goal is at the heart of the EU's regional policy, which originated in the 1970s, and which uses its financial instruments, the structural and cohesion funds, to effect economic and social cohesion by 'narrow[ing] the development disparities among regions and Member States' (European Commission, n.d.-d; Shankar and Shah, 2009). The instruments most relevant to social policy, the European Regional Development Fund (ERDF) and the European Social Fund (ESF), finance a variety of projects, largely in member states with GDPs well below the EU average. These programmes are designed by the Commission and regional and national authorities based on member state priorities and according to Commission guidelines, with member states choosing 'concrete projects' and taking responsibility for their implementation

(European Commission, n.d.-c; Falkner, 2007; Hantrais, 2000; O'Connor, 2005; Shankar and Shah, 2009; Threlfall, 2007).

While the structural funds have not directly financed social insurance schemes, they help protect EU citizens against social hazards by building up their human capital. The ESF database documents a wide range of programmes. Three on-going examples, chosen simply to give a flavour of the initiative, are:

- a programme co-funded by the ESF's Cohesion programme and Cornwall's Federation of Young Farmers Clubs which provides training in business leadership and management skills to Club office-holders;
- a programme co-funded by the ESF and the Latvian Ministry of Welfare, which provides 18- to 24-year-old unemployed Latvians with 6 to 12 months of practical training in participating companies, a monthly 120 lat scholarship, and crèche facilities for the children of young unemployed parents on the programme;
- a Swedish job-centre project co-founded by the ESF, Volvo Cars, AB Volvo, and suppliers that updates employees' car manufacturing skills. (European Commission, 2010)

The shared motivation for these programmes is that increased employment skills protect against unemployment, by two mechanisms. Skilled workers keep businesses afloat, thereby protecting their jobs; but should the business fail, they are more easily re-employable.

The EU's indirect social insurance also extends to building up community assets. For example, the Danish north Jutland region uses ESF funds to recruit and train more male health care workers (European Commission, 2010). In Bulgaria, the ERDF and the European Cohesion Fund (ECF) fund 80 per cent of improvements to key infrastructure such as roads and railway lines, targeting sustainable economic growth and the creation of 'more and better jobs' (European Commission, n.d.-a). By developing health care, transport, and other facilities such as schools, the EU indirectly insures citizens against social risks such as ill health, lack of jobs, and lack of education, although it does not provide direct cash payments should these risks occur.

The subnational involvement in projects that are co-funded by the structural funds and a regional, national, or local body, which also administers them, could be viewed as a democratic leavening of supranational officialdom. However, this is a narrow view. More holistically, the EU could be considered as a (con)federal democracy whose national parliaments have ceded considerable local power without an increase in democratic control at the federal level. This leavening does not fill the gap.

The expanding EU

As we have seen, the EU is indirectly involved in the social protection of its citizens. It spends money on social services that avert unemployment and sickness, but tends not to compensate people financially when these risks occur. However, the Maastricht and Lisbon treaties specified that the member states would share competency in the social and employment field with the EU (Craig, 2010; Goetschy, 2009),[4] which therefore is empowered to at least co-lead its member states' social affairs (although EU social security decisions must be unanimous).

The 2004 and 2007 accession of ten Central and Eastern European states appeared set to challenge the cohesion of the EU member states' employment and social policies. As Sissenich (2007, p. 1) explains, the 'wealth gap' between the new and old member states sparked fears that low-wage competition from the East might 'do away with the "European social model"', of high wages, sector-level collective bargaining, safe-guards against redundancies, 35–40 hour work weeks, generous holiday allowances, 'and the social peace that Europeans associate with these arrangements'. Similarly, Orenstein (2008, p. 88) notes that, prior to the accession, EU officials worried that low social spending levels by the new member states would induce their citizens to move west, or 'to export their social and medical problems'. These fears of 'social dump-ing' caused the EU to encourage candidate countries strongly to maintain affordable, sustainable, 'European' levels of social protection (Orenstein, 2008, pp. 88–89). Even recent Slovakian, Baltic, Portuguese and Greek austerity programmes have only lowered social spending by a few percentage points – for example, Portuguese social contributions are projected to decrease from 12.2 per cent to 11.4 per cent of GDP between 2011 and 2015 (Directorate-General for Economic and Financial Affairs, 2011a, 2011b; Government of the Republic of Lithuania, 2011; Republic of Estonia Stability Programme, 2011; Slovak Republic Minis-try of Finance, 2011; Vilks, 2011).

The maintenance of welfare spending in the accession countries did not of course prevent post-accession East-West migration. Yet, interest-ingly, van Oorschot and Uunk (2007) found that although immigrants are attracted to states with generous welfare policies, the more immigrants who arrived, the less threatened and more solidaristic the existing population felt towards them, and the more comfortable they felt about distributing social spending, equal to their own, to needy immigrants and their families. And indeed, coordinating social security arrangements between member states is another area where the EU leads in social and employment matters. Since 1971, it has guaranteed the equality of EU citizens in terms of social welfare treatment although in practice it can be difficult to define what 'equal social protection' for citizens and immigrants entails (see, for example, Sainsbury, 2006).

MODELS OF SOCIAL INSURANCE IN THE EU AND THEIR GOVERNANCE AT THE MEMBER STATE LEVEL

A substantial body of scholarship has identified different models of European welfare. In previous work (Lyons and Cheyne, 2011) we have explored three different social insurance models found in the EU. With the sovereign debt crisis and attendant pressure on fiscal policies, there will be implications for the evolution of social insurance in the EU at precisely the time when social insurance is more important than ever. The effect of these implications can be illustrated through the four models of European welfare systems that are widely recognized: Continental, Anglo-Saxon, Scandinavian, and Southern.

As we have seen, the EU has encouraged its newest members to maintain 'European' levels of social protection, even when implementing austerity measures, and it could be even more direct in persuading its members to grant intra-EU migrants a degree of social protection similar to that enjoyed by their own citizens. Yet, although EU mechanisms help fund some social protection schemes to foster social cohesion throughout the EU, most social insurance schemes operate entirely at the member state level. It is therefore worth investigating how social insurance is administered in the EU member states. Although the governance of member states' social security bodies is not within this chapter's scope, the general design of their systems is an important indicator of their degree of democratic governance.

Continental Model of Social Insurance

Social insurance in the Continental members of the EU, as outlined in Lyons and Cheyne (2011) in relation to pensions, maintains status differentials and is based on employment history rather than need. In Germany, a social security tax deducted directly from employees' salaries helps fund health, unemployment, pension and accident insurance, while in France, it contributes to sickness/maternity/paternity insurance, old-age pensions, disability insurance, and death insurance. In Austria, employment-related social security contributions paid by insured people and their employers fund health, pension and accident insurance (unemployment insurance is funded by similar employment-related contributions) (Austrian Museum for Social and Economic Affairs, 2009). The social insurance system is regulated by the state but managed independently by representatives of various groups of insured employees and their employers (Austrian Museum for Social and Economic Affairs, 2009; Main Association of Austrian Social Security Institutions, n.d.). These insurance institutions vary in the number of types of social insurance they provide – there are health-only, pension-only, health-and-pension, health-pension-and-accident schemes – but in all cases the fund managers are nominated by the groups they represent (Austrian Museum for Social and Economic Affairs, 2009; Main Association of Austrian Social Security Institutions, n.d.).

The Continental system's use of union-managed insurance institutions seems a smart compromise between state and private-run insurance funds. People have democratic input into the state's social insurance policies and the specific practices of their own occupational funds. Private non-union insurance funds exist but do not dominate the market; their governance issues are therefore not a strong concern here.

Anglo-Saxon Model of Social Insurance

In the Anglo-Saxon EU – the UK – social insurance tends towards socialist universalism strongly tempered by liberal notions of self-help (Carmel and Papadopoulos, 2009). This means that basic, means-tested statutory income guarantees exist for the unemployed, the old, and the sick, with higher, non-means-tested sums available to people with contribution histories or memberships of private schemes (Social Security Administration and International Social Security Association, 2010). The statutory payments are funded through general taxation, and governed by the state, with the Department for Work and Pensions managing and administering unemployment, sickness and pension benefits. The department also administers government policies such as ensuring that individuals are looking for work and stopping benefit payments when appropriate. Each of the four countries in the UK has its own version of the National Health Service (NHS), and a department to administer it. UK citizens can vote in general and health board elections, but their democratic link to the governors of their insurance is clearly weaker than that of their Continental European counterparts.

As outlined in Lyons and Cheyne (2011), workers belonging to the state's contribution-based pension scheme may opt out into private schemes which meet certain state-set criteria. As in the Austrian schemes, the state regulates but does not manage; however, unions are not generally involved in management.[5] Supplementary privately managed insurance is also available to UK citizens. Private insurance is widely used, but not democratically managed, so any decisions that these institutions make contrary to the wishes of their members may affect society as a whole. Certainly, the fact that less-risky individuals may opt out of state-run insurance increases the risk for the public scheme. Congleton's (2007) suggestion that 'good risks' will move back to state institutions if private insurers are perceived to be making poor decisions only holds as long as there is reliable, transparent information about insurers' decisions.

Scandinavian Model of Social Insurance

Scandinavian social insurance is regarded as the most solidaristic in the EU (Moene and Wallerstein, 2008). Tax-funded and contributions-based benefits both redistribute money between income and class brackets, although since the 1990s there has been a greater focus on income-related pensions, and redistribution has decreased accordingly (Goul Andersen and Carstensen, 2009). Social insurance governance is largely conducted by the state or unions, which individuals are able to influence democratically.

In Denmark, Sweden, and, to a lesser extent, Finland, social insurance is typically funded by the state (Social Security Administration and International Social Security Association, 2010). In Denmark, taxes fund, and government departments govern, basic pensions and health costs, as well as maternity/paternity leave, and sickness benefits after two weeks (those weeks being covered by employer-paid insurance contributions). For example, the Ministry of Social Welfare supervises and provides national-level administration for the universal basic pension and sickness and maternity benefits, and municipal governments provide local administration. The arrangement for medical benefits is similarly divided between the Ministry of Health at national level and municipal and regional governments locally. Danish unemployment benefits are funded by employee (and sometimes employer) contributions, plus small government subsidies, to recognized union-established unemployment insurance funds.[6] As in Continental Europe, while the government provides general supervision through the Ministry of Employment and the National Directorate of Labour, these funds administer themselves nationally, collecting benefits and making payments. Insured people influence the governance via their elected union representatives. The ATP (*Arbejd-markedets Tillaegs Pension*), Denmark's main statutory pension scheme, is similarly funded; employees, employers, and the government contribute to occupational funds, which make payments based on the contributor's contribution history. The ATP is government-supervised, through the Danish Financial Supervisory Authority, and administered by an independent organization, the Labour Market Supplementary Pension Institution, headed by a bipartite board of directors.

Southern European Model of Social Insurance

The Southern European welfare model emphasizes the family's role in providing social protection much more than the other models (Karamessini, 2008; Rhodes, 1996). In Portugal, Greece, and Spain, insurance benefits commonly accrue for both directly insured people and their dependent relatives. State funding of social insurance is lower than in Scandinavia, and union involvement is lower than in the Continental welfare states (Ferreira, 2003; Social Security Administration and International Social Security Association, 2010). As in the other models, basic, means-tested, statutory benefits are available to those who would otherwise not be covered. Above this baseline safety-net, Southern social insurance resembles that of the Continental welfare states, as it maintains status differentials, with contribution and benefit levels dependent on income, and different social insurance systems for different occupational classes. Many Greek workers are covered by the general scheme administered by the Social Insurance Institute (IKA), but several groups have their own special schemes for pensions, health costs, and so on (European Commission, 2011a; Social Security Administration and International Social Security Association, 2010). Spain is similar, though in Portugal the separate schemes are being unified (Social Security Administration and International Social Security Association, 2010).

Social insurance in the Southern member states is generally overseen by a government ministry but administered by secondary organizations (for example, Spain's National Institute of Social Security). In Spain, those organizations are managed and supervised by general councils and executive committees, with union representation (Lagares Perez, 2000). Similarly, in Greece insured people, employers and the state are all represented on public social insurance organizations' administrative boards (European Commission, 2011a). Uptake of private pension schemes, to which this may not apply, is low in Portugal and Greece (OECD, 2009a), and while a fairly high proportion of Spaniards are members, the OECD (2011, p. 13) records subdued contributions, probably because of the 'generous benefits offered by the public system'. The OECD (2009a) does argue that occupational private pensions will become more important due to benefit-reducing reforms in the public pension system; if so, it will be important to ensure scheme-members' representation in these schemes. Indeed, growing privatization of pensions heightens the importance of governance (Ebbinghaus, 2011).

As mentioned regarding the Anglo-Saxon model, privately insured people can only exercise 'market governance' (to the degree that they are able to select the specific scheme they belong to) if they can easily access clear information about each scheme. Occupational schemes may limit market governance further, as only one scheme may be available. If their popularity does increase, insured people will need to be represented on the schemes' governing boards.

The other potential form of representation for insured people is by electing the legislature that drafts the guidelines governing social insurance. Various EU and international bodies and member states have pushed for more influence over some member states' budgets following their sovereign debt crises (see, for example, Baetz, 2012; Spiegel and Hope, 2012). This would decrease the influence of the individual governments and the citizens most affected by the crisis. The challenge for the EU in responding to the crisis is to maintain if not enhance democratic governance in the Southern EU member states' social insurance whilst pursuing a new fiscal compact.

The challenge for the EU is to find the appropriate balance of supranational and national-level governance. At the supranational level, Fischer and Hoffman (2012, p. 16) emphasize the need for the European Commission to give priority to fighting social exclusion and poverty in the wake of the economic crisis beginning with requesting member states to conduct social impact assessments of fiscal consolidation measures 'in order to draw up additional country-specific recommendations on how to enhance social cohesion'. As well, Fischer and Hoffman propose the introduction of a '"Social Investment Pact" or "Social Stability Pact" ... to achieve a more balanced relationship between short-term fiscal consolidation, on the one hand, and long-term social investment requirements' (p. 19). EU leadership is needed to ensure that those member states that are able to maintain social investment policies and expenditure do so, recognizing that such investment can stimulate growth whereas spending cuts in social insurance will weaken the ability of member states to respond to the economic crisis and, indeed, may exacerbate the crisis. It is now widely acknowledged that crisis management and response focused on fiscal austerity will not deliver an economically and politically viable long-term solution. Where member states have not placed social investment policies at the fore of their social and economic agenda, EU leadership and assistance is needed for the reason that a social investment approach, according to Hemerijck (2012, p. 21) 'has proved more resilient in the face of the new fiscal austerity' and because there are no serious alternatives. In light of this, key EU initiatives, such as the Lisbon Strategy and its successor the Europe 2020 Strategy, and EES must be maintained to provide momentum for social investment. With regard to the specific matter of social insurance, the promotion of models that incorporate strong regulation of private providers and financial markets, rigorous analysis of the trend towards privatization, and a focus on design of schemes to foster solidarity between the social partners are specific areas that should receive attention at the EU level. At the EU level and at the member state level, a particular focus must be on reform of public pensions. With fiscal conditions now significantly altered, there are profound challenges that need to be addressed in order to ensure that, with increasing pension privatization, further financial market failures do not increase exposure to poverty (Ebbinghaus, 2011; Holzmann, 2013). A critical element in pension reforms is improved governance of schemes to ensure participatory stakeholder rights.

CONCLUSION

As argued by Vandenbroucke et al. (2011, p. 4) 'long-term goals of social and economic policy in the EU must not fall victim to short-term policy orientations prompted by the banking crisis that hit the global economy in 2008 and the subsequent financial and fiscal problems affecting the Eurozone and the EU at large.' It is more imperative than previously that EU leaders advance the concept of Social Europe. While member states may need to transfer power to the European level, the EU, in turn, will need to ensure that democratic governance is enhanced.

Social insurance, in the narrow cash-benefit sense and the broader social-investment sense, pools society's risks, converting disastrous events like job-loss, which may become chronic unemployment, into a relatively minor financial drain on those less susceptible to such events. Sharing this insurance burden appeals to solidaristic notions of redistributing resources from richer to poorer; it can also protect society as a whole from the adverse effects of economic and other crises. While the expanding and deepening economic crisis in Europe and subsequent fiscal compact pose significant challenges to social insurance, nevertheless it is at such a juncture that public, and properly regulated private social insurance, become even more critical. The challenges and the responses to these challenges differ, reflecting the particular orientation and focus of different models. It is increasingly emphasized that models which favour public over private management are 'particularly relevant to the economic circumstances of the early twenty-first century, given the failure of the financial services industry to generate outcomes that are compatible with generalized economic and social well-being' (Mohan, 2012, p. 91).

EU member states' social insurance systems generally fall into one of four categories: Continental, Anglo-Saxon, Scandinavian and Southern. Continental and Scandinavian social insurance are the most democratically governed; Germany and Austria have systems designed by elected officials and managed by representatives of the groups they serve. Sweden and Denmark have systems designed and implemented by elected officials in central and local government, or by union representatives. In both Continental and Scandinavian models, private social insurance exists, but does not dominate the market. This contrasts with the UK where, although elected politicians designed the social insurance system, and government departments administer basic means-tested benefits, the main way individuals can influence their social insurance programmes is through the limited and possibly unattractive option of exiting the scheme. This is a much more indirect form of democracy. While, in most cases, the privately administered pensions will be there when people retire, the less-direct representation and participation in scheme governance reduces transparency and accountability, and increases the opportunities for corruption and ineffectiveness.

In the Southern EU member states, such as Spain and Greece, the governance of social insurance is currently similar to that of Continental social insurance, although recent reforms may lead to increased use of private pensions, where again it is important to allow citizens some influence over the schemes' governance.

At the EU level, the member states' cash-benefit-style programmes are supported by a broader conception of social insurance which involves social investment in human and social capital. Spending on infrastructure such as schools and hospitals, and training programmes designed to ensure people's skill sets and employability, protect the EU's people against social risks, or help them recover quickly when they occur. The governance of these projects is shared between the EU and various country-level bodies, which may be seen as providing some democratic leavening that raises the EU's accountability.

But if we think of the EU as a (con)federal democracy, we must admit that this democratic leavening at supranational level does not compensate for the member states' loss of national sovereignty. The challenge for the EU in addressing the causes and effects of the sovereign debt crisis will be to ensure that goals of democratic governance and risk-pooling are not compromised in the quest to end the debt crisis and stimulate growth.

NOTES

1. For a full discussion of social insurance mechanisms in the EU see Lyons and Cheyne (2011).
2. Similar insights were differently formulated by the 'professorial' socialists (*Katheder-sozialisten*) in Germany in the late nineteenth century (see Dawson, 1973 [1890]; Haney, 1911).
3. The preamble of the 1957 Treaty of Rome refers to reducing regional disparities in the 1970s. Community financing for this was increased and national instruments were coordinated, while the 1986 Single European Act made social and economic cohesion an objective alongside completing the single market; but the policy was not incorporated into the EC Treaty until the 1992 signing of the Maastricht Treaty (European Commission, n.d.-b).
4. The exact boundaries of which parts of social policy are not always easily discerned however; see Craig (2010).
5. Unless the scheme is union-based.
6. Membership of such funds is voluntary, and municipal governments may provide social assistance to people ineligible for benefits who have no other means of support.

4.   Active social policies, inclusion and democracy in the European Union

Mark Thomson

INTRODUCTION

Social policies are an important feature of democracy. In many instances, they have developed into social rights that are seen to deepen the 'hollow' character of democracy (Giddens, 1996). Without social policies that invest in children's education or workers' pensions, or provide a safety net in times of personal crisis (e.g., unemployment or illness), levels of abject poverty and social exclusion grow. Social policies hence try to contain the adverse effects of human difference by compensating for inequalities that exist between people at different stages in their lives. They are intended to be welfare enhancing, especially for more socially vulnerable individuals, and to keep people attached to their local and national communities.

Yet, the outcome of social policies is not always positive. Social policies can be socially divisive when they are seen to benefit some people over (or, indeed, at the expense of) others. They can also cause harm to the very same people they are supposed to help if they lead to dependency on social support instead of personal autonomy. These associated risks are increasingly recognized in the case of social policies for the unemployed. Long-term dependency on state benefits has been identified with diminished work skills, lack of self-respect, and loss of confidence and motivation (Sen, 1997), all of which increase the likelihood of permanent exclusion from the labour market – of particular concern when considering the high incidence of youth unemployment in many European countries. It is also identified with social friction and diminishing support for welfare institutions.

How then are societies to mitigate these risks to the individual and to society without undermining social rights or the democratic legitimacy of policies (Eriksen and Fossum, 2007)? This chapter discusses new policy trends in Denmark, the UK and France towards the unemployed, in particular those perceived to be furthest from the labour market, most in need of employment assistance and most at risk of social exclusion. This 'new governance of activation' emphasizes local solutions to ensure that policy interventions are more responsive and sensitive to individual needs. Decentralizing the delivery of employment or active social policies has taken two main forms: the engagement of a broader set of welfare actors (public, private and third-sector) in policy design and implementation; and, the individualization of activation services to the unemployed through one-stop job centres where all jobseekers (both the insured and uninsured) are entitled to receive professional help with their job searches, advice about suitable educational or training opportunities, or support to overcome non-vocational barriers to work such as health problems.

This chapter considers how far these more locally sensitive ways of delivering active social policies adhere to basic democratic norms. These norms include treating people fairly and equally, ensuring that processes are transparent and that those making decisions remain accountable. The chapter asks if this new governance of activation fulfils these conditions for democratic governance, paying particular attention to the interactions between the unemployed and their employment advisors, and between the new and old welfare actors that are now engaged in designing and implementing active social policies. Drawing on theories of deliberative democracy and Amartya Sen's capability approach, it is argued that the democratic legitimacy of active social policies lies in treating all those involved in the activation process as key stakeholders. The aims of this more participatory form of democracy are twofold: to inform better policy and decision making by recognizing people's diverse needs and capabilities; and to limit instances where coercion rather than persuasion is adopted to make the unemployed accept job offers.

The chapter is hence less concerned with how effective policies are in improving employment rates, and more with the ways in which this is achieved. This is why, as explained in the following section, the term 'active social' policies is used instead of the more usual 'active labour market' policies. The chapter then discusses the benefits of adopting Sen's capability approach and ideas of deliberative democracy in legitimizing state interventions. A comparison of activation trends in three distinct welfare states, Denmark, the UK and France, follows. All three have decentralized the governance of active social policies, but it is not clear if this has helped policymakers to engage better with people's barriers to work or simply allowed them to devolve the costs of 'activating' hard-to-reach groups to local welfare actors. The chapter concludes by drawing some lessons for the wider democratic system.

ACTIVE LABOUR MARKETS OR SOCIAL POLICIES?

Especially in times of fiscal austerity, high unemployment and flexible labour markets, the challenge for policymakers is to find ways to reconcile economic aims with the objective of social policy – that is, improving the welfare of citizens. The growing incidence of 'in-work' poverty due to low wages and casual contracts means that employment is not always welfare-enhancing or a route into more regular and stable job opportunities (see, for example, Kenway, 2008). Indeed, there is a risk that activation measures such as subsidized employment or job trials lead to exclusion trajectories (Enjolras et al., 2001), and in effect provide employers with a source of cheap and highly flexible labour.

In order to mitigate these risks, and avoid distorting the primary goal of welfare actors to assist the unemployed into independent work, the preference here is to use the term active social policies to emphasize broader welfare goals over short-term job or labour market outcomes. Work remains a policy objective (hence the notion of *active* social policy), but it is an objective that needs to be adapted to the local context as well as to individual circumstances. This is important given that current approaches to unemployment tend to shift explanations of the cause of benefit dependency away from structural factors (for example, the state of the local economy) and on to individual characteristics (Drøpping et al., 1999). As a result, it has become much easier for governments to justify changing the status of social rights into a contractual arrangement (Handler, 2003) that spells out jobseekers' responsibilities if they are to avoid benefit sanctions or cuts.

Social rights have to an extent been refashioned as instruments of labour market activation, especially in countries adopting a stricter work-first approach to long-term unemployment. At the same time, however, an emphasis on more local solutions suggests possibilities for acknowledging wider barriers to employment better, especially as it is people furthest from the labour market who are increasingly the focus of policy interventions: for example, the long-term unemployed, young people with few qualifications and limited work experience, people impaired by disability or sickness, and residents of economically deprived areas.

Because these groups of unemployed do not usually belong to trade unions, their interests have not been well represented in the democratic process. In this respect, the involvement of third sector welfare actors such as charities in designing and implementing active social policies is a promising development. But whilst local actors can bring better know-ledge and experience, much depends on the level of resources and flexibility available to provide long-term solutions for people who can require significant investments of both time and money. The challenge is to develop policies that are adaptable and flexible as a one-size-fits-all approach is unlikely to adequately address the range of employment barriers faced by the hard-to-reach unemployed.

THE BENEFITS OF A CAPABILITY APPROACH AND DELIBERATIVE DEMOCRACY

As Robert Salais puts it, policies will often need 'to struggle against inequality of capabilities' (Salais, 2003, p. 317). Drawing inspiration from Amartya Sen's writings on the capability approach (Sen, 1999), the objective of active social policies should be to promote effective or substantive freedoms (what Sen calls 'capabilities') by asking how much agency people have to do or be what they value, thus echoing calls for activation policies to empower individuals (Bonvin and Orton, 2009; Dean et al., 2005; van Berkel and Roche, 2002). The capability approach is explicitly anti-utilitarian, arguing that people should 'be in charge of their own well-being; it is for them to decide how to use their capabil-ities' (Sen, 1999, p. 288), not others. The way to enhance effective freedoms, from the perspective of both Sen's capability approach as well as the model of deliberative democracy, is through more consensus-seeking and inclusive dialogue; that is, through more democratic chan-nels of inclusion. Those most affected by policies must have opportunities, free from coercion or exploitation, to impart local know-ledge and 'lived experience' as a way to contextualize problems that otherwise might remain unknown or abstract to policymakers or panels of experts – the idea of 'situated public action' as a way of empowering and giving voice to local communities (Salais and Villeneuve, 2004, p. 8). Given the diversity of individual circumstances, Sen emphasizes the value of learning from others (Sen, 2003, p. 31) through democratic participation in the production of knowledge. Through public deliber-ation, participants have the opportunity to publicly transform others' 'preferences, interests, beliefs and judgements' (Young, 2000, p. 26).

Two sets of criticism might be levelled at this form of participatory democracy. The first is that it is too individualistic and focuses on local solutions alone. Yet, the above discussion has already pointed to social or institutional barriers as impediments to effective freedoms, and thus to the importance that social policies play in empowering both individuals and social groups. It is precisely at the local level that it is possible, by adopting participatory methods, to capture the issues affecting individuals better and to uncover the wider structural causes of inequalities (Frediani, n.d.), hence serving to inform policymaking and local initiatives better. More individualized employment services as a way to 'activate' the unemployed offer opportunities to achieve forms of social inclusion that are sensitive both to local context and individual needs.

The second set of criticisms is that this form of participatory democracy is simply too idealistic, as it neglects imbalances of power due to status, class, race or gender that routinely distort human interactions. The model of deliberative democracy is criticized for not adequately reflecting on the social preconditions necessary to reach the ideal of deliberative democracy (Toens, 2007). But by identifying norms of discussion and argumentation, a deliberative approach is explicit in seeking to avoid reinforcing existing imbalances of power that participants might otherwise exploit as a way to dominate proceedings through coercion, intimidation or disregard for alternative views. It is hence important that activation policies do not, by design, allow or encourage participants to take advantage of others (for example, employers who use trial jobs as a source of casual and cheap labour) or lead to perverse incentives (for example, employment agencies that, to meet job-related performance targets, focus their efforts on the most employable to the neglect of people with more complex needs, or allow the threat of benefit sanctions to define their relationships with their unemployed clients).

Whilst across Europe there has been a growth in more personalized employment services (van Berkel and Valkenburg, 2007), it is not always clear that more *deliberative* norms of discussion (reciprocity, mutual respect, equality, freedom of expression, openness to persuasion and transparency) always apply in discussions between the unemployed and their personal advisors. Nor is it always clear how far these interactions contribute to the wider content design, evaluation and reform of activation measures by means of appropriate feedback mechanisms to policymakers, for example through key stakeholders such as trade unions, civil society actors, employers' representatives, labour market authorities and political representatives. As Parkinson argues, the 'legitimacy [of policies] is enhanced by numerous deliberative forums interacting in a wider deliberative system, not simply within individual deliberative moments' (Parkinson, 2003, p. 188).

A deliberative system, conceived initially by Mansbridge (1999), thus relies on a degree of flexibility being built into the formal relationships between actors involved in the activation process. If local employment advisors, for example, are not to resort routinely to coercion or to exploiting power imbalances, then they need to have and use the resources to adapt to the diverse needs of their clients. Otherwise, the outcomes achieved are unlikely to contribute to the longer-term goals of raising people's capabilities and social inclusion, and may turn out to be harmful or discriminatory. Similarly, actors involved in the design of activation measures must be receptive to how the unemployed, local employment advisors and employers experience activation in their local context. In sum, what is required is a 'democratization of the activation process' (van Berkel and Roche, 2002, p. 209). The following case studies consider the contribution of recent changes in the governance of activation to this democratic aim.

NEW GOVERNANCE OF ACTIVATION IN DENMARK, THE UK AND FRANCE

There is substantial evidence that European governments are changing how they design and deliver activation policies as a way to provide more locally sensitive and cost-effective welfare services.[1] Two common features of new governance stand out: a rise in the contracting-out of welfare services, not just in liberal welfare regimes,[2] to engage a broader range of private and civil society actors in the design and implementation of activation measures; and a growing emphasis on local solutions, but with the state retaining much control over the administration of activation services, in some cases referred to as 'centralized localism' (Lødemel, 2001).

Denmark, the UK and France are chosen as good examples of 'active' welfare states (Lindsay and McQuaid, 2008). All three have put a degree of faith in more locally sensitive responses to unemployment, but whereas contracting-out in the UK reflects a continuation of its liberal approach, activation policies in France and Denmark represent a break with their respective Jacobin and corporatist traditions. The chapter considers the impact of new governance through case studies of: 'centralized localism' and the diminished role for traditional social partners in Danish activation policies; the contracting-out of activation services to the private and voluntary sectors in the UK; and a growth in local policy networks in French activation policies.

Reflecting the chapter's main concern with the conditions for legitimate democratic governance, the following two questions guide discussion of the case studies:

1.   Do the new modes of governance deliver welfare services in ways that promote genuinely cooperative partnerships akin to the model of deliberative democracy (based, for example, on the sharing of knowledge, resources and expertise)?
2.   Do they improve the welfare of the unemployed through better recognition of the diversity of individual capabilities?

Denmark

Labour market reforms from the early 1990s saw Denmark switch from a passive to an active welfare state. The reforms emphasized individual *rights* to receive employment support and *responsibilities* to actively seek work (see Table 4.1 for a summary of these changes). Until 2007, Danish social partners (trade union and employer representatives) were – within the parameters set by the national government – able to influence both the content and scope of activation measures by their presence in regional-level councils. According to Damgaard and Torfing (2010, p. 256) this had helped to establish important 'processes of mutual learning and trust building' among key stakeholders. Reforms in 2007, however, devolved power from the regional to the local level. Responsibility for how and where to spend activation funding moved to managers in new job centres, whilst the traditional social partners were assigned a mainly advisory and monitoring role within the new governance structures. The reform also integrated services for both insured and uninsured jobseekers in these one-stop job centres.

The development of one-stop job centres has potentially given recipients of social assistance (that is, the harder-to-reach unemployed) access to the same level of employment assistance as the insured jobless entitled to unemployment benefits. Under the previous arrangements, the regional bodies focused their activation plans on the insured unemployed, whilst the municipalities took care of the uninsured. It is suggested that the presence of the social partners within the old regional bodies contributed to better activation offers because policies could be suitably adjusted to meet the needs of both employers and the unemployed (Lindsay and Mailand, 2009, p. 1051; Walker and Sankey, 2008, p. 1042). Indeed, Danish firms were found in 2004 to have participated more in the active labour market than British companies, and to have valued it as a way to gain access to more highly skilled labour, in contrast to British firms which more often used it as a means to get cheap labour (Martin, 2004).[3]

There are two reasons to be cautious about how much recipients of social assistance will benefit from the expertise and knowledge of social partners. The first is that the social partners have less reason to participate in the new local governance structures as they now have a more reactive role and limited avenues to influence policy. Indeed, there have been problems in recruiting employers' representatives to sit in the new local employment councils (Damgaard and Torfing, 2010). The second reason to be cautious is because the 2007 reforms continued Denmark's growing emphasis on a work-first approach in activation policies. One motive behind the governance changes was to make municipalities more responsible for meeting nationally set employment targets (Damgaard and Torfing, 2010, p. 251). Hence there was a push towards more 'centralized localism' as it had long been felt that munici-pality autonomy from central government led to inefficient and expensive activation programmes and dependence on social assistance (Bredgaard and Larsen, 2008). Indeed, one of the issues since the reforms has been with experienced municipal officers in the new job centres who continue to see their role more in terms of social work (Walker and Sankey, 2008).

There are risks associated with the governance reforms. From the perspective of deliberative democracy, it is feared that the new local councils will not benefit from the knowledge, contacts and resources that were previously held within the regional structures (Lindsay and McQuaid, 2009). Whilst observations of discussions within the new local councils note how they act more as a deliberative than a bargaining forum, the new 'municipality agenda' of getting people off social assistance and into work tends to dominate discussions (Damgaard and Torfing, 2010). From the perspective of the capability approach, Damgaard and Torfing (2010, p. 254) note that those with more complex barriers to employment risk being 'internally excluded' (Young, 2000) whenever the wider social context of unemployment is insufficiently recognized. As a result, the reforms may well lead to the increased use of benefit sanctions by local job centres to compel people to take up activation offers. Whilst evidence of this effect is not yet available, the municipalities have shifted their employment policies towards a work-first approach in order to meet the short-term job targets that are set and monitored by central government (Bredgaard and Larsen, 2008).

On this cautionary note, the next section turns to another hard-to-reach group – people on incapacity (that is, sickness) benefits in the UK.

UK

Since the late 1990s, the UK has invested much more in policies to support the unemployed back to work (see Table 4.2.). One innovative approach has been to contract out employment services for the un-employed to private and not-for-profit companies. The 'Pathways to

Work' programme, designed to assist people on incapacity benefits (IBs) back into work, was delivered by private and voluntary-sector providers in 60 per cent of regions – with a private company most often acting as the lead or 'prime' provider and voluntary groups usually as specialist subcontractors. It followed a payment-by-results model with 70 per cent of public funding[4] to providers tied to moving clients into work, with an ambitious target of moving one million people off benefits between 2005 and 2015 out of a total of more than 2.5 million. The aim was – using language that echoes sentiments expressed in the capability approach – to 'empower people back into work' by delivering a better and more personalized customer experience.

The payment-by-results model, often referred to as an outcome-based, contracting model (OBC), led to concerns that many private providers did little to help IB claimants with more complex needs; in fact, the focus on job outcomes in contracts raised no expectation that providers would work with clients further from the labour market (Nice et al., 2009), and clearly there were financial disincentives for them to do so. But as all new IB claimants considered as having some future work capacity were required to attend mandatory work-focused interviews to avoid benefit sanctions,[5] it is legitimate to expect that clients would have been offered some activation services – and, given that these social interventions were supposed to be client-led, that these offers be appropriate and recognize the diverse needs and resources of clients.

This underlying tension in the OBC model led to the 'parking' of more difficult clients (offering them only a minimal service) whilst personal advisors focused their efforts ('creaming') on the more job-ready.[6] Research findings showed that these were fairly common practices, and ones that were justified in the eyes of advisors by the need for them to meet individual performance targets as well as by the formal use of a traffic-light system to gauge job readiness (Hudson et al., 2010). Although a lack of engagement by some clients may well have contributed to their own exclusion from activation services, especially when ongoing medical treatment or deteriorating health prevented them from contemplating a return to work (Barnes et al., 2010), the OBC model was unable to deliver adequate support for clients with more complex needs, for example people with mental health conditions or Asian women with limited English and little to no work experience (Hudson et al., 2010). These support gaps led provider managers to call for greater (financial) recognition of 'soft outcomes', such as completion of a training programme or a work trial, and to criticize their contracts as insufficiently long to allow them enough time to build clients' employability (Hudson et al., 2010).

There was also a concern, expressed by both academics and politicians (Hudson et al., 2010), that the OBC funding model distorted formal working relationships between the lead or 'prime' provider and its subcontractors. Prime providers were often found to cherry-pick the more job-ready clients and refer the harder-to-place ones to subcontractors. This worked against the formation of genuine partnerships based on trust rather than a sense of competition. It also made it difficult for subcontractors to deliver equitable services to their own clients as they too had to prioritize the more job-ready in order to remain financially viable under the funding model (for a similar argument related to English-language support for refugees in the UK, see Shutes, 2010).

From the perspective of the capability approach, it is evident that the payment-by-results philosophy, most explicit in the OBC model, led to new forms of exclusion for some IB claimants, either because they are seen as too far removed from the labour market to benefit from activation services or because a work-first approach means that they are more likely to end up in an unsuitable job. From the perspective of deliberative democracy, the rigid contractual arrangements did not contribute to genuine partnership-building or a sense of shared ownership in the activation process, since the payment-by-results model led to more competitive than collaborative relationships between organizations. The lack of mechanisms for client feedback about activation services was another concern with the OBC model as it does not allow for clients' voices to be heard in the design and reform of activation policies (Hudson et al., 2010) – an obvious prerequisite for more participatory and deeper forms of democratic governance.

The 'Pathways to Work' programme was wound up in 2011, and was replaced by a general Work Programme. Again it is based on a payment-by-results funding model, and early findings are mixed. On the one hand, there are longer, five-year contracts and agencies are paid more to work with more challenging clients. A code of conduct has also been introduced to bring greater openness and transparency in the relationships between prime providers and their subcontractors, with those failing to comply risking the loss of their contract. On the other hand, competitive tendering of government contracts under the Work Programme has meant that many small, specialist charities who work with the most disadvantaged unemployed are still not able to compete with larger commercial firms, some of which are newcomers to welfare-to-work programmes and are seen to have simply undercut their competitors on price.

France

The concept of employability, or lack of it, is central to understanding the evolution of French activation policies. Successive governments over the past three decades have invested heavily in job-creation schemes, especially aimed at the young unemployed to help them gain valuable work experience and skills (Table 4.3). Subsidized jobs have enabled some to move into regular employment but others have gone from one subsidized job to the next. The danger has been that such jobs operating outside the market economy become 'exclusion trajectories', especially when employers do not value the work experience gained under a subsidized contract or if society attaches a stigma to such work (Enjolras et al., 2001, p. 44).

Recent reforms have encouraged the development of local policy networks in an effort to address persistently high unemployment rates in France.[7] A wider set of policy actors, including traditional social partners and not-for-profit agencies, now have greater opportunities to participate in initiatives addressing local labour market issues (van Gestel and Herbillon, 2007). Two examples of local partnerships in France are given here: the Local Plans for Inclusion and Employment (*Plans Locaux pour l'Insertion et l'Emploi,* PLIE); and employment agencies that actively attempt to change employers' hiring practices outside the provision of subsidized contracts.

PLIEs operate at the lowest administrative level, the *communes* or local municipalities,[8] and have expanded nationally since their origins in northern France in the 1990s following the closure of many textile and steel factories. Most of the current 190 PLIEs are joint partnerships between different municipalities, and include a range of public, private and third-sector actors in collaborative platforms to assist disadvantaged populations at risk of social exclusion.

PLIEs offer insertion programmes tailored to the needs of individual jobseekers. Each PLIE, though, has different sets of objectives, both qualitative and quantitative, to reflect local circumstances in terms of the scope or content of insertion programmes and the number of jobseekers to be helped. In this way, PLIEs offer a flexible approach to meet individual needs in the context of local labour-market opportunities and demands, and can offer employment advisors enough scope in line with the capability approach to ask how much freedom people have to do or be what they value, and empower individuals.

By forming local policy networks of support, PLIEs also attempt to bring together prospective employers and jobseekers. Whilst the most concrete example is the organization of employment fairs, the day-to-day work within the PLIE framework involves tapping into local knowledge about job vacancies, training requirements for these posts and identifying, then advocating on behalf of, suitable jobseekers to fill these vacancies. Local training providers are often a good source of this knowledge given their existing contacts with employers and other educational establishments.

One criticism levelled at PLIEs is that they can reproduce labour-market selectivity. Those jobseekers most likely to satisfy the ideal-worker profile as defined by employers are more likely to be assisted than the least employable (Benarrosh, 2000, p. 21), undermining to some extent the very purpose of PLIEs to assist those furthest from the labour market. This will shape, perhaps distort, partnerships within the framework of PLIEs in favour of employers if public actors adopt an overly subservient role to business interests. It is employers alone who then define the notion of employability as an objective fact. For jobseekers to be employable requires prior investment in human capital; yet, those most in need of assistance may not receive this support if they are seen as too far from the labour market.

An alternative approach is to consider the notion of employability more as a social construct than as an objective fact. This is the core belief of the 'Intervention sur l'Offre et la Demande' or IOD method that has been adopted by around 80 recruitment agencies across France as well as by a few PLIEs.[9] It is employers' standard hiring practices that pose significant work barriers to some people because, on paper, they do not have the required or ideal qualifications, or are stigmatized by their status as recipients of social assistance, by employment gaps in their CVs or by their ethnicity (e.g. because their name identifies them as being of foreign origin). Employers, especially in France, are seen to be overly prescriptive and demanding when setting out their ideal job-candidate profiles (Salognon, 2007, p. 716). Instead of a focus on investing in human capital, through training or subsidized jobs, agencies using the IOD method actively mediate with prospective employers to counter negative attitudes towards the least employable and to encourage firms to be more realistic in their expectations. One of the aims, given the tendency towards over-qualification in menial jobs, is to reclaim unskilled posts for the least qualified.

It is this mediation role with employers that sets the IOD method apart. IOD teams first build up then maintain partnerships with local businesses, eliciting information about their real (as opposed to ideal) needs. In doing so, the IOD teams try to build a collaborative platform and commit local firms to more stable job offers for groups seen to face discrimination in the labour market. They explicitly avoid subsidized contracts and, instead, directly propose one suitable candidate who is interested in the vacant post, thus discouraging firms from going through the usual competitive hiring process based on a selection of CVs that often excludes the most disadvantaged due to poor work history (Castra and Pascual, 2003). Their mediation role extends to attending the initial meeting between the jobseeker and employer, and then following up regularly with both to resolve any difficulties and prevent a premature end to the contract.[10]

The IOD method, by trying to assuage firms' selective hiring practices, brings active social policies closer to the ideals of deliberative democracy, notably the stated aim that public deliberation should lead to transforming 'preferences, interests, beliefs and judgements' (Young, 2000, p. 26). In doing so, IOD teams aim to redress the inevitable imbalances of power between the most vulnerable groups and employers who are reluctant to hire, or even interview, those seen as the least employable. Figures for 2005 show that 67 per cent of jobseekers assisted by an IOD team in France found work, of which 41 per cent later became permanent contracts (Salognon, 2007, p. 727).[11]

Table 4.1   Overview of Danish welfare policy changes, 1993–2007

1993	Labour Market Reform
	Duration of unemployment benefits (UB) reduced from 9 to 7 years
	Individual plans of action for long-term unemployed
	Decentralized corporatist labour market policy
1994	Check up
	Right and duty to activation after 4 years
	Stronger availability requirements and sanctions
1995	Labour Market Reform II
	Duration of UB reduced to 5 years
	Right and duty to activation after 2 years
	Duty to accept 'appropriate job' after 6 months and 4-hour daily commutes
1998	Labour Market Reform III
	Duration of UB reduced to 4 years
	Right and duty to activation after 1 year
	Duty to accept 'appropriate job' after 3 months
	'Law on Active Social Policy' stressing everybody's duty to be active and to accept any 'appropriate' job
2000	Duty to actively seek job for social assistance claimants whose only problem is employment

2002	'More People to Work' (*Flere i arbejde*) reform Rules for people on UB and social assistance (SA) harmonized Duty to take 'appropriate job' from day one for people on UB and SA
2006	Welfare Reform Agreement Interview with unemployment insurance fund after 4 weeks Controls every 3 months of the obligation to be available for work Right and duty to activation after 9 months of unemployment Abolished prolonged right to unemployment benefit for 55–59 years Right and duty to activation for 58–59 years old
2007	Danish Municipal Reform Five regions replace the former 16 counties Municipalities reduced in number from 270 to 98 Creation of 91 new one-stop Job Centres for UB and SA claimants Local Employment Councils replace Regional Labour Market Councils

Source: Andersen and Pedersen, 2007.

Table 4.2   UK welfare policy changes, 1996–2011

1996	Jobseekers' Allowance (JSA) introduced Brought together UB and Income Support for people on social assistance Claimants must be available to work for at least 40 hours a week and be actively seeking work Sanctions for leaving employment voluntarily without just cause, for refusing employment or refusing to attend work programme without good cause, or for losing employment through misconduct Means-tested after 6 months
1997	National Traineeships for young people
1997–98	'New Deal' programmes including: New Deal for Young People (NDYP): aged 18–24 and unemployed for 6 months or more; benefits conditional on participation in 1 of 4 options (subsidized work in the private or public sector for 6 months, education or training up to 12 months, or self-employment) New Deal 25+: compulsory for adults over 25 unemployed for more than 18 months and may include work experience, occupational training and help with workplace skills New Deal for Lone Parents: voluntary for parents of children under school-leaving age and includes help and advice on finding work, training and childcare New Deal for the Disabled: voluntary and delivered through various 'job brokers' to assist with finding training opportunities, job vacancies and applying for work
1998	National Childcare Strategy Target of child care places for all 3- and 4-year-olds by 2004

1999	Introduction of the UK's first national minimum wage
2002	Creation of Jobcentre Plus (merging the Benefits Agency and the Jobcentre) Work-focused and supporting a broader range of benefit recipients to move from welfare into work Aimed to offer a more personalized service
2003	'Pathways to Work' reforms To help people living with illness or disability back to work Up to 6 compulsory work-focused interviews with a personal employment advisor for all but the most sick or disabled; assistance to manage illness or disability (the Condition Management Programme) or to find training opportunities A Return-to-Work credit of £40 a week for up to a year 2003–06: pilot phases led by Jobcentre Plus 2007–08: national roll-out engaging private and voluntary-sector providers to lead programme delivery
2007	Welfare Reform Act Employment and Support Allowance (ESA) to replace Incapacity Benefit and Income Support paid on incapacity grounds for new claimants 13-week Work Capability Assessment phase during which ESA paid at basic JSA rate Stricter medical assessment for ESA claimants; people assessed as being able to work required to attend work-focused interviews and develop, with their advisers, a plan of action to help them
2011	Welfare Reform Bill Universal Credit as a 'single streamlined benefit' proposed to replace most existing in- and out-of-work benefits (JSA, ESA, housing/child-tax/ working-tax credits etc.) Work Programme introduced and replaced previous programmes for the unemployed including 'Pathways to Work' whilst 'Flexible New Deal' replaced New Deal programmes A partnership between the state and public, private or third-sector providers Payments to providers largely based on results achieved

Table 4.3   Welfare reforms in France, 1984–2009

1984	Travaux d'Utilité Collective (TUC) Part-time, community service jobs with elements of vocational training A 'training' contract for young people but without employment rights of a standard contract
1988	Revenu Minimum d'Insertion (RMI) Created due to large numbers of unemployed not qualifying for other forms of social assistance A right to social inclusion but without any benefit conditionality Minimum eligibility age of 25

1990	Contrat Emploi Solidarité (CES) Replaced TUC and extended to include all long-term adults and RMI recipients A formal contract but remained part-time (20 hours per week)
1997	Emploi Jeunes Full-time, subsidized work in the public or voluntary sectors for a minimum of 5 years
1998	Trajet d'accès à l'emploi (TRACE) A 18-month personalized plan to help young people (16–25) back to work Access to various insertion programmes for participants; e.g. training or education, subsidized contracts, apprenticeships
1998 & 2000	'Aubry' laws on reduced working hours Aimed to create new jobs as well as achieve a better work-life balance Statutory working week reduced from 39 to 35 hours but employers given more discretion over work time More exemptions for employers' social contributions and a move from national to sectoral and firm-level collective bargaining
2001	Prime Pour l'Emploi (PPE) In-work benefit for low-income households Plan d'Aide au Retour à l'Emploi (PARE) Reform of unemployment insurance into a more contractual basis, with increased obligations to demonstrate work-related activity, for the (insured) unemployed
2002	Contrat Jeune en Entreprise (CJE) Three-year subsidies to private-sector employers hiring young unemployed
2004	Revenu Minimum d'Activité (RMA) Targeted recipients of RMI for at least 2 years Stricter obligations to find work
2009	Creation of Pôle emploi Integrates employment services for the insured and uninsured unemployed in a one-stop job centre Offering a personalized service to the unemployed Revenu de Solidarité Active (RSA) Integration of RMI and the single-parent allowance Opens up eligibility rules for under 25s Increased benefit conditionality; jobseekers cannot refuse two 'reasonable' job offers

DISCUSSION AND CONCLUSIONS

Nonetheless, the motivation behind this chapter was not to see how effective active social policies are in getting the unemployed back to work. The Danish governance reforms, for example, are difficult to assess because they occurred shortly before the global economic crisis and a subsequent steep rise in unemployment. The motivation, instead, was to consider whether the trajectory of active social policies, with more localization and greater involvement of private and third-sector organizations, fulfilled a normative set of conditions for legitimate democratic governance.

The capability approach and the model of deliberative democracy provide a framework for considering the democratic legitimacy of active social policies. The capability approach makes us think about what people can do given their diverse circumstances. It points to the need to develop a range of policies that are sensitive to individual need, as well as to local context. Despite a discourse of empowering jobseekers in the UK, recent experience has shown that private companies that deliver employment services according to a payment-by-results philosophy tend to focus attention on the most job-ready. This tendency is confirmed in other countries that have contracted out welfare services to the market. Both Australia and the Netherlands abandoned price competition for this reason (Finn, 2008).

Part of the problem, as Dean et al. (2005) point out, is that in discourses of activation the notion of people's capabilities has been conflated with the idea of human capital or their 'employability'. But if we are to treat human beings as more than just 'means of production' (Sen, 1999), then it is important to recognize that paid work, though important, is only one means of enhancing capabilities – and not, in the case of people with multiple health or social problems, always the most immediate means of raising their effective freedoms.

Without this recognition, job utility or the argument that any job is better than none may prevail in discussions with harder-to-place clients to the neglect of issues of job quality and suitability. The Danish reforms towards a work-first approach are worrying because they are likely to undermine the legitimacy of activation measures in the eyes of the unemployed, noting the finding that three out of four people were satisfied with their activation offer prior to the reforms (Kvist and Pedersen, 2007). Alternatively, simply neglecting harder-to-place clients undermines the principle of universal coverage of social policies. A way to avoid this is through service guarantees to promote more transparent and equitable services for all.

The capability approach helps to avoid framing the issue of unemployment in narrow terms of just individual work-related deficiencies. One way to shift the focus away from the individual is to question the validity of the employer-driven concept of employability. The IOD method in France reminds us that people's capabilities are affected by other people's perceptions and prejudices which, to a large extent, are beyond the control of jobseekers. The method adopted by some French recruitment agencies, albeit small in number, points to a need to challenge such attitudes as a way to raise people's effective freedoms.

This takes me to the model of deliberative democracy. The French case allows us to think about how to develop more effective partnerships with the private sector. PLIEs in France have had some relative success in achieving more permanent outcomes for the largest number at risk of social exclusion.[12] But where they reproduce labour-market selectivity, employers can distort the local partnership models that are at the core of local policy networks in France. It is the growth and influence (albeit still limited in scope) of the IOD method that potentially makes local partnerships in France more reciprocal and genuine. By working on firms' selective hiring practices, IOD teams are shown to have been effective in narrowing some of the perceived gaps between employers and people deemed the least employable.

This reminds us, rather obviously, that private firms are a critical part of the solution to unemployment. A simple conclusion from the UK study is that financial incentives are necessary to make it commercially viable for private companies to work with the most disadvantaged. This would encourage them to form more genuine and collaborative partnerships with charities. But questions remain about how to engender a better sense of responsibility in the private sector for the unemployed. In Denmark, prior to the 2007 reforms, the views and concerns of employers were well represented in the design of activation policies. Employers, as a result, were more committed to ensuring that work placements or work-subsidy training programmes were effective, notably by addressing key skills shortages (Lindsay and Mailand, 2009). As the Danish study indicates, the transfer of power to the Danish municipalities may well diminish levels of commitment among employers.

What lessons can be drawn for the wider democratic system? The scope and trajectory of active social policies reveal a lot about how societies cope with social inequality. Compared to more autocratic systems of governance, democracy is better equipped to recognize that people have different capabilities. Indeed, an aim of democracy is to understand difference better by widening access to institutions whose decisions affect people's lives. Active social policies, by promoting local employment solutions and more personalized services, seem to offer better opportunities for this, both for the individual unemployed and for new welfare actors. In turn, they may provide avenues for better appreciation of local context as well individual circumstance.

For these reasons, the ways in which active social policies are being implemented are a wider democratic issue. In asking if the new governance arrangements adhere to democratic norms, we can also draw lessons from a democratic perspective for policies dealing with other social issues. The first is that policies are implemented in ways that acknowledge the social context of disadvantage. Against the tendency to point to individual traits to explain disadvantage, the structural causes of inequality remain an important consideration. Without this recognition, it may appear justified to treat individuals as unequal and neglect those with more complex problems.

It is hence also important to be wary of rigid policy targets that are inflexible and fail to adapt to local context. Approaches that adopt a payment-by-results philosophy, for example, need to recognize 'soft outcomes' for the most disadvantaged target groups. In other words, social policies must avoid creating incentives to work only with easier target groups.

Neither should policies lead to further social disadvantage. Using cuts in social benefits to change behaviour is not a long-term option because it will cause additional hardship, not just for the individual but also for his/her dependents. Care must also be taken that policies do not channel people into 'exclusion trajectories' (Enjolras et al., 2001, p. 44), either through passive dependence on social benefits or due to marginal and low-status jobs that contribute minimally to social inclusion.

To mitigate the negative effects of social policies, this chapter set out to show the benefits to the policy process of adopting values consistent with the capability approach and the model of deliberative democracy. The most important is the value of learning from others, which requires that there is mutual respect among key policy stakeholders. Policies can then evolve better and adapt to new social challenges. Without this ability to be self-reflective, policy responses will not fully recognize people's different capabilities and, as a result, will be less well placed to address barriers to social inclusion.

NOTES

1. Two special issues of the *International Journal of Sociology and Social Policy* in 2007 focus on 'new modes of governance in activation policies' (issues 7/8 and 9/10).
2. The Dutch experience of contracting out public employment services has served to inform other countries' experiments with introducing competition and quasi-markets into the delivery of activation, notably the UK. See Finn (2008).
3. More recent findings from the UK on Local Employment Partnerships (LEPs), introduced in 2007, again found little emphasis on job quality. See Bellis et al. (2011).

4. 50 per cent was for initial job entry and 20 per cent if a client remained in a job of at least 16 hours a week for a minimum of 13 of the previous 26 weeks. The remaining 30 per cent was paid up front as service fees.
5. Figures for new IB claims show that fewer than a quarter of people who applied between October 2008 and August 2010 for the new Employment and Support Allowance (ESA) qualified following their medical assessment – only 6 per cent were assigned to the Support Group (SG) for people deemed unable to work due to serious illness or disability, and 16 per cent to the Work-Related Activity Group (WRAG) for people with some future work capacity. Most (39 per cent) were either deemed Fit For Work (FFW) or (36 per cent) closed their claim before assessment was completed. See http://www.dwp.gov.uk/newsroom/press-releases/2011/apr-2011/dwp043-11.shtml. Existing IB claims are currently being reviewed (from October 2010 until 2014).
6. Other national experiences of contracting-out also note these tendencies – on the Netherlands, see van Berkel and van der Aa (2005).
7. On average around 9.5 per cent since the early 1980s with up to and over 40 per cent made up of the long-term unemployed.
8. There are more than 36,000 communes in France, a huge number largely because the number of inhabitants in communes ranges from two million in Paris to ten people living in a hamlet. Nearly 21,000 communes have fewer than 500 inhabitants.
9. The IOD method (*Intervention sur l'Offre et la Demande*) has been developed locally in France over the past 25 years by a non-profit organization called *Transfer* based in Bordeaux (www.transfer-iod.org). It is the intellectual property owner of the IOD method, and trains agencies (funded by the *département*) wanting to adopt it as a way to help the unemployed back to work. According to their website, teams adopting the IOD method have helped more than 10,000 people back into stable employment and have mobilized more than 6,000 companies.
10. For a more detailed description of the work of an IOD team based in Evry, south-east of Paris, in the *département* of Essonne, see Salognon (2007).
11. The author notes the relative cost of the IOD method at €2,400 per person and €5,500 per person when they return to permanent positions. The costs, particularly to help people back into permanent work, are relatively high compared to privately operated back-to-work programmes (€2,300 per person) and those operating for insured jobseekers within the PARE scheme (€750 per person for a three-month programme).
12. 46 per cent of jobseekers helped by a PLIE found stable employment (that is, of at least 6 months) between 2000 and 2006 (OECD, 2009).

5. Democratic boundaries in the US and Europe: inequality, localization and voluntarism in social welfare

Tess Altman and David G. Mayes

INTRODUCTION

Recent global changes have had a pronounced effect on the nature of social welfare. Ageing populations, increased immigration and mobility, changes in technology and communication, increased inequality, voluntarism and decentralization all create new conditions and new risks. Most advanced industrial countries have experienced changes in the nature of the welfare state. There has been a general shift away from the state as the sole provider of welfare and an interest in other kinds of welfare providers and forms of governance, as exemplified in the 'disorganized welfare mix' (see Altman and Shore, chapter 6 for a discussion of this term). Civil society and private actors have become more central to welfare provision. For some, such changes constitute a radical 'crisis of the welfare state' (Jessop, 1999), while others claim that changes are regime-specific.[1] Either way, such changes raise questions about how social welfare is being reformed and reshaped, and what the implications of such reforms might be for conceptions of democracy and citizenship.

Our aim in this chapter is to examine three of these trends which have emerged in recent years and are contributing to important changes in the way both social welfare and democratic decision making over its form and content interact. These trends are:

- growing inequality,
- an increase in devolution of powers to local authorities and institutions, and
- a rise in voluntary provision and contributions.

These trends have important consequences for social welfare. The traditional welfare state was fundamentally concerned with providing protection and addressing inequality through decommodification and redistribution of wealth (Esping-Andersen, 1990). However, inequality is now being redressed through a range of different and more active rather than passive means. How or whether localization and voluntarism enhance or diminish inequality is unclear. On the one hand, increasing localization can permit a much better focus on the needs of local communities and improve incentives and efficiency, while on the other it can facilitate increasing polarization according to income and preferences. The match between decision making and democratic control can alter, either positively or negatively. The rise of voluntarism may be a reinforcing or offsetting factor. These trends appear strongly in the US and Canada. This chapter explores them and considers in particular their consequences for European countries and the evolution of democratic relationships in the European Union (EU).

While there has been considerable concern over the challenges globalization places on the traditional welfare state (Snower et al., 2009), a social, political and economic trend toward decentralization has also been taking place in the same period (Rodríguez-Pose and Gill, 2003). Local authorities and jurisdictions, grassroots movements, and local communities have been receiving increased emphasis in many countries. This localization entails devolving responsibilities traditionally associated with the state, such as social provision, economic stability and growth, and the smooth functioning of society, to local authorities and communities.

An emphasis upon the local is related to a further trend: the rise of a discourse of 'civil society' and a renewed interest in and visibility of volunteering and charitable giving. Though voluntarism is not a new phenomenon, the value and recognition bestowed upon volunteering and the voluntary sector has increased almost exponentially on both local and global levels (Salamon, 1999). Globally, this has been manifested through ideologies of humanitarianism, the development of global volunteer networks, global social movements, the rise of 'civil society' and a proliferation of celebrity do-gooders. Locally, volunteers have continued to work for social causes but have also become more involved in social service provision through working for voluntary social service providers and through charitable giving/donations to local social services such as education and health.[2] However, such voluntarism is not necessarily focused on the disadvantaged. It can also be a response to elitist concerns related to cultural activities, quality education, health care, and environmental protection (Horstmann and Scharf, 2008).

Our overarching concern is with the effects of localization and voluntarism on equitable and democratic welfare provision. Equality of access, opportunity and treatment is one of the defining characteristics of a socially inclusive democracy. However, the current global climate is one of increasing polarization or inequalities (Pontusson, 2005). Indeed, some have argued that 'global times' bring 'good times' only to certain localities rather than all regions (Amin, 1994, p. 25). Disparities occur both between countries and within countries, with the rich tier of society becoming richer and the poor relatively poorer. These inequalities have been exacerbated by the recent global financial crisis.

The chapter is divided into two sections. The first section explores the three trends, both theoretically and empirically. First we outline definitions of inequality, localization and voluntarism in order to delimit our scope. Second, we examine the interrelationships between the three trends. We discuss linkages between localization and inequality in the context of the Tiebout (1956) hypothesis which claims that people form like-minded local communities based upon income and preferences, and hence that localization may encourage social stratification. We also discuss the social science literature on localization which draws a strong connection between localization and democracy. Some critics have termed this 'the local trap' and have argued that there is nothing inherently democratic about the local level (Purcell, 2006). We then assess the links between localization and voluntarism, and voluntarism and inequality. We discuss the pitfalls and potentialities of voluntarism as a means to 'fill the gaps' in social welfare provision and as an avenue for increased citizen involvement and participation.

In the second section, we explore the trends in specific regions empirically. We follow de Vries (2000) in noting the lack of empirical studies on localization, and argue that it is important not to generalize about processes of localization and rather to examine such processes in specific contexts. We compare the trends of the US and Europe through examining case studies of workfare, Business Improvement Districts (BIDs), and education. The US provides a clear example of the relationship between localization, voluntarism, and inequality; indeed, it appears from the US that the nature of the framework for social welfare is changing (Horstmann and Scharf, 2008). Localization and voluntarism are pronounced in the US, and have been strengthened through legislation such as the *Serve America Act 2009*, employment policies such as workfare and local community initiatives such as Asset-Based Community Development (see Altman and Shore, Chapter 6). The US is also characterized by general processes of competition among regions/cities and, perhaps more importantly, competition within cities between the centre and the suburbs over taxes and benefits related both to insurance and quality of life.

The European situation is less clear cut. While there is certainly scope and support for localization, the situation is necessarily more complex due to the varying approaches of member states. Those who support the move towards devolution and decentralization have argued that it may provide a means of alleviating the potentially alienating effects of integration (and, relatedly, globalization).

Through comparison between the US and Europe, we seek to highlight the tensions and trade-offs involved in social welfare provision more generally. We are also interested in exploring the possibility of 'policy transfer' (Cook, 2008) from the US to Europe. We are particularly interested in the implications of increasing localization and voluntarism for inequality and democracy in Europe; in other words, do these trends mitigate or contribute to rising levels of inequality, and hence to levels of social exclusion from the democratic process?

INEQUALITY, LOCALIZATION AND VOLUNTARISM: DEFINITIONS, SCOPE AND LINKAGES

Inequality

Definitions of inequality have increasingly moved away from conceptions based on measures of poverty and deprivation, to include social concerns such as equality of opportunity, social exclusion, and affording the disadvantaged the capabilities for exiting their problems (Sen, 1997). Inequality has historically been a central concern of the welfare state. A challenge for redressing inequality through welfare provision has been the need to negotiate the relationship between equality, redistribution, and social protection, on the one hand, and economic efficiency, growth, and employment on the other (Pontusson, 2005, p. 2). This tension is a key feature of modern capitalist democracies, as 'while capitalism generates inequality, democracy is a source of egalitarian pressure' (Pontusson, 2005, p. 2).

In recent times inequality has been increasing (Pontusson, 2005; Sen, 1997). We might assume therefore that somehow the relationship between these factors has become unbalanced. However, this conclusion depends on two widespread assumptions. The first is that equality and efficiency/growth are somehow conflicting; however, recent notions such as flexicurity[3] attempt to illustrate they can be compatible, though this is as yet inconclusive (Madsen, 2008). The second assumption is based on how inequality is measured. Often, inequality is measured by income.[4] However, as we demonstrate, there are more factors involved in measuring inequality than income alone.

When measured by income, inequality has a seemingly easy remedy: increased inequality of pre-tax incomes in the higher quantiles could easily be consistent with increased post-tax redistribution of wealth. Following the median voter hypothesis, the majority in society, who will tend to determine the government (providing they vote), will be on lower and medium incomes given the shape of the skew of the distribution of incomes. They hence in theory have the power to raise taxes on the higher earning group. Moreover, even without those on lower incomes exercising the ability to raise taxes, tax revenues will increase because income tax rates are progressive and a larger portion of the population will get drawn into paying the higher rates.[5] This argument suggests that taxation systems are, in their pure form, disposed towards a redistributive model. It would appear that inequality can be resolved in one way or another by redistribution. Nevertheless personal income tax systems have become less redistributive in some countries, in part responding to the worries over the disincentive effects of high rates and the increasing ability of those on high incomes to avoid them by moving.

However, there are problems with using only direct income to measure inequality. Differences between welfare regimes may in fact be less pronounced than they seem, depending on what is used to judge the extent of the inequality. Some cross-national studies have ignored the effects of in-kind transfers provided by the state and only measured direct taxes when there are many indirect (value-added, sales and property) taxes (Garfinkel et al., 2006). When measured this way, some countries are not as unequal as they might have appeared without taking into account these factors (see Garfinkel et al., 2006, Figure 2). There are also issues with the somewhat idealistic notion that pre-tax inequality will be solved by post-tax redistribution. Often this will depend on context. For instance, Bjorvatn and Cappelen (2003) argue that the more unequal a system is, the more likely that this will be mirrored in unequal post-tax redistribution. By contrast, they argue that the more egalitarian the system is (that is, the more equal pre-tax incomes are), the greater the trend is to redistribution. This may be due to the effects of social and geographical segregation between rich and poor in unequal societies which lowers the propensity for the rich to support redistribution. Moreover, some authors (for example, Borck, 2007) have complicated the median voter hypothesis by noting that the majority in society (earning low to medium incomes) are not necessarily the ones voting. This majority does not necessarily possess political influence or a strong political voice. Being in the majority is not the only source of political power – access to resources and exclusive networks are other means of political influence available only to an elite few. This is particularly likely to be true when some of the decisions are administrative rather than democratically determined and the richer can be more effective in lobbying the appropriate officials.

We hence take into account the complexities of welfare provision, taxation, and other non-monetary factors when assessing inequality. Inequality is, as Sen (1997) points out, a difficult thing to measure, and ought not to be defined in terms of income differentials alone. Other factors affecting levels of inequality include the ease of access to public goods, such as schools and doctors, and the quality of a person's living and working environment. A pertinent question for this chapter is how, and to what extent (if any), devolving powers to the local level has affected levels of inequality as well as democratic accountability.

Localization

It has been widely noted that a major problem with attempting to define or label the local level is that the very concept of 'the local' is shrouded in ambiguity (Brodie (2000) quoted in Boudreau, 2003, p. 793). Many terms have been used to define social, economic, political, and cultural initiatives or processes which emphasize the local or sub-state level, such as decentralization, devolution, federalism, regionalism and localism.[6] Some authors link these processes to new forms of urban governance, citizenship, and civil society (see Purcell, 2006). Literature on localization is generally concerned with two principal groups involved in processes of localization: local authorities, who are linked to political and fiscal devolution, and local communities, in relation to civil society and voluntarism.

A further problem stems from differences in the nature of subnational layers of government, where some countries have regions, states or provinces with very extensive powers and others do not. Most have two levels of more local government and some more. Since nation states vary very considerably in size, so do their component lower levels of government. Each of these levels is subject to some of the forces of localization, so we attempt to be as inclusive as possible in our discussion. It does, however, impede generalization and requires more detail from time to time.

Most definitions and studies of localization raise questions about democracy. Dating back to Tocqueville, 'there has been a strong normative argument within political theory that local self-government is a

fundamental component of broader democratic structures and practices'
(Pratchett, 2004, p. 358). This assumption is linked to the nineteenth
century ideas of theorists such as J.S. Mill, who claimed that local
institutions are the most effective and accessible for political participation
and facilitate social inclusion. More recently, local government has been
touted as an avenue for participatory democracy (Pratchett, 2004, p. 360).
It has been argued that local democracy enhances participatory citizenship and is in fact a necessary prerequisite for facilitating representative
democracy (Pratchett, 2004, p. 361). In fact, the rights and duties
encompassed by citizenship are most significant at the local level, for this
is where they are concretely exercised (Boudreau, 2003, p. 73). Local
democracy has hence been viewed as an important characteristic of a
wider democratic society and culture (Pratchett, 2004, p. 161).

Recently, however, the conflation of the local (or more specifically
local autonomy) with democracy has been questioned. Pratchett (2004,
p. 368) notes that the relationship between local autonomy and local
democracy represents a paradox:

> On the one hand, strong local autonomy is essential to maintaining the local
> democracy practices that underpin broader democratic cultures within the
> polity. On the other hand, local autonomy threatens the viability of demo-
> cratically supported national priorities. Too much local autonomy, in this
> sense, can destabilize the national institutions of democratic government.

Here, local autonomy can represent a threat to the sovereignty and hence
the democratic legitimacy of the nation state. The most extreme form of
such autonomy would be secession from the state which can take place in
a democratic or undemocratic fashion and depending on this can either
enhance or diminish inequality (see Boudreau, 2003).

There is of course the long-standing debate between James Madison in
The Federalist No.10 in 1787 and the anti-federalists about the merits of
having a broader democracy to avoid the capture of smaller areas by
interest groups. Hayek's (1944) *The Road to Serfdom* also provides a
very vivid picture of how a minority can become tyrannical.

Other theorists have argued that 'there is no necessary or obvious
linkage between the local and the democratic' (Brodie (2000) quoted in
Boudreau, 2003, p. 793). Purcell (2006) has termed this assumed linkage
'the local trap'. He assesses a wide range of literature and concludes that
'the local trap' rests on a wide range of assumptions: localization is
presented as synonymous with democratization; 'local people' are conflated with the wider 'people', as in the popular citizenry of a democracy;
'community' is conflated with 'local-scale community'; local

community-based development is conflated with participatory development; and the term 'local' is used as a euphemism for other terms such as
'indigenous', 'poor', 'rural', 'weak', or 'traditional'.

However, localization could just as easily lead to an inferior application of democracy; 'the people' and 'community' can be defined at a
number of levels; local community based development does not necessarily give way to wider political participation and there is nothing
inherently local about the poor, the rural etc. (Purcell, 2006, p. 1924). In
short, there is both analytical imprecision and idealization surrounding
the notion of the local. Yet as Purcell (2006, pp. 1925–27) points out,
there is nothing inherent about scale. Scales are contingent strategies,
dependent on particular agendas, and are only partially fixed at any given
time (Purcell, 2006, p. 1928). Further research into the local, and scale in
general, should 'interrogate how the interrelationships among scales are
continually fixed, struggled over and reworked by particular social actors
pursuing specific political, social, economic and ecological goals'
(Purcell, 2006, p. 1929).

De Vries (2000) has similarly noted that there are no inherent qualities
or characteristics attached to centralization and decentralization, the
assumed polar opposites of scale. Taking the UN definition of decentralization as 'the devolution of power and responsibility over policies from
the national level to the local level, and centralization as transformation
in the opposite direction' (de Vries, 2000, p. 196), De Vries notes that the
arguments made for decentralization are very similar to those made for
centralization. For example, metaphors such as 'increased efficiency',
'democratization of policy processes' and 'effectiveness' have been
attributed to both decentralization and centralization in different contexts.
What is needed when analysing the development of de/centralization
policies is a comparative and historical perspective, as well as an
awareness of the importance of the opinions of actors directly involved in
such processes (de Vries, 2000, p. 204). In this case, the opinions of local
elites who may seek to benefit from increased devolution should be taken
into account.

There are hence potentialities and pitfalls in both localization/
decentralization and centralization/statism. There is nothing inherently
democratic or equitable about the local level; but neither is the local level
inherently undemocratic or inequality-inducing. Therefore though some
commentators, such as Prud'homme (1995), have warned against the
decentralization and fiscal federalism as inequality inducing, these same
dangers could arise in a centralized system.[7] De Vries (2000) has also
questioned whether decentralization is actually occurring to the extent it
is claimed to be. Instead of seeing decentralization as a linear, hegemonic

trend, he views centralization, decentralization and recentralization as caught in 'ongoing cycles in which trends and taking sides in the discussion succeed one another continuously' (de Vries, 2000, p. 194).

Voluntarism

Voluntarism is by no means a new phenomenon but its role in social welfare provision has shifted and become more pronounced since the relatively recent move from an 'organized' to a 'disorganized' welfare mix (Bode, 2006; Altman and Shore, chapter 6 this volume). This shift has entailed both a larger role for the voluntary sector in welfare provision, and an increase in volunteering, charitable contributions, and civil society participation in the social services arena (Salamon, 1999; Wolch, 1990; Fyfe and Milligan, 2003).

Paralleling the growth of voluntarism has been a burgeoning literature expounding upon its value. This literature comes from many different disciplines, and variously describes the positive effects of voluntarism as fostering social capital (Putnam, 2000), creating a 'warm glow' of giving (Diamond, 2006), increasing civic participation, and facilitating participatory democracy (see Purcell, 2006 for examples). Often, a link is drawn between voluntarism and local communities. Indeed, the non-profit sector is seen as an important player in the new local 'urban governance' landscape (Pincetl, 2003).

Such literature has been termed 'neo-Tocquevillean' (van der Meer and van Ingen, 2009). Tocqueville saw voluntary associations as 'schools of democracy' and, by drawing a causal link between voluntary participation and wider civic participation, the neo-Toquevillean literature does the same. However, in primarily focusing on the positive potentialities of civil society and voluntarism, this literature has largely ignored the possibility of new risks and dangers that could arise with the growth of voluntarism. Those studies which do provide a more critical analysis of the role of voluntarism in social welfare provision note that it is possible for the voluntary sector and volunteers to be co-opted by state and market forces (Wolch, 1990), that the voluntary sector is dynamic yet volatile (Bode, 2006) and that 'geographies of voluntarism' can be uneven and may 'reinforce rather than alleviate social and spatial welfare inequalities' (Fyfe and Milligan, 2003, p. 400). We hence take a cautious approach to assessing the role of voluntarism. Furthermore, we recognize that voluntarism is a broad term, what Kendall and Knapp (1995) call a 'loose and baggy monster', and mainly use it to denote the social services and facilities that are provided through voluntary donation and participation in the fields of education, health, welfare and culture. We follow this approach and do not use voluntarism simply to denote the non-public sector as much of that is clearly for profit.

Linkages

Horstmann and Scharf (2008, p. 427) argue that although the three trends have independent determinants they also have a clear mutual link. They argue that people differ in both income and preferences and that localization enables them to obtain more of what they want. Thus services tailored to local demands are likely to be less costly, and incentives for success and voluntary participation will be greater.

The framework Horstmann and Sharf use to discuss linkages between localization, voluntarism and inequality is the Tiebout hypothesis (1956). The Tiebout hypothesis, based on empirical observation in the United States, argues that people will tend to sort themselves into like-minded communities based upon income and preferences. In some instances the reason for choosing a particular locale is financial. For example, in situations where pressure exists for the wealthy to pay increasing taxes, a common response, according to the Tiebout hypothesis (1956), is simply for them to 'vote with their feet', and move. People can move to lower tax jurisdictions or move their activities to those locations. Indeed, this is one of the objections to high rates of tax for high income individuals because tax yields actually fall as a result. Wealthy individuals or families can move between or within countries.

Concentration in particular areas will affect the demands for local goods and services. Greater polarization through mobility leads to a greater matching of overall demand and the wishes of those who will be paying taxes in any particular local area. This has been revealed in the drift to the suburbs, the rise of lifestyle blocks and even in the gentrification of inner city areas once unpleasant industry has left. Horstmann and Scharf (2008) have also suggested that devolution leads to an increase in the supply of local 'public goods',[8] partly because the objectives of expenditure fit better with the needs of the local community but also because some of the responsibility will devolve on the local area for finance if the federal funds are insufficient. Thus people have an incentive to ensure that the local labour market works as they will bear a proportion of the cost if it does not.

These processes are principally designed to ensure greater efficiency and to try to make sure that local preferences and differences are addressed. Nevertheless, such attention to local needs can encourage people to move. It is well known that people will move in order to make sure that their children are in the catchment area for better schools.

Property prices will rise in those areas as a result and fall in the areas serving the worse schools, thereby exacerbating the problem. Those with higher incomes and the ability to support additional activities in the schools will gravitate to the good area. Those with limited resources cannot move home or commute long distances and hence may find they cannot exercise their preferences. The Tiebout hypothesis hence suggests that social stratification or polarization is likely to occur.

The Tiebout hypothesis thus requires two dimensions of difference: income and preferences. If preferences are fairly homogeneous then the incentive for the rich to seek out places where their preferences predominate will be smaller. However, the greater the inequality, and hence the tax pressure on the rich, the more they will be inclined to seek out a lower tax regime.[9] One of the most obvious concerns relates to the costs of property and the rates of property taxation. If it is possible to move to get substantial reductions in property taxation, this will influence those with higher valued properties or wishing to upgrade, given the substantial transaction cost involved.[10] Thus the property values in the higher tax regime will tend to fall and those in the lower tax regime rise. The former will therefore tend to see falling tax receipts and the latter rising; in the second case possibly allowing the authority to cut tax rates further. Raising tax rates for the higher tax area may be impractical and hence a reduction in services may be the only solution, thus tending to increase inequality.[11]

Fiscal federalism is based upon such findings that localization may encourage polarization. Policies of fiscal federalism advocate redistribution from the richer areas to the poorer ones if the provision of public goods is to be equitable, as mobility will not solve the problem. Germany, Italy and Spain, for example, use inter-regional transfers to try to keep public spending reasonably equal across the country. In the UK the block grants to local authorities from central government reflect both the revenue raising capability of the area and the needs of the area relative to the national average. This conclusion is particularly important at the EU level, where the extent of fiscal federalism is strictly limited, with total EU level expenditure only a little over 1 per cent of total GDP. Certainly the EU's structural funds are firmly based on the notion that such fiscal federalism is essential, especially since EU enlargement in 2004 and 2007. However, the size of these funds has gone down in relative terms in recent years as the new member states tend to be recipients rather than adding to the pool of providers.

The Tiebout hypothesis is discussed frequently in terms of capital tax competition (Perroni and Scharf, 2001) as other taxes tend to be more economy wide. Clearly the appropriate choice of the taxes over which competition takes place depends on the tax system of the country concerned. Taxation of real estate is a more common source of local funding than income taxation, which is used in Sweden and Finland for example. In the US use is also made of sales taxes but in Europe a common rate of VAT is the norm across each country.[12] Competition is quite complex, because it is not just a matter of who can be more efficient and offer the lowest tax rate for a given bundle of services but also has to reflect the variety of preferences that exist over the bundle of services to be provided. In Finland, for example, much of the competition among local areas relates to attracting employers on the assumption that population will follow if the employment opportunities exist. This interaction can be quite complex. In the Helsinki region, one of the peripheral authorities was reluctant to agree to the extension of the metro system as, inter alia, this would make it easier for its residents to go and work in central Helsinki hence reducing the incentive for businesses to relocate nearer the growing suburbs. (They were happy for the metro to extend from Helsinki as far as their own centres of employment to encourage the reverse flow of workers.)

So how does this provide evidence of the linkages between our three trends? The Tiebout hypothesis rests on a broad understanding of localization, taking into account a range of factors for why and how localization occurs, as well as its effects. Yet the key interest is the relationship between localization and inequality or, in other words, whether localization fosters cohesion or polarization. Tiebout's hypothesis also presents a distinctive understanding of voluntarism, meaning charitable contributions to social welfare. People make these contributions for a range of reasons. They can be altruistically motivated, but they can also be driven by the consumption preferences of the donor (Horstmann and Sharf, 2008). The poorer majority often do not vote to provide the sorts of public facilities that many of the richer group want.[13] However, many tastes do not reflect income. Since such activities cannot in the main survive on a purely commercial basis they require donations to make them viable. Thus in supporting cultural, recreational, educational and other activities the richer are ensuring that these activities take place and are available to all those who wish to use them at a price which many of the poorer majority can usually afford. However, though cash contributions are dominated by the wealthy, social capital contributions are not only made by the rich tier of society but by people from all income groups, particularly the retired. People can make contributions in the form of utilizing skills and simply providing the services.

Voluntarism has been presented by policymakers and in academic circles as a 'panacea' to social and political issues faced by contemporary liberal democracies (Fyfe and Milligan, 2003, p. 397). However, though a wide range of socioeconomic groups engage in voluntarism, links have still been drawn between voluntarism and inequality (Fyfe and Milligan, 2003). Though voluntary activity and voluntary associations can 'fill the gaps' in social welfare provision, the quantity of volunteers/associations and the effectiveness of their efforts can depend upon already existing resources and capabilities. Moreover, often voluntary activities are driven by the private allegiances and interests of the volunteers, rather than by actual needs (Fyfe and Milligan, 2003, p. 400). Fyfe and Milligan have referred to this phenomenon as 'uneven geographies of voluntarism', which privilege some and not others and exacerbate existing inequalities. Localization may be a contributing factor, as illustrated by comparison between the US and the UK (Fyfe and Milligan, 2003). US welfare reforms which emphasize the local level have stimulated non-profit sector growth and allowed for more space for local differences and preferences, but have also contributed to inequalities between different places and locales – for example, wealthy urban areas versus deprived rural areas as exemplified by the lack of volunteers in the 'sunbelt' region of the US (Fyfe and Milligan, 2003, p. 399; Wolch, 1990). In the UK, a centralized government has also emphasized the importance of voluntarism but its implementation has been more formalized and controlled by the state (Fyfe and Milligan, 2003). Whether the centralized or localized model leads to more inequality is difficult to assess, but it is clear that localization has some effect on the form voluntarism takes.[14]

EMPIRICAL EVIDENCE: CASE STUDIES FROM THE UNITED STATES AND EUROPE

Establishing or refuting the various generalizations made thus far clearly requires empirical evidence. Yet empirical investigations of the specificities of localization are strongly affected by the particular area in which the study takes place. Country size and satisfaction with existing arrangements can influence perceptions of decentralization – the smaller the country and the more satisfied they feel with existing arrangements, the less need for decentralization policies (de Vries, 2000). Those who occupy positions of power are often averse to change, and hence may affect decisions to centralize or decentralize governmental structures. It has also been argued that the suitability of decentralization policies depends on specific context. Decentralization should hence not be adopted just because it has worked well in another area (de Vries, 2000, pp. 219–20). This would appear to be an argument for caution in the use of benchmarking and best practice lessons.

Evidence is also insufficient for drawing clear conclusions even concerning the most basic hypotheses. For example, though the Tiebout hypothesis is easy to set out, it is much more difficult to test empirically (Epple et al., 1978; Epple and Sieg, 1999). Tiebout's initial discussion assumes that migration is costless. This is clearly not true in reality and relaxing this assumption has little impact on the validity of the argument, although it complicates the algebra. The effect of transactions costs is first that there has to be a minimum differential in preferences before people will be prepared to move. But we also have to recognize that moving location is not something that normally occurs very frequently, although it is easier in the US than in Europe. To get the full benefit from any particular location people need to build up social capital and get themselves fully included in the new society. This takes time.[15] Therefore local authorities may have the ability to move faster than migrants in changing local conditions, and the mover cannot be certain that the authorities will not change provisions and tax rates to their disadvantage.

On the other hand, one of the most obvious verifiable characteristics of the Tiebout hypothesis is the movement of house prices which acts as a clear indicator of preferences (Oates, 1973). This has been substantiated in the case of schools where people will move even quite short distances to get into the catchment area of what they regard as better schools. This in turn tends to emphasize the difference between the schools, because those who are prepared or able to pay to get their children better education are also likely to pay for extra activities and facilities. Such schools will also be able to attract the better teachers. It requires very strong corrective action to provide resources to schools with poorer performance or in disadvantaged areas, something which may prove beyond the resources of the disadvantaged. Driving up house prices will in itself increase the rateable values of the area and hence the local tax take. Indeed with raised values it is possible for the tax rate to fall despite providing increased revenues. Hence there is a danger of polarization.

Universities offer a different aspect to the problem. Though students and staff are usually mobile and hence all can compete, universities are attractors for other local activities, for example through science parks. Similarly, the general public can participate in many university activities. Success tends to be reinforcing. The alumni from the better universities tend to become wealthier and provide greater resources for their alma mater. In some countries, these marginal funds have a major effect on the ability to pay staff more than competitors and finance research. However, in other countries, France, Italy and Spain, for example, academic salaries are set nationally with little scope for local variation. Thus voluntarism in the case of universities contributes to inequality.

The same incentives will of course apply if local taxation is based on incomes as it is the richer who will be able to move. Epple and Sieg (1999) show that house values do rise with the median income of communities in the Boston metropolitan area (as measured in 1980) and that education expenditure also rises with median income. Crime rates, on the other hand, fall slightly with income of the community. Not surprisingly, population density also falls as median income rises.

Many other characteristics which make one area more desirable than another may be based on characteristics that are inherent, such as low density housing, parks or seashore and cannot be provided by others. However, much of the Tiebout hypothesis is based on competition among growing municipalities. The argument is that there is a minimum efficient scale, which will encourage authorities to compete very vigorously until they can reach that scale, otherwise their costs will be uncompetitive. However, there are limits and beyond that scale increasing concentration may make the area unattractive to the higher income residents if density is an issue for example. Tiebout uses the example of beaches. People will tolerate increasing density up to a point after which they begin to look for somewhere else to go. However, location is relevant in a different sense as commuting time and cost to areas where jobs are concentrated will also affect the attractiveness of a locality.

We make our own empirical contribution in this section by exploring three aspects of welfare – workfare, Business Improvement Districts, and education – that exemplify linkages between localization, voluntarism and inequality in the US. We then compare and contrast this with the experience in European countries.

The three trends we examine are very obviously exemplified in the US but rather differently in Europe. Both regions have been exposed to the same global shifts and changes, and have sought to adapt or amend their welfare systems. This has especially been the case in the US, where changes in the framework for social welfare have been advocated in quite a radical form, as illustrated in the 1996 statement by then-President Clinton that 'welfare has ended as we know it' (Handler, 2004). The US welfare reforms clearly encompass the three trends we are examining. Strong emphasis has been placed on local level social provision and voluntary contributions; clear links can be drawn between these and inequality. The intersection of the three trends is less clear cut in the European case. Generally, there have been similar shifts towards devolving responsibility to local authorities in Europe, and EU-wide legislation such as the European Charter for Local Self-Government 1985 and the establishment of the Committee of the Regions (CoR) have further legitimized both regional and local levels. However, forms of localization vary between member states. Voluntarism is present but less pronounced, and it is more difficult to draw direct casual links from localization and voluntarism to inequality. Nevertheless some have posited that localization and voluntarism are linked to segregation along socioeconomic lines in both the US and Europe (Sellers, 1999). We turn to our case studies to test this hypothesis. We have deliberately chosen three examples which illustrate strong localization in the US to investigate the extent of potential policy transfer to Europe.

Workfare

Most OECD countries have institutionalized active welfare programmes that are to varying extents classified as workfare (see Handler, 2004; Lødemel and Trickey, 2001). Workfare has a 'broad and elastic meaning, both as a pithy, generic label for work-enforcing welfare reform and as a rather vague umbrella term for a wide range of welfare-to-work policies, job-training and employability programmes, and active-benefit systems' (Peck, 2001, p. 1). We take the view that there are different variants of workfare, and want to establish to what extent European countries have adopted US-style (often labelled Anglo-Saxon although it has not generally been adopted in other Anglo-Saxon countries including the UK) workfare as this variant embodies our three trends.

Workfare encompasses the general shift from passive, benefit-focused welfare regimes, which have been criticized as encouraging cultures of dependency, to active welfare regimes, which require the welfare recipient to engage in employment, job training and job seeking. The prevalence of such active welfare/workfare programmes has implications for our three trends. Firstly, workfare regimes or programmes deal with inequality differently from traditional social welfare policies. Workfare policies accept a certain level of inequality, and are more concerned with the 'work disincentives' fostered by the welfare state than with wage inequality (Handler, 2004, pp. 7–8). Workfare is also more concerned with equality of opportunities than equality of outcomes (Handler, 2004, p. 7). Secondly, local authorities, agencies and economies are the key actors. Workfare entails the 'decentring of welfarism', a move from nationally based welfare regimes to locally based workfare regimes (Peck, 2001, p. 11). Thirdly, there is a move away from the state, and its so-called 'culture of dependency', to private and civil society actors such as employers, agencies, and communities. This shift entails an increasing reliance on voluntarism as a first step to improving the employment prospects of participants. Therefore the spread of workfare indicates the increase of and potential linkages between localization, voluntarism and inequality.

The literature on workfare can be divided into two schools: the regulation literature and the mainstream welfare state literature (Vis, 2007). The regulation literature sees workfare in broad terms as the subordination of social policy to the demands of a competitive and flexible labour market. The mainstream welfare state literature sees workfare as a mandatory supply-side programme aiming for full employment combined with market flexibility and reduced public expenditure. While the regulation literature claims that there has been a radical global shift from a Keynesian welfare state to a Schumpeterian workfare regime, the mainstream welfare state literature argues that such shifts correspond to specific regimes classified using Esping-Andersen's (1990) typology of liberal, conservative and social democratic regimes.[16] Both literatures identify three key principles of workfare which distinguish it from broader activation programmes: the obligation to work; the aim of maximal labour market participation; and minimal income protection (Vis, 2007, p. 109). Workfare reforms also represent a wider shift from status to contract, from a language of rights and entitlements to one of obligations (Handler, 2004). It is worth noting that while most countries do follow workfare programmes, there is a difference between a country having a workfare programme and it constituting a workfare regime (Vis, 2007, pp. 118–19).

The United States
In the last thirty or so years, workfare has proved to be a policy field of immense dynamism, especially in the US (Peck, 2001, p. 1). The US workfare system exemplifies the 'work first' approach to Active Labour Market Programmes (ALMPs) (Daguerre, 2004). The work first approach is often juxtaposed with the 'human capital' approach which is prominent in Scandinavia and some other European countries (discussed in the next section). The former approach uses both carrots and sticks to achieve the ultimate aim of full employment. This form of workfare has been criticized as entailing exclusion and a narrow understanding of inequality which focuses only on providing equality of opportunity, not outcomes (Handler, 2004).

The most prominent legislation to date which enabled the growth of workfare programmes through fiscal and administrative devolution is the Personal Responsibility and Work Opportunity Reconciliation Act (PRWORA) of 1996. The logic behind the Act is straightforward. There is an incentive for both the unemployed and the local authorities to get the former back into work. Local authorities receive strictly defined funds in the form of block grants, and are no longer able to increase funding simply on the basis of the number of unemployed. Thus their focus is going to be on getting as many people into work as possible rather than on those with the greatest disadvantage. Local authorities focus on means of improving the opportunity for people to find jobs (and employers to fill vacancies) including self-employment.

The incentive structure of benefit payments has also changed to encourage welfare recipients to seek employment actively. Higher-rate benefits are time limited; benefits are dependent on the recipient making demonstrable efforts to obtain a job, whether through search or retraining; and the reward to working is increased by lessening the taper of the removal of benefits once earning starts (Horstmann and Sharf, 2008). This is in contrast with some of the older systems in which all benefit was immediately cut once a person started earning again. Given that there are increased costs from having to go out to work, from commuting, child care and the potential loss of medical benefits (Dulmus et al., 2000), the effective tax rate in the past has sometimes been more than 100 per cent on the extra income, thereby acting as an effective disincentive to work. Tax credits act as an effective remedy by enabling those who have successfully made the transition from welfare to work to pay less tax on the new income.

The US welfare system is a unique mixture of public and private welfare provision which relies on government as well as non-state actors (Handler, 2009, p. 79). These non-state actors include private companies who are often directly involved in contracting the unemployed, as well as a large number of non-profits and religious charity organizations (Dostal, 2008; Handler, 2009). This encourages a tighter relationship between local authorities and employers, and there has been a large role to play for voluntary or non-profit providers and the community in general (Handler, 2009). The role of the community and voluntary sector is further strengthened by the fact that workfare programmes offer local subsidized jobs, often related to community projects that enable people to have many of the characteristics of employment even if they cannot get back into the fully competitive market (Horstmann and Sharf, 2008). Pay is low and subsidized by state benefits to bring it up to a 'living wage'. Furthermore, where people are not deemed 'job-ready' due, for example, to health problems or drug addiction, they may be required to do unpaid work experience as a transitional step towards employability. Welfare recipients under this arrangement engage in work that, similar to subsidized jobs, is seen to benefit the wider community (such as care work or working in a thrift store). This is sometimes described as 'coerced voluntarism' from the point of view of the employee. However, it strengthens the role of the voluntary sector in the system. Furthermore such community jobs can be inherently localized.

There is of course a difficulty in making sure that the next step of moving to a normal job takes place, but where training and work experience are involved the chance is increased, especially if the initial unemployment was cyclical. Most new employment under the PRWORA is not subsidized from the point of view of the employer but it is easy for the jobs to be more marginal and for these workers to have a fragile employment position. To gauge the full effect on welfare it is therefore necessary to appraise such schemes over a reasonably long period, in case it is disproportionately the more vulnerable group that goes back into unemployment at the next adverse shock.

The combined measures ensure that employment becomes the key objective for authorities and welfare recipients, and in tight economic times, this work first approach could represent a practical solution to strained national and local budgets. However, an emphasis on employment is also related to the stigmatization and radicalization of welfare in the US and a belief in some quarters that certain groups of poor people have an ingrained low work ethic. Hence some forms of welfare, such as social security programmes, are seen as routine and normalized, while others, such as food stamps and Temporary Assistance for Needy Families (TANF), are stigmatized (Daguerre, 2004). An artificial divide has been created between a 'deserving' and 'undeserving' poor (Handler, 2009). Within workfare programmes themselves, some are also more disadvantaged than others. The most employable are prioritized and less emphasis is placed on the most difficult or disadvantaged cases. These problems are referred to in the literature as the 'cherry picking' or 'creaming' of the best clients by job agencies, and the 'parking' of difficult clients in dead-end, low paid positions or unemployment (Bredgaard and Larsen, 2007). This reinforces existing inequalities as those who are most in need often do not receive the extra aid and resources they require to find better paid, skilled employment.

Sole discretion for the implementation of the work first model is at the state rather than the federal level (Daguerre, 2004). Authority at the state level has been formalized to the point where the federal level has been unable to interfere or to intervene in the policies and practices of state programmes. This has had an impact on inequality in the US. For example, in the case of the TANF programme, the federal government wished to ensure that all recipients were granted equal access to child care services. Clinton stated that affordable, good quality child care was essential to the success of welfare reforms. However, this proved impossible to enforce in practice as state authorities were responsible for administering the programme (Daguerre, 2004).

Much depends on the local context, and on the range of opportunities that exist for job-seekers to find work in the local economy. In Hasenfeld and Weaver's (1996) study of welfare-to-work programmes in four Californian counties, the authors uncovered distinct differences in the approaches adopted by programme staff in rural/agribusiness and urban/ suburban areas. Given the discretion allowed to county governments in the ways each chose to implement the state's welfare programme, there was a greater emphasis on improving the work skills of welfare recipients living in the more affluent suburban and urban areas. In contrast, the emphasis in the rural/agribusiness areas was primarily on getting the unemployed off welfare and back into work.

These distinct approaches owed much to the local political economy and how it shaped attitudes to welfare (Hasenfeld and Weaver, 1996). In the urban/suburban areas where unemployment and poverty levels were relatively low and where skilled labour was in greater demand, welfare recipients were more likely to be identified as in need of training and education to help them compete in the local labour market. In the rural/agribusiness counties where the labour market was less reliant on skilled workers, there was less incentive for programme staff to offer clients the opportunity to improve their job skills. The higher incidence of unemployment in these counties also meant that staff had a heavier caseload of clients and had less time to discuss long-term options with them. Furthermore, it is likely that the local authorities were more restricted by funding limits on welfare spending. This situation contributed – most notably in the rural county – to greater tensions between staff and job-seekers as staff-client relations became more about compelling people to work, through the use of threats, and less about counselling or advocacy. This reinforced the stigma attached to being on welfare, and increased feelings of hostility on both sides.

Hasenfeld and Weaver's study painted a mixed picture of workfare.[17] It nonetheless illustrates how regional inequalities may be further widened by different approaches to implementing workfare. The rural and agribusiness cases offer another perspective into the reasons why some welfare recipients find it difficult to escape the poverty trap, particularly in regions hit by cyclical unemployment during periods of economic downturn. It is precisely these welfare recipients who might benefit from appropriate training and work experience in order to break the cycle of being in and out of work. Yet, the 'work-first' approach to welfare reform limits their long-term prospects by failing to assess the suitability of the work offered, assuming that any work is better than none. As Handler (2004, pp. 74–5) writes:

> The more successful welfare-to-work programmes [have] a flexible, balanced approach that offers a mix of job search, education, job-training and work activities. They have more individualized services, a central focus on employment, ties to local employers, and are intensive, setting high expectations for participants. Some of these mixed strategies have not only increased employment but also succeeded in helping welfare recipients find better jobs.

These 'success' stories appear, however, to be relatively few in number. Even programmes that emphasized education and training were not found in a national evaluation of welfare-to-work strategies to have lifted participants out of poverty (Hamilton, 2002). Several studies quoted by Handler (2004, pp. 36–7) concluded that welfare reforms, whilst bringing net gains for government through cuts in welfare payments, had not raised the standard of living of workfare participants. The loss of some benefits upon taking up a job, even when these are not cut entirely but steadily reduced, was not sufficiently compensated by the wages earned. Workfare participants were simply unable to access higher-paying jobs.

The structure of the modern US economy in part explains this lack of upward mobility. With a distinctive 'hourglass' form in which there are far fewer mid-level jobs than low or highly skilled positions, the labour market offers few opportunities for workfare participants, most of whom are low-skilled and on low wages, to move into better-paid jobs. In another study (Scott et al., 2000), working mothers engaged in workfare had quite modest work expectations about their future job prospects. Most were unable to see beyond the type of positions that they had previously held: unskilled or semi-skilled jobs that were highly gendered, offered only low pay, no medical benefits and little flexibility at times of family crises or illness. A lack of affordable child care, limited welfare support and the workfare mandate to go to work once their infant was three months old ruled out training, education or alternative job options. To quote the authors, the women's perspectives had been 'profoundly shaped by the structural constraints of class, gender, motherhood and the labour market' (p. 733).

Whilst the decentralization of welfare policy in the form of workfare may offer local authorities the opportunity to help people move from passive welfare recipients to more independent workers, interviews with workfare participants often suggest otherwise. Particularly when welfare recipients are employed in subsidized jobs, workfare can contribute to other, more precarious, forms of dependency and to greater financial and personal insecurity. In research by Collins (2008) into women employed in Community Service Jobs (CSJs) in Wisconsin, they remained dependent on welfare such as food stamps because their jobs did not pay a living wage. The mandate to go out to work in return for state aid brought additional dependency on jobs that offered little employment protection and few benefits such as sick leave or health insurance. Whenever crises occurred in their lives, many felt that they had no choice but to quit or, in some instances, were dismissed from their jobs. The interviews also revealed that some workfare participants suffered downward mobility when they were assigned to inappropriate jobs that were not commensurate with their skills or past experience.

Workfare in such cases appears to be more akin to a policy response to labour shortages in marginal jobs, reinforcing wage inequalities in the US labour market. It is about creating 'workers for jobs that nobody wants', according to Peck (2001, p. 6). It can entail exclusion from the private welfare benefits that are attached to more stable, flexible and higher-paid work, and an ongoing dependence on state aid that becomes acute during times of personal crises. At the same time, tighter welfare criteria, strict time-limits and sanctions coincided with cuts in welfare rolls but also with strong economic and employment growth in the United States.[18] Since the recent global economic crisis, however, welfare rolls have only increased slightly despite the unemployment rate more than doubling in the last two years to over 10 per cent of the labour force in early 2010. The slower rise in welfare rolls may suggest that fewer are eligible to claim benefits, and instead people are turning to charity to meet their basic needs. It may be that the willingness to claim benefits has also declined but this is not likely to be such an important determinant. The US's largest food bank network, Feeding America, noted in its 2010 report a 46 per cent increase since 2006 in the number of people – or one in eight Americans – who sought food assistance in 2009 from food banks, soup kitchens and emergency shelters (Mabli et al., 2010).

It is also worth exploring the impact of workfare on mobility as *prima facie* one might expect that, since workfare offers greater discretion to states in the way that they implement welfare reform, the more generous states will attract welfare recipients from states that have adopted stricter welfare policies. Echoing Tiebout's hypothesis, this would lead to competition between states to lower their welfare provisions to avoid becoming welfare magnets. On the other hand, welfare benefits are time-limited in all states; so migration is therefore unlikely to bring sufficient lifetime gains to people on low income to induce them to move. Indeed, Kaestner et al. (2003) found no evidence that low-income women had moved to another state in search of better benefits, in fact noting a small decrease in interstate migration. More noteworthy was their claim that the effect of welfare reform was to 'motivate' people to relocate within the same state in search of better employment prospects. As an unintended consequence of the reforms, it emphasizes the perverse effect of enforcing strict workfare mandates in a local labour-market context that lacks appropriate job opportunities. Where people are for personal or financial reasons unable or unwilling to move, workfare offers few alternatives to lift the most disadvantaged out of a cycle of dependency on state aid and marginal employment. One might expect this to be a greater problem in Europe where mobility is noticeably lower. However, the recent fall in house prices in the US has made moving more difficult for many as they have negative equity.

Europe
In Europe, ALMPs are common practice. However, they are not often explicitly defined as workfare. There are connotations attached to the label 'workfare' which have made certain countries uneasy or opposed to the term (Daguerre, 2004). Workfare has been widely labelled an Anglo-Saxon phenomenon, prominent in the US, Canada, the UK, and Ireland (Peck, 2001; Vis, 2007). An exception is Denmark, which exemplifies one of the most radical workfare regimes outside this cluster (Vis, 2007; Thomson, chapter 4 this volume). Yet despite this, workfare-style programmes were implemented in most European countries in the 1980s and 1990s, and have become a feature of European welfare.[19] Often types of welfare/workfare programme adopted vary across member states, or can be regime-specific (using Esping-Andersen's typology) (Vis, 2007). European welfare reforms also continue to differ from those in the US due to uniquely European concerns, histories of welfare and understandings of social citizenship (Handler, 2004). Such differences continue to be clear in the policy choices the EU makes today; for example, Europe appears to be more concerned with wage equality than the US as exemplified in the EES's call for better as well as more jobs.

Workfare programmes in the UK incorporate many elements of the US 'work first' approach, to the point where some have heralded the 'Americanization of British social policy' (Daguerre, 2004, p. 53). The US-style work first approach was promoted in the UK as a way to focus on Third Way empowerment rather than dependency and to end the 'something for nothing' culture (McDowell, 2004). This approach was implemented through the 'New Deal' legislation of 1997, which took the form of six new policies targeted at youth, unemployed, lone parents, disabled, partners of unemployed, and elderly (Daguerre, 2004, p. 49).

Through the New Deal policies, the emphasis on achieving full employment was key. This occurred through a combination of job retraining and subsidized employment. The resemblance between the US and British systems can be attributed to Anglo-Saxon ideological climates as well as similar labour markets (Daguerre, 2004, p. 52). British opposition to an overarching European social policy may be another factor (Daguerre, 2004, p. 52).

However, some differences can be found between the British and US approaches (Daguerre, 2004). Dostal (2008) has labelled US workfare as socially conservative, and UK workfare as labourist. The British system is much more centralized, with programmes being subject to national eligibility criteria; some New Deal policies remain voluntary; and the UK aims to incorporate human capital elements to combat social exclusion (Daguerre, 2004). Spending on job retraining in the UK is also higher than in America, but is still much less than in other European countries. Hence whilst in some senses the US and the UK do exemplify a distinctive Anglo-Saxon workfare approach, in other ways UK workfare is milder than workfare in the US. Some scholars have grouped the UK not with the US but with the Netherlands and Denmark as one of the European centralized programmes which emphasizes universalization of welfare benefits, standardization, and strongly codified sanctions (Trickey, 2001). Whilst the codification of sanctions does leave less room for compromises, it can also be a potential deterrent to the problems of 'creaming' mentioned in the US decentralized system by clarifying participants' rights and accommodating heterogeneity (Trickey, 2001, p. 288).

The 'human capital' approach to ALMPs is more common in other European countries and is most prevalent in Scandinavia (Dostal, 2008). This approach seeks to reskill the labour force through training and education to improve their chances of long-term employment, rather than focusing on getting people into work as quickly as possible (Daguerre, 2004, p. 42). Sweden provides a classic example. Sweden has a long tradition of ALMPs dating back to the 1950s and currently spends the most out of all the EU countries on ALMPs and training programmes (Daguerre, 2004; Dostal, 2008). Swedish ALMPs make strict demands of welfare recipients, but balance these with high levels of benefits and high quality labour market training programmes (Daguerre, 2004). Therefore though there is pressure to find employment, this is balanced social protection and support, as well as national coordination.[20]

Countries on the continent exemplify different mixes of the work first and the human capital approaches. France and Germany occupy a middle ground, having undergone 'buttressed liberalization' (Vail, 2008). This process has seen liberalization of labour market regulations accompanied by supportive, 'buttressing' ALMPs and subsidies. ALMPs are administered in a decentralized manner in Germany, while in France there is more coordination between central and local levels (Trickey, 2001). Also in France, unemployment benefits are not conditional upon participation in work programmes and the French are careful to distinguish themselves from Anglo-Saxon workfare (Daguerre, 2004; Rees, 2000). However, recent reforms have brought the country much more into line. For spending on labour market training, France falls somewhere in between Sweden and the UK/US (Daguerre, 2004).

In terms of our three trends then, European welfare systems do incorporate elements of Anglo-Saxon workfare to some degree. However, whether workfare is administered centrally or locally is dependent on the country (Trickey, 2001). Voluntary or non-state actors are important, but are not relied upon to the same extent as in the US, where there is a whole private welfare system (Handler, 2009). Finally, equality and social inclusion are key priorities in European social policy and welfare regimes, though in practice there continue to be a number of marginalized and excluded groups (Handler, 2009, p. 84).

Business Improvement Districts

Originating in Canada and the United States, Business Improvement Districts (BIDs) are 'self-assessment districts that are initiated and governed by property or business owners and authorized by governments to operate in designated urban and suburban geographic areas' (Morçöl et al., 2008, p. 2). BIDs have been variously described as new forms of urban governance, as public private partnerships, private governments, and tools of public policy (see Morçöl et al., 2008, p. 4). Taxation is a distinctive and fundamental component of BIDs as they derive their funding from compulsory taxation of commercial property owners (Cook, 2008, p. 774). Commercial property owners vote to establish a BID in a certain locale and upon its establishment are legally required to pay the tax (Brooks, 2008). BIDs then use the levies to provide a range of local services which are designed to promote urban regeneration (Brooks, 2008, p. 389).[21]

BIDs are becoming an established feature of local governance in the US, and aggressive marketing has also led to the policy transfer of a US-style BID model to Europe and more globally. The spread of BIDs is of relevance to our interlinked trends because they provide an example of radical localization. BIDs provide a fascinating example for our purposes as they encompass both voluntary and involuntary localization. They occupy a middle ground between voluntary participation in the BID organization and involuntary taxation (Caruso and Weber, 2008). BIDs could hence be construed as entailing a kind of coerced voluntary donation. For those residents of the local area who are not business owners and are hence excluded from the decision making process, BIDs are an example of forced localization. This means that BIDs also have implications for inequality as they may promote exclusion and hence polarization. BIDs are often undemocratic in the way they are established as only a small section of the population is involved in the voting and decision making process.

Proponents of BIDs (often using rational choice theories) see them as efficient and effective due to their private, unbureaucratic nature (Morçöl et al., 2008, p. 4). Critics (often taking social constructionist or political economy approaches) point out the undemocratic ramifications of the neoliberalization or privatization of public space (Mitchell and Staeheli, 2006). A major issue is that BIDs are unaccountable as the wider public do not have the power to either participate directly in their activities or to vote on their establishment in the first place (Cook, 2008; Briffault, 1999). As commercial property owners fund BIDs through taxation, they are the only ones able to vote on the establishment or dissolution of a BID, and on decisions about its activities. In effect, this means that the voices of residents and citizens are ignored (Ross and Levine, 2006).

From another perspective, BIDs have been cited as a potential solution to the collective action problem of free-riding. In order to solve this problem, economists have tried to determine the optimal size for efficient extra-governmental provision of public goods (Alesina et al., 2004; Tiebout, 1956; Brooks, 2008). There are two ways to get around this difficulty in large-scale settings (Olson, 1971). One is to exclude non-members from the benefits of the public good, and the other is to coerce all members into making a contribution. BID legislation draws on the second principle by providing all neighbourhoods with the opportunity to provide themselves with local public goods (Brooks, 2008, p. 393).

The United States
BIDs have a history spanning at least thirty years in Canada and the US. They became a widespread and well-known phenomenon in the 1980s and 1990s (Mitchell, 2008). As of 2008, between 800 and 1200 BIDs existed in the US and Canada in a variety of geographical locales (Morçöl et al., 2008, p. 2). The proliferation of BIDs in the US in the 1980s may have been a response to economic decline in cities combined with the tightening of federal funds made available to local governments

(Morçöl et al., 2008, p. 8). The strong privatist tradition in the US may have further enabled their development (Morçöl and Zimmerman, 2008). Legislation for BIDs in the US is passed at the state level and is then enacted by local authorities (Brooks, 2008). The local authorities legally establish the BID, collect the taxes, and then pass them on to the BID organization to use as they see fit within the agreed framework for action (Mitchell, 2001). BID initiatives have in general been concerned with boosting the local economy through downtown renewal and revitalization (Mitchell, 2001). This has occurred through the provision of services such as cleaning, security, and consumer and events marketing (Mitchell, 2001, p. 116). Most BIDs are not directly involved in the provision of social services (for example, homeless shelters), but some bigger BIDs like the Grand Central Partnership in New York City operate social service units (Mitchell, 2001, p. 121).

BIDs diverge in form and legal status depending on the state in which they are established. For example, in New York, where BIDs are most numerous, not to mention wealthiest and most established, BIDs are incorporated as non-profit organizations (Morçöl and Zimmermann, 2008, p. 37). However, in Pennsylvania they are treated as public authorities; in the District of Columbia, they are non-profit corporations; in California they are public-private partnerships; and in Georgia they are local governments (Morçöl and Zimmermann, 2008, p. 37). This places BIDs at different points along the continuum between public and private entity, ultimately blurring the distinction between public and private completely. BIDs also vary in size and budget, and this influences the kinds of services and/or activities they provide (Gross, 2008). The status of residents and home owners in relation to BIDs also varies between states, but is always problematic (Morçöl and Zimmermann, 2008, p. 39). The major issue is that BIDs are not legally obliged to consult with everyone who falls within their district, and therefore the decisions they make may suit some members of the community more than others. In such situations, it is often those most in need who miss out, as Cook (2008, p. 789) points out, '... the US BIDs ability (or inability) to improve either employees' work conditions and pay or the public space and "shopping experience" for those with low or no consumer power [are] rarely, if ever, of interest to on-looking policy makers and advocates'. Moreover, this inequality extends to the areas in which BIDs are established too:

> BIDs in low-income communities are faced with a wider range of needs, a wider range of stakeholders, and limited resources (revenue and expertise) to respond with ... conversely, BIDs in high-income neighbourhoods face fewer

socioeconomic problems, have fewer stakeholders, and have greater resources that enable increased investment in the physical infrastructure of the area. (Gross cited in Kreutz, 2009, p. 315)

There is great potential for BIDs to affect community development positively if they so choose. The problem is that under the current legislation there is no way to ensure any kind of consistency across BIDs in different states and locales. Too much of the quality of BID delivery is dependent on already established local resources and interests, and hence the positive outcomes of BIDs are entirely uneven. Due to such issues, BIDS have experienced varying success in the US. The East coast district BIDs (for example, New York, Philadelphia and Washington) have been labelled the 'success stories' (Cook, 2008). In New York, BIDs have statistically reduced crime and increased the cleanliness of streets. Times Square is held up as an example of the success of BIDs. A study of BIDs in the Los Angeles area also showed that they have been successful at reducing serious crime (Brooks, 2008). However in more rundown areas of the US such as Detroit and Camden, New Jersey, downtown areas have not undergone an 'aesthetic transformation' under BIDs (Cook, 2008). An important point is that although BIDs can indeed contribute to improving local conditions, they are 'not a magic wand for urban regeneration', and areas with 'chronic unemployment, high crime rates and urban blight' will generally need multiple sources of funding and resources (Symes and Steel, 2003, p. 311). If this fact goes unacknowledged, BIDs could contribute to further polarization and inequality by creating an illusion of local sufficiency and hence blocking other much needed funding.

Europe
BIDs in Europe are a very recent phenomenon, and are by no means as widespread as in the US. At this early stage it is hence difficult to assess how they will develop and what kind of outcomes they may yield. Yet even so, some scholars argue that over the past ten years a steady process of BID policy transfer from the US to Europe has been occurring (Cook, 2008; Ward, 2006; Peel and Lloyd, 2005). Since 2002, Germany, Ireland, Serbia, Albania, England, and Wales have implemented BIDs (Cook, 2008, p. 774). Austria and the Netherlands are considering the prospect (Morçöl et al., 2008). These European BIDs have been modelled on the US-style BID, even though other countries with BIDs such as Canada, New Zealand, Jamaica and South Africa could easily have been selected as blueprints (Cook, 2008).

The implementation of an American-style BID model has been clearest in the UK. UK BIDs have been openly branded by the UK government as 'New York-style schemes' (Ward, 2006, p. 68). BID legislation was introduced in the UK in 2003 through the passing of the Local Government Act (Cook, 2008; Peel and Lloyd, 2005). Under this Act, 22 pilot BIDs were set up in different locations around the UK (Ward, 2006). In the lead-up to this legislation, a concerted effort was undertaken to orchestrate policy transfer from the US to the UK. A number of visits, conferences and seminars were organized by the Association for Town Centre Management and the Local Government Association which featured BID policy experts from cities on the East Coast of the US. These East Coast BIDs were promoted and marketed as the most 'successful' and therefore 'appropriate' for introduction into a UK context. They were regarded as successful due to their perceived success at urban regeneration through reviving economies and public space and reducing crime (Cook, 2008, p. 782). The variety of services they provided and their sheer numbers and pervasiveness also made them more attractive (Cook, 2008, p. 781).

However, significant differences in the 'welfare regimes, scalar divisions of the state, and urban political–economic trajectories' in the two countries have resulted in differences between UK and US BIDs (Ward, 2006, p. 69). The UK has a much more centralized governmental system, and BIDs have been implemented from the top down, in contrast to the decentralized US system where BIDs were pursued as a bottom-up solution to the perceived failings of government (Ward, 2006). A need to adapt and respond to local contexts and relations when introducing BIDs in the UK has been increasingly recognized in their implementation (Cook, 2008, p. 788).

In Scotland too, responses to a 2003 Consultation Paper which sought to elicit views from organizations, authorities, trade unions, and business owners on how BIDs could be implemented indicate a need to tailor BIDs to national and local contexts. In particular differences from the US in tax regime and institutional capacity were cited (Peel and Lloyd, 2005, p. 94). Additional points of concern were that BIDs are resource intensive to initiate and manage, may not be as effective in rural contexts (i.e. may be sensitive to spatial economic context), and may accrue benefits only to those retailers who funded them (Peel and Lloyd, 2005).

In Germany, BID legislation was implemented in 2004 (Kreutz, 2009). In 2007, a Neighbourhood Improvement District (NID) model was adapted to make BIDs more applicable to suburban contexts (Kreutz, 2009).[22] BID laws in Germany are highly decentralized, similar to their US forerunners. They are administered at the state level and there is no federal policy on BIDs except for a general regulation in the Federal Building Code (Kreutz, 2009, p. 307). So far, six out of the 16 Länder have chosen to implement BID legislation (Kreutz, 2009). Kreutz (2009, p. 306) notes that BIDs are part of a 'general policy turn to less public provision and more private initiative, individual responsibility and self-help supported through public regulations'. Using Hamburg as a case study, Kreutz notes that the four BIDs currently active in Hamburg are uneven in size, funding, and priorities. Unlike the UK and US versions, German BIDs are funded by real estate proprietors rather than local businesses. BID law clearly states that they are to supplement rather than replace public services (Kreutz, 2009). However, Kreutz notes that a problem with this caveat is that the standard of public services to begin with is not clearly defined. This means that adding another provider to the mix may cause declining standards unless issues of jurisdiction and responsibility are sorted out between local authorities and the BIDs. Furthermore, ensuring BIDs are successful in Germany will be more than a matter of simply 'copying and pasting' from the US (Kreutz, 2009, p. 315). Unlike the US with its strong privatist tradition, post-war Germany invested much weight in the sovereignty and rights of the state.

In Europe more generally, Town Centre Management (TCM) has constituted the common framework for urban revitalization (Coca-Stefaniak et al., 2009). Most encompass some form of public private partnerships, with various levels of voluntary and community involvement, and a majority are retailer led (Coca-Stefaniak et al., 2009). Coca-Stefaniak et al. have come up with a classificatory model which shows their differing characteristics. Some exhibit characteristics of a US-style BID while others do not. In general privatizing space has become the norm, as have various retailer-led initiatives for economic revitalization, but it remains to be seen to what extent these initiatives will shape urban governance in Europe and if so how much they will draw from the US and how much will be adapted to national and local contexts. At the very least it appears that the approach in most European countries (with the exception of Germany) is more centralized.

Education

Education provides a poignant example of the intersection of our three trends. First, since the late 1970s educational provision in many countries has undergone radical decentralization and localization (Karsten, 1999; Power et al., 1997; Zajda, 2006). Decentralization originally gave greater power to local authorities, but has recently been focused right down to the level of the school itself in the form of school based management programmes (Power et al., 1997). In the social science literature, the move towards decentralized education has commonly been described as part of a globalizing neoliberalism, entailing processes of marketization and privatization (Astiz et al., 2002; Davies and Quirke, 2007; Zajda, 2006; Jones et al., 2008). Hence the issue of decentralization in the field of education has become highly politicized. The neoliberal reforms 'dismantled centralized educational bureaucracies and created in their place devolved systems of education entailing significant degrees of institutional autonomy and a variety of forms of school-based management and administration' (Whitty et al., 1998, p. 3 in Karsten, 1999, p. 303). However, often this purportedly neoliberal decentralization has also been accompanied by new forms of centralization, making the current process a complex interaction between centralizing and decentralizing forces (Power et al., 1997).

Second, voluntarism often plays a large part in education, whether through donation, community and family involvement and participation in schools, or voluntary relocation in order to attend certain schools. Third, as is the case in the literature on decentralization more generally, the education debate centres on questions of equity. Schools are sites for the production and reproduction of social and cultural capital (Bourdieu and Passeron, 1977). Education can hence act to reinforce and/or perpetuate existing divisions, class and ethnicity being the most commonly referred to. Differences in the funding and perceived quality of education become particularly pronounced at the level of higher education, where prestigious universities often attract students who either are from wealthy families or possess high earning potential, and perpetuate the institutions' prestige by going on to become alumni with the ability to make generous donations. In some countries this is limited by state control of universities. However, education can also provide opportunities for class mobility though equality of opportunity. Hence the perpetuation of inequality is not a fixed outcome.

Our key concern is not the decentralization of education per se but rather what such localization might facilitate. Has the decentralization of education led to greater polarization and segregation? Or has it indeed fulfilled its aims of being:

> democratic, efficient, and accountable; more responsive to the community and to local needs; empowering teachers, parents, and others in the education community while improving the effectiveness of school reform; and able to improve school quality and increase funds available for teachers' salaries through competition? (Astiz et al., 2002, p. 71)

United States

The US system represents a radical case of decentralized education, with 50 separate state education departments and approximately 15,000 semi-autonomous school districts in 2002 (Astiz et al., 2002). Education has been decentralized in terms of both funding/resources and decision making. However, such decentralization has always coexisted with centralization. In fact, over the past two decades, there have been two simultaneous and contrasting forces – the first being the centralization of national curricular goals and the second being the decentralization of curricular implementation (Astiz et al., 2002, p. 77). Recently, a greater emphasis has been placed on individual schools at the same time as centralized policy, indicating the extreme ends of the continuum. Some schools, called charter schools, have circumnavigated the state system altogether and have a direct relationship with the federal government (van Langen and Dekkers, 2001).

Decentralization in the US has been enabled by the political and administrative federal system, but also by American cultural norms. For example, there is a strong emphasis placed on the importance of parental and student choice (McDermott, 1999). The prevalence of choice is related to American individualism, but also to notions of equal opportunity as a means to achieve equality. Another push towards decentralization has come from what Plank and Boyd (1994) term 'the antipolitics of education'. By this they mean that Americans have become disillusioned with direct democratic governance, so they have begun to advocate alternative institutional arrangements outside the realm of the 'political' (e.g. legislatures, school boards), in favour of more 'authoritative' arenas such as courts and markets (Plank and Boyd, 1994, p. 264). This 'antipolitics' has arisen out of continuing conflicts over the structure and content of education (Plank and Boyd, 1994). Some advocate increasing the power of parents and local communities through decentralization, privatization, local control, and parental choice. Others seek to defend larger communities by equalizing resource distribution and regulating educational practices to create more equitable conditions for the disadvantaged (Plank and Boyd, 1994, p. 267).

In this sense, support for educational decentralization in the US is by no means unanimous. In fact, over the past two decades decentralization has been found to have its problems. The 1980s saw great polarization between the states in terms of financing, with some school districts finding it easier to mobilize local resources though property taxes etc than others (Bray, 1999, p. 224).[23] Problems also occurred in the realm of decision making. In NYC, decision making was decentralized to community boards in the hope that they would be more democratic and representative, but they turned out to be at least as factionalized and exclusionary as city politics (Bray, 1999, p. 225).

Perhaps as a response to some of these issues, in some states authority was rescinded from local boards to state legislatures in the 1980s (Plank and Boyd, 1994, p. 265). This had the appearance of somewhat reversing the decentralization but still in effect retained the decentralized system. Recently, in a climate where 'the achievement gap on standardized tests increasingly is viewed as the most significant educational change facing American society in the 21st century' (Kim and Sunderman, 2005, p. 3) there have been more overt centralized attempts to remedy educational inequality.

The most significant of these is the No Child Left Behind Act 2001 (NCLB). The NCLB Act, an updated form of the Elementary and Secondary Education Act 1965, has institutionalized a standardized accountability system which uses high stakes testing and adequate yearly progress (AYP) assessments to reward or punish school districts, schools, and teachers for the academic performance of their students (Dworkin, 2005, p. 170). It sets national targets to close the gaps in test scores among racial/ethnic, socioeconomic, home-language, and special education students by the year 2013–14 (Dworkin, 2005).[24] A school can fail to make AYP if a single subgroup does not meet the performance target or participation requirements. Schools that fail to make the targets for two consecutive years are identified as 'in need of improvement' (INOI) and are subject to sanctions that become more severe the longer the school retains this status (Kim and Sunderman, 2005, p. 3).

In this way the Act embodies the polar relationship mentioned earlier, where extreme centralization of policy is accompanied by extreme decentralization (to the level of the school) of implementation. Advocates of the Act argue that such high expectations are needed to tackle the learning needs of public school students who have been segregated by low expectations, and to create incentives to address this under-achievement (Kim and Sunderman, 2005, p. 4). Others have argued that the Act actually hinders and stigmatizes those high-poverty schools that it is trying to help (Kim and Sunderman, 2005, p. 4; Dworkin, 2005). Supporting this conclusion is a study by Kim and Sunderman (2005) of the effects of the NCLB Act in six states who note that 'an accountability system based on mean proficiency is likely to over-identify many high-poverty schools as underperforming schools' (Kim and Sunderman, 2005, p. 8).[25] They hence recommend the use of multiple indicators and some state specific performance goals. Widespread opposition to these 'one size fits all' elements of the NCLB Act indicate that it appears to have moved too far in the direction of centralization, punishing rather than accommodating diversity.

Europe

In many European countries, a concerted effort was taken post-war to universalize and democratize education provision (Jones et al., 2008). The method of universal provision has generally been cited as a means of combatting inequality; however, in the first instance it may lead to a widening of inequalities as middle and upper classes are able to use their cultural capital to take advantage of the new opportunities (Paterson and Iannelli, 2007). The trend towards decentralizing education gained momentum in the 1970s, with England leading the way. Devolution in England took place through Local Education Authorities (LEA), which remain the key executive body in the education field (Teelken, 1999, p. 286). However, decentralization of finances and resources in England was also accompanied by increased centralization of curriculum (Daun, 2006). Throughout the 1980s and 1990s, the process of decentralizing education in England became part of a modernizing and neoliberalizing project, leading to quasi-marketization (Jones et al., 2008, pp. 20–22). This had the effect of 'strengthening competition and differentiation within the school system, empower[ing] middle-class parents with "school choice" and, via the decentralization of financial control, creat-[ing] a new class of school managers' (Jones et al., 2008, p. 17). This effect can be witnessed with the empowerment of individual schools through the Local Management of Schools (Teelken, 1999), which has provided a challenge to the LEA's authority. Legislation allowing schools to apply for funding directly from the national level, similar to US charter schools, has provided another avenue for schools to opt out of LEA control (Teelken, 1999, p. 286).

Throughout the rest of Europe, decentralization of education has also occurred, though the process varies between countries. In many countries, decentralization has been accompanied by the notion of educational choice (Teelken, 1999; Ambler, 1994; Power et al., 1997), which some critics have labelled empty rhetoric that intensifies class segregation (Ambler, 1994). The Netherlands took an approach to restructuring education that was labelled by some as a middle ground between the fairly decentralized systems in England and the USA and the more centralized continental systems of France and Germany (Cummings and Riddell, 1994; Karsten, 1999, p. 304).[26] The Municipal Educational Disadvantage Act 1998 provides an interesting case study from the Netherlands. This Act was devised at the central level with the objective of decentralized implementation (van Langen and Dekkers, 2001). The aim of the Act is to combat educational disadvantage stemming from economic, social and cultural factors, with a focus on native Dutch pupils from lower socioeconomic background as well as ethnic minorities (van Langen and Dekkers, 2001, p. 368). The education minister constructs a 'national policy framework' every four years, which is then used as a guideline by local municipal authorities when they draw up their own four yearly plans. These local plans involve consultation with local state and private school governing bodies and are based on an analysis of local problems (van Langen and Dekkers, 2001, p. 368). Resources are also allocated to local authorities who are expected to distribute them equitably amongst local stakeholders.

Decentralized reforms in the Netherlands were subject to debate. The education minister claimed that decentralization would enable an integrated policy, would be tailor-made for local conditions, would allow for greater decisiveness and efficiency with regard to changing conditions, and would allow for better prioritizing based on local analysis (van Langen and Dekkers, 2001, p. 368). Others argued that the factors that create educational disadvantage are not necessarily local or even national, and that a centralized programme would be more effective. There was also concern over the loss of money through fragmentation across local municipalities, and that local authorities lacked the expertise to implement policy. Of most relevance to our study is the observation that due to the different starting points of localities decentralization could result in a two-tier system, with some wealthy local authorities producing affluent schools and poor authorities reinforcing poor schools (van Langen and Dekkers, 2001).

In the Czech Republic and Sweden, decentralization occurred rapidly and radically (Daun, 2006). In Sweden, the reforms moved away from a central and regulated system traditionally associated with the social democratic model to one which gave increased freedom and responsibility to the local level, particularly to teachers and school leaders (Lundahl, 2002, p. 626). These reforms included establishing independent schools, introducing vouchers, and providing state subsidies to municipalities (Lundahl, 2002, p. 626). The changes have introduced new social risks and costs, including particularism, polarization, and social differentiation (Lundahl, 2002). Nevertheless, the changes are seen by most as necessary and reasonable, and it has been argued that the Swedish system is still much more equitable than any other European national education system (Paterson and Iannelli, 2007).

Education in Sweden is representative of the Nordic approach more generally. In comparison with the rest of Europe, the Nordic countries still present a distinctive social democratic approach to schooling (Arnesen and Lundahl, 2006). However, as the process of Europeanization gains speed, education has become a key priority and hence educational approaches may become more and more integrated. This has been expressed through EU social policy objectives such as the competitive knowledge-based economy (Jones et al., 2008). At this level, educational policy becomes caught up in wider tensions in Europe between the forces of the market and those of social inclusion and protection.

DISCUSSION

The three sectoral comparisons show that Europe has adopted many of the main characteristics of the US approaches to workfare, business improvement districts and education, reflecting the interactions of the concerns of inequality, localization and voluntarism. However, in the European environment the approaches have been 'softened' in key respects, which has resulted in many of the negative aspects being left out (Table 5.1). Thus while 'workfare' has placed a greater emphasis on an active localized approach to getting people back into employment and has limited the costs of income support, minimum wage legislation has helped to maintain standards and the stigma about 'undeserving' groups has been avoided to a greater extent. BIDs are much less developed in Europe but even in education, where localization and voluntary efforts may have contributed to some inequalities it has usually been a stimulus for intervention to provide special encouragement for the most deprived. Thus as a generalization, Europe has accepted the incentive advantages of some of the US approaches but has attempted to use them in a way that reduces rather than increases inequality.

Table 5.1   Cross-sectoral comparison between the US and Europe

	US	Europe
Workfare	LOCALIZATION States/local authorities/ businesses granted more authority than Federal ✔ Face-to-face programmes ✔ VOLUNTARISM Strong private welfare system ✔ Emphasis on community and self-help, voluntarism ✔ INEQUALITY Work first approach ✔ Coercive, involuntary sanctions ✔ Uneven implementation ✔ Problems of creaming, cherry picking ✔ Some forms of welfare routinized while others stigmatized ✔ EVIDENCE OF TRENDS: YES	LOCALIZATION 'European Centralized Programmes' ✗ Localized (Germany) ✔ Centralized (UK, Scandinavia) ✗ Mixed (France) ✗ Face-to-face programmes ✔ Some policy transfer from US to UK ✔ VOLUNTARISM Strong public welfare systems ✗ Empowerment/active citizenship (UK) ✔ INEQUALITY Human capital approach ✗ Voluntary sanctions ✗ Emphasis on social inclusion ✗ Some groups excluded/ marginalized ✔ EVIDENCE OF TRENDS: MIXED
BIDs	LOCALIZATION Formed by local businesses ✔ State legislation ✔ VOLUNTARISM Established voluntarily ✔ INEQUALITY Success appears dependent upon high socioeconomic status in area ✔ Exclusive (decision making process only available to business owners) ✔ Can improve quality of life for communities and neighbourhoods ✗ EVIDENCE OF TRENDS: YES	LOCALIZATION Established and legislated locally (Germany) ✔ Established locally, centralized top-down legislation/ implementation (UK) ✗ ✔ Town centre mgmt, centralized (Europe) ✗ VOLUNTARISM Established voluntarily (UK, Germany) ✔ Some pressure from the government to introduce BIDs (UK) ✗ INEQUALITY Exclusive ✔ Issues with US model noted (Scotland, Germany) ✗ Can improve quality of life for communities and neighbourhoods ✗ EVIDENCE OF TRENDS: MIXED

	US	Europe
Education	LOCALIZATION Centralized curriculum ✘ Focus on school level, school managers ✔ VOLUNTARISM Parents and community involvement ✔ Emphasis on choice ✔ INEQUALITY No Child Left Behind Act creates polarization, punishes diversity and poor performing schools ✔ EVIDENCE OF TRENDS: YES	LOCALIZATION Local Management of Schools (UK) ✔ Municipal Educational Disadvantage Act (Netherlands) ✔ Decentralization (Scandinavia, Czech) ✔ VOLUNTARISM Parents/other organizations more involved ✔ INEQUALITY Universalization of provision can lead to inequalities (rich having more opportunities to use cultural capital) ✘ ✔ EU competitive knowledge economy can create tensions between market/social protection ✘ ✔ EVIDENCE OF TRENDS: YES

CONCLUSION

We have seen over recent years in the US that three trends have combined to alter the nature of the welfare environment.

1. Inequality has been increasing (Horstmann and Scharf, 2008). However, this has largely been achieved by the richest few getting relatively richer rather than the poor getting poorer relative to some absolute standard. Redistribution of wealth may have been a reasonable description in the Clinton era and again with the Obama administration, but taxation over much of the recent period has been characterized by Republican presidencies where the emphasis has been more on tax reduction.
2. Charitable giving has been increasing much faster than incomes, so at least some of this new wealth is being redistributed. Yet some of this increase comes from making 'voluntary' contributions to schools and to elitist purposes, such as opera, so the public goods that are being produced are not necessarily consumed by the poorest groups in society.
3. Responsibility for more of social spending is being devolved to more localized levels, which has had mixed consequences.

In many respects this US experience has been positive, with improvements in employment and welfare. A focus on the local level has improved both delivery and incentives. However, employment has not always ensured a reduction in inequality, poverty, or deprivation. Some of the policies have been controversial and even the name 'workfare' has had adverse connotations to it.

In this chapter we have explored the evidence both for the success of these US changes and also for their implementation in Europe. We use three pertinent examples: workfare, business improvement districts and education. These ideas have indeed been adopted in Europe but there has been care to avoid some of the most negative features and to focus on the improved incentives, greater effectiveness and greater efficiency that these initiatives can offer.

As a result there has been a clear manifestation of the trend towards localization that is observed in the US but the trend towards voluntarism is rather weaker. What has been actively resisted, at least in the dominant policy rhetoric, is the consequences that either of these might have for increasing inequality. Yet this does not mean that inequality has been completely circumvented, as Handler (2009, p. 84) notes.

Some authors are cautious of the risks to equitable and democratic provision posed by the trends. Forces of globalization and neoliberalism are closely linked to all three trends and they also inject a politicized element.

However, at least in the case of localization, outcomes are not fixed. Bray (1999, p. 223) says: 'In general, decentralization is likely to permit and perhaps encourage social inequalities. Conversely, centralization provides a mechanism for reducing inequalities; but whether that mechanism is actually used depends on goals and willpower at the apex of the system'. Here what really matters are the political agenda and goals of those in positions of power, and the ends to which they seek to employ spatial arrangements. As Purcell (2006, pp. 1925–7) has argued 'there is nothing inherent about scale' in and of itself.

The Tiebout hypothesis offers further insights into the uses to which scale can be put. The hypothesis represents a non-cooperative equilibrium (Perroni and Scharf, 2001) and hence endogenously determined jurisdictions will be somewhat smaller than optimal. It is in any case observable from recent years that the ability for people to set their own jurisdictional boundaries tends to lead to secessions (Alesina and Spolaore, 1997) and, if boundaries could be freely chosen, jurisdictions would be inefficiently small. As a result it is possible by redistribution to improve welfare but it is not clear whether this would be delivered by a majoritarian system. To some extent this can happen in so far as both labour and capital are mobile. Tax competition will then encourage such movements (Edwards and Keen, 1996).

The underlying trade off is between the benefits of increased size and the costs of heterogeneity, up to the point that diseconomies of congestion and over-crowding cut in (Barro, 1991). However, the redrawing of geographical boundaries by democratic consent in the EU is on the whole only possible within member states. A Europe of the Regions (De Rougemont, 1966; Hepburn, 2008) is likely only in terms of devolved responsibilities, such as those in the UK and Spain and in overtly federal countries such as Germany. National boundaries between member states are not on the agenda and in so far as they might be, relate to readily identifiable groups and not the choice of the demarcation of municipal boundaries, which can follow geographic, fiscal and other considerations. The number of cross-border workers is of course increasing with the accession of the new member states.

What is noticeable is that municipal boundaries are often not determined by local democracy, except in so far as people vote with their feet. The new boundaries for the Auckland region have been introduced against the wishes of many of the areas involved. The main arguments advanced for the larger area are not efficiency but the inability of a group of independent authorities to agree on essential major projects that will benefit the whole region. Evidence from Canada[27] suggests that similar agglomeration in both Winnipeg and Toronto have led on the one hand to higher tax rates than in competing cities and on the other to a slower rate of economic growth, not simply in terms of income per head but through emigration and lack of population growth.

There are thus many issues for democracy still to be addressed. Our analysis suggests that the selective adoption of the better facets of the US experience are enabling European countries to obtain a greater net benefit and that the facets of localization will continue to appeal. The key implication of the three trends as seen in the US and applied in Europe for democratic arrangements are thus rather more muted and relate primarily to the increase in localization. Localized delivery does not imply localized democracy. Nor indeed does the rise in voluntary motivation. What is most pertinent is in fact an old question reflected in Tiebout's (1956) discussion. Where people are relatively mobile they can move to neighbourhoods of the like-minded. It is the richer in society who find that easier and hence they will tend to do better, if they can afford to move into the catchment areas for the better schools or hospitals or can move to pleasanter neighbourhoods. Of course this can be offset to some extent by central provision to the less fortunate but not entirely.

To some extent the framework has been upset in recent years by the enlargement of the EU. The income differentials between the new and the older member states are sufficient that there is encouragement to move, even temporarily, on a scale not seen in earlier enlargements. A wide range of income and skill groups are taking up this opportunity. Further research is needed to assess these newly developing spatial relationships and their implications for social welfare in the EU.

NOTES

1. They are linked to the type of welfare cluster a country belongs to, using Esping-Andersen's (1990) typology of social democratic, conservative, or liberal.
2. Since the 'roll back of the state' encouraged during the Thatcher and Reagan years, the voluntary sector has been afforded the room to become a more prominent actor in the delivery of social services (Wolch, 1990).
3. The policy of flexicurity as a central part of the EES aims to demonstrate that the concepts of *flexible* labour markets and job *security* need not be mutually exclusive, and can be complementary through regular and up-to-date training of workers, and improved mechanisms of job search to allow a smoother transition between jobs. Thus continuity of employment can be obtained for an employee without continuity with any one employer.
4. Cross national comparisons of income inequality use Gini coefficients (see Pontusson, 2005, Table 1), and have observed disparities between different regimes in terms of welfare transfers. The US is found to have the highest level of inequality (Garfinkel et al., 2006, p. 4).
5. Much of the debate in the UK for example has been characterized by 'stealth taxes', whereby taxation has risen from a low of 31.8 per cent of GDP in 1993–94 to a high of 36.4 per cent in 2007–08 without much in the way of increases in actual tax rates (data retrieved from HM Treasury statistics http://www.hm-treasury.gov.uk/psf_statistics.htm). The tax–GDP ratio was even higher in the early 1980s, however, at over 38 per cent.
6. The mainstream economics literature tends to discuss localization in terms of tax competition, fiscal federalism, public goods and inequality. Mainstream political science literature, on the other hand, is concerned with localization in terms of local governmental authorities, local autonomy and democracy.
7. For example, Besley and Coate (2003) discuss problems with centralization in terms of public good provision.
8. They have in mind quite a soft definition of what constitutes a public good, so it may be in limited supply and at a price that excludes some potential consumers.
9. This is assuming that greater inequality does lead to tax pressure on the rich.
10. It would also make sense for those who wanted to release equity.
11. The effects are documented in the tax competition literature (Prud'homme, 1995).
12. The level of the local authority for tax purposes varies considerably.
13. Again this assumes that the poor actually have some political influence which may not be the case.
14. However, in the current 'mixed economy' of welfare provision other actors besides the state (such as the private sector) also need to be taken into account when making such observations.

15. Clearly the temporary migration that has been taking place from the new to the older EU member states in search of employment and higher incomes does not fit into this framework.
16. Others have suggested that workfare can take social democratic, labourist, and socially conservative forms (Dostal, 2008).
17. Albeit a blurred one as we do not know the long-term employment outcomes of the job-seekers who participated.
18. The number of people in receipt of Temporary Assistance to Needy Families (TANF) benefits in 2008 was cut by a third in a decade (data retrieved from http://www. acf.hhs.gov/programs/ofa/data-reports/caseload/caseload_recent.html). The decline in the welfare rolls has also been attributed to the expansion of the Earned Income Tax Credit (EITC) which can be claimed back by low-income workers (see Meyer and Rosenbaum, 1999).
19. See Lødemel and Trickey (2001) for a list of workfare programmes in Europe.
20. However, there has been increased localization in the implementation of ALMPs in some other Scandinavian countries, notably Norway (Trickey, 2001).
21. The range of services BIDs provide has expanded over time, and includes marketing and economic development assistance to local businesses; policy advocacy; traditional local government services such as cleaning and maintenance, safety and security; land-use planning and regulation; and the running of community courts (Morçöl et al., 2008). BIDs are publicly sanctioned through the passing of legislation (Brooks, 2008).
22. Together, BIDs and NIDs are referred to as Urban Improvement Districts or UIDs.
23. For example, in 1989–1990, Alaska had average per pupil expenditures of US$7918 while Utah's were $2606 (Bray, 1999, p. 224).
24. The Act labels such students as 'subgroups', and requires 95 per cent of students overall and 95 per cent of each subgroup to take the standardized reading and mathematics tests.
25. The six states in the study were Arizona, California, Georgia, Illinois, New York, and Virginia.
26. Though the extent to which these latter two systems can be classified as centralized is debated (Daun, 2006).
27. Peter Holle '"Supercity" – what New Zealand might learn from local government amalgamation in Canada', paper presented at LEANZ, Auckland, February 2010.

6. Privatizing welfare. Changing the face of social protection and democracy in Europe

Tess Altman and Cris Shore

INTRODUCTION

In their publication entitled 'A Done Deal? The EU's Legitimacy Conundrum Revisited', Eriksen and Fossum (2007, p. 17) conclude by outlining the profound challenges that are haunting contemporary Europe. These range from 'overcoming nationalism without doing away with solidarity' and 'establishing a single market ... without abolishing the welfare state', to 'achieving unity and collective action without glossing over difference and diversity' and 'achieving efficiency and productivity without compromising rights and democratic legitimacy'.

This chapter takes up the last of these conundrums by exploring the democratic challenges for Europe raised by attempts to reconcile European welfare systems with the dictates of Economic and Monetary Union (EMU) and the European Single Market. It also examines the intractable and often contradictory goals of those European welfare regimes themselves. The principle objective of welfare has traditionally been to provide basic economic security for citizens by protecting them from market risks associated with unemployment, old age and sickness. However, norms about the need for protection have shifted significantly since the 1980s and new risks have emerged, particularly with the global financial crisis of 2008. 'Social inclusion' or the ability to participate and be fully included in society has also become an important objective for the EU and many of its member states. Yet the extent to which these different goals are achievable, or indeed compatible, remain issues for debate.

This study analyses some of the unanticipated consequences of the increased role of the private and voluntary sectors in the welfare regimes of OECD countries. It links these issues to the wider tensions between increasing flexibilization and privatization of social welfare provision on the one hand and, on the other, the continued need for state regulation and social protection in Europe. As governments throughout Europe have embraced the principles of economy, efficiency, deregulation and flexibility typically associated with neoliberalization, there has been a notable shift towards the marketization of social welfare provision. According to critics of neoliberalism, the fundamental principles of the single market – which include the unfettered free movement of capital, goods, services and labour – are incompatible with the welfarist goals of comprehensive economic and social security (see Huffschmid, 2005; Preece, 2009). But is achieving efficiency with equity really a 'zero-sum game' as these authors suggest?

This chapter sets out to address this and the following related questions:

- What are the costs and benefits of increasing private and voluntary sector involvement in welfare provision?
- Can the private and voluntary sectors contribute to the democratic goals of equal access, openness, transparency, and socially inclusive citizenship?
- What lessons do the case studies of Anglo-Saxon or neoliberal-inspired reforms offer for social policy in the EU?
- How can the current 'welfare mix' regime ensure democratic accountability?

As Eriksen and Fossum (2007) observe, democracy is an immensely complicated concept and there is a vast literature examining different models of democracy and their theoretical, procedural and philosophical connotations. In the context of European integration, a key issue has been the problem of democratic legitimacy across multiple levels (Scharpf, 1997, 1999). In this chapter we use the term democracy in its traditional sense as a system of 'government by the people as a whole (Greek: *demos*), rather than by any section, class or interests within it' (Scruton, 1982, p. 116). What this means in practice is a system that promotes not only the principles of full social inclusion, but also the ability of the people to 'have their say' and hold their rulers to account (Giddens, 1996). Welfare regimes are complex and have always comprised many different actors, both statutory and non-statutory (Ascoli and Ranci, 2002; Bode, 2006, p. 348; Esping-Andersen, 1990). Though private and voluntary sector involvement in European welfare provision was overshadowed by the creation of the welfare state in the postwar period (Poole, 2007, p. 235), Bode (2006, p. 349) has observed that welfare provision throughout the 20th century was in fact an 'organized welfare mix' involving both public and private providers.[1] Competitive structures and market relations played virtually no role within this organized public-private collaboration. Yet a recent shift from 'organized' to 'disorganized capitalism' in the 1980s has heralded the rise of what have been termed 'disorganized welfare mixes' (Castells, 1996; Lash and Urry, 1987; Offe, 1985). These new 'disorganized welfare mixes'[2] reflect shifts in Europe from the Keynesian welfare state model towards ever-more 'commoditized' and free-market approaches. They also reflect a broader movement from 'government to governance ... on all scales' (Jessop, 2002, p. 35, cited in Bode, 2006, p. 346). This entails a shift from traditional hierarchical systems of authority to more de-centralized, multi-level, network-based forms of decision making.

The normative stance taken in the literature on governance is that policy networks have enriched democracy by creating partnerships, plural access to influence, flexibility and reciprocity, yet some authors advocate a more cautious and empirical investigation (Greenaway et al., 2007, p. 719; Grimshaw et al., 2002; Shore, 2011). New modes of governance can lead to greater innovation and dynamism, but can also be volatile, highly flexible, informal, easily manipulated by powerful actors, and hence exclusive (Hay and Richards, 2000). They thus present both opportunities and challenges. Ascoli and Ranci (2002) have termed these inherent tensions 'the dilemmas of the welfare mix'. Our hypothesis is that the fundamental dilemma, which subsumes the others, is between efficiency and democratic accountability. On the one hand, a market-oriented emphasis on innovation, efficiency and competition provides a solution to the inefficiencies and rigidities of state monopolies. On the other, the new welfare mix introduces its own inefficiencies based on increased volatility and variability which may undermine accountability and consistency. Can equitable and democratic social provision be sustained under such volatile conditions, or does such a climate create new social risks and vulnerabilities?

The new 'disorganized welfare mix' also raises larger political and philosophical questions: Are monopolies in health and social welfare provision necessarily a problem? Is competition the best way to improve public services and is the private sector necessarily more efficient? Even if competition helps to break up monopolies and encourage efficiency, can 'for-profit' organizations be trusted to serve the public interest? Does commodification of health and welfare provision undermine the ideals of democracy and partnership? And what role can the voluntary sector play in mitigating some of these problems?

We present three empirical case studies in order to analyse the impacts of increased voluntary and private sector involvement in social welfare provision. Our case studies exemplify the risks and problems with increased private and voluntary sector involvement. Of course, this is not always the case. Historically there have been some appalling public sector botch-ups in welfare provision. However, this point is largely irrelevant to the problem addressed here. Our aim is not to romanticize the traditional welfare state model but instead to question the *a priori* assumption that the private sector is necessarily a more responsive, cost-effective and efficient service provider. In doing so, we identify the risks for a European social policy arena based upon such assumptions.

We have specifically chosen countries that have progressed further down the Anglo-Saxon path towards 'modernization' and efficiency to which the EU increasingly appears to aspire: the UK, the USA, and New Zealand. The UK case study concerns the Norfolk and Norwich University Hospital Private Finance Initiative (PFI), which during the 1990s became a flagship policy initiative for forging partnerships between public and private sector bodies. The USA study examines the Asset Based Community Development (ABCD) scheme, a community social welfare initiative aimed at mobilizing citizens and the non-profit sector. Lastly, the New Zealand study discusses the 'new contractualism', which claims to provide a new model for organizing social policy, employment relations and labour markets.

Our aim in presenting these examples is to map some of the recent trends towards the increasing marketization of social welfare. More specifically, we examine the implications of this for democracy in Europe and for the competing policy priorities that underlie attempts to define a more coherent European social model. We present examples of current developments in European social policy – including the European Employment Strategy (EES), 'flexicurity' and attempts to regulate European labour standards – to assess the extent to which these initiatives promote or inhibit the democratic process and the goals of a more open and inclusive society.

'ORGANIZED' AND 'DISORGANIZED' WELFARE MIXES

Under the 'organized welfare mix' regime which was common in Europe for most of the 20th century, the key actors involved in welfare provision were the public sector, the private sector, the voluntary sector, and the family. For clarity we provide some working definitions. We define the public sector as the state and the private sector as the market.[3] We view market actors as non-state organizations such as companies, firms, and for-profit organizations. The voluntary sector is harder to define.[4] Most agree that a key characteristic of the voluntary sector, and volunteering itself, is its heterogeneity and diversity (Musick and Wilson, 2008; Poole, 2007). It is commonly labelled a 'third sector' located somewhere between the state (first) and the market (second) (Anheier, 2001, pp. 1648–9). We include voluntary, civil society, non-profit, and community organizations in this definition, but distinguish between the voluntary sector and the family.

Similarly to the voluntary sector, the family has functioned to 'fill the gaps' in external welfare provision, especially regarding care for children, the sick and the elderly. The notions of familialization/defamilialization have been used to gauge the extent of family provision in different member states (Esping-Andersen, 1999). Some argue that a reliance on the family exacerbates traditional social and gender inequalities (Wall et al., 2001) and is no longer viable (Bahle, 2003), while others view family involvement as essential for building communities and social capital (Kretzmann and McKnight, 1993). While we recognize the importance of this debate, this study focuses on the role of the private and voluntary sectors in welfare provision and debates over the effects of marketization.

The 1980s brought profound changes to the existing 'organized welfare mix' model as deregulation and privatization programmes progressively sought to roll back an interventionist welfare state. One of the most crucial changes was dwindling public faith in the state's ability to act as the main provider of welfare (Bode, 2006; Deakin, 2002; Poole, 2007). In addition, the breakdown of Fordism, ageing populations, and the growing instability of traditional family structures left large sections of the European population subject to 'new social risks' including homelessness, intolerance, and social isolation (Ascoli and Ranci, 2002, p. 1). 'Disorganized capitalism' gave rise to 'a more flexible world economy and the end of direct state interventionism', not to mention 'the pluralization of class structures and altered cultural representations' (Bode, 2006, p. 350).

These combined changes contributed to the development of the new 'disorganized welfare mix' (Bode, 2006, p. 349). Under this new mix, the actors have remained the same, but their roles, objectives, and relationships have changed. The boundaries separating public, private and voluntary sectors have become increasingly porous. The new mix has also been viewed as part of the New Public Management (NPM) reforms of the 1980s which signify a trend towards marketization and commodification (Christensen and Lægreid, 2001; Ramia, 2002; Pollit et al.,

2007). For yet others, the new disorganized welfare mix is part of the 'passage to privatization' (Ascoli and Ranci, 2002; Gray, 2004).

Such welfare restructuring has had varied and sometimes unforeseen consequences in different sectors. For example, the introduction of market principles into the voluntary sector in the UK has led to an increasing polarization between larger, more formalized, and more professionalized voluntary organizations and those that are smaller, more informal, and more reliant on volunteers and community effort (Poole 2007, p. 234). It has been argued that tough competition for state funding and contracts may encourage the voluntary sector to become reactive as opposed to proactive, conservative and cautious instead of innovative, and exclusive rather than socially inclusive and empowering (Poole, 2007, p. 237). Yet social needs still remain a key driver of provision in Europe. An equal emphasis on not only *efficient* but *effective* social provision has been enshrined in political rhetoric (Poole et al., 2007, p. 239). For example, New Labour in the UK often invoked a 'Third Way', drawing on the neocommunitarian discourse of 'active citizenship' and 'civil responsibilization' as a means to counterbalance their neo-liberal agenda – although its presumed benefits have been critiqued (Cruikshank, 1999; Rose, 1996).

Restructuring invariably poses a series of choices and challenges for all actors involved. Ascoli and Ranci (2002) have termed these the 'dilemmas of the welfare mix':

1. Delegation *or* sharing of responsibility
2. Cooperation *or* competition
3. Organizational efficiency *or* quality of the service
4. Stability of cooperative relationships *or* the chance to innovate
5. Central *or* marginal role of volunteering
6. Identity *or* service provision
7. 'Customers' *or* 'citizens' to be involved
8. Conservation *or* disappearance of a public sector role in the delivery of services
9. Uniform *or* diversified services

Following Mörth (2008) we suggest a key dilemma that subsumes all of these is the tension between 'efficiency' and 'democratic accountability', although some may question whether this is necessarily a 'zero-sum game'. Market-led efficiency versus democratic accountability becomes a dilemma in public-private collaborations because the prerequisite for democratic accountability is transparent decision making and clearly defined chains of responsibility. These are often lacking in the more complex and diffuse 'disorganized welfare mix' which blurs boundaries between public and private sectors. Hence private-sector actors often remain outside the democratic chain, and 'democratic accountability becomes a problem when public authority is shared with rather than delegated to private actors' (Mörth, 2008, p. 3). Another tension arises from the fact that accountability is often conceptualized differently in the public and private sectors: for the former, it entails accountability to voters, while the latter are answerable not to the general public but to institutional stakeholders and investors. This difference is sometimes expressed in terms of the rights of 'citizens' versus those of consumers.

In the end, each sector has its strengths and weaknesses when it comes to welfare provision. We attempt to illustrate these in Tables 6.1 and 6.2.

Table 6.1   Characteristics of social welfare providers

Is it:	Efficient?	Cost Effective?	Competitive?	Monopolistic?
State (Public)	?	✔	✗	✔
Market (Private)	✔	✗	✔	✗
Voluntary	?	✔	✔	✗
Family	?	✔	✗	✗

Table 6.2   Democratic tendencies of social welfare providers

Does it offer:	Equity?	Account-ability?	Trans-parency?	More social inclusion?	More choice?
State (Public)	✔	✔	✔	✔	✗
Market (Private)	✗	?	✗	✗	✔
Voluntary	✔	?	✗	✔	✔
Family	?	✔	✗	✔	✗

CASE STUDIES FROM ADVANCED LIBERAL OECD COUNTRIES

In what follows, we present a series of empirical case studies to observe how some of the 'dilemmas of the welfare mix' translate into action. Our first case concerns the UK Private Finance Initiative and is paradigmatic of private sector involvement in social welfare provision. This case study illustrates how the attempt to break up monopolies advocated in a competitive market approach often recreates or amplifies them. Our second case study investigates the US Asset Based Community Development (ABCD) initiative as an example of voluntary sector and 'community involvement' in welfare provision. Through this example we illustrate how voluntary and community interests can indeed 'fill the gaps' in welfare provision. However, there is a fine line between the *aligning* of voluntary sector and community interests with those of state and market providers, and the *co-option* of those interests by state and market agendas. Our final case examines the 'new contractualism' in New Zealand as an example of the commodification of employment relations and the ramifications of this for social relations and democratic participation. Taken as a set, these three case studies provide important lessons for Europe by offering a transversal analysis relevant to Eriksen and Fossum's (2007) models for reconstituting European democracy. They also challenge the assumption that private-sector involvement necessarily provides the best solution to the challenges faced by advanced liberal societies.

The Private Finance Initiative in the UK

The Private Finance Initiative (PFI) is part of the realization of successive British policies seeking to move activities and services from the public to the private sector. Some authors view the PFI as part of the government's 'modernization' agenda and a form of New Public Financial Management (NPM) (Broadbent and Laughlin, 2005; Mayston, 1999). Others see PFIs as a way to overcome financing and other bottlenecks associated with traditional provision, to relieve financial risks and costs from the public sector, to engage private sector principles of efficiency and innovation whilst ensuring accountability (Mayston, 1999, p. 249), and to ensure Value for Money (VFM) (Blanken et al., 2009, p. 123; Shaoul et al., 2008, p. 1).[5]

The British government formally launched its PFI policy in 1992 (Spackman, 2002, p. 285). The number of PFI projects increased substantially after the introduction of a universal testing rule in 1994 required that private financing be made an option for every public sector project. In 1997, the New Labour government added further support to PFI schemes by instating legislation holding the public sector to PFI contracts. They also abolished the universal testing rule in favour of a new 'Public Private Partnership' policy, under which PFIs were subsumed (Spackman, 2002, p. 285).[6] As of March 2008, 627 PFI schemes had been signed in the UK, delivering private finance of £58.2 billion (HM Treasury cited in Hellowell and Pollock, 2007, p. 13).

The National Health Service (NHS) is the biggest exponent of PFI contracts in the UK (Blanken et al., 2009, p. 124).[7] PFI projects in the NHS are funded through financial markets by groups of investment banks, builders, and service contractors who own, 'design, build, finance and operate' (DBFO) the new health facilities and manage them once they are completed (Broadbent and Laughlin, 2005, p. 77; Hellowell and Pollock, 2007, p. 8). This is in contrast with a 'conventional public procurement model', where the public sector finances the building through taxation and 'Treasury gilts' as well as owning and operating the finished product (Hellowell and Pollock, 2007, p. 8). Between April 1997 and April 2007, 85 out of 110 (87.3 per cent) new hospital contracts were PFI schemes[8] (Hellowell and Pollock, 2007, p. 8).

The Norfolk and Norwich University Hospital

Phase 1: Decision making through governance and networks   The Norfolk and Norwich University Hospital was one of the earliest and most important NHS PFI projects. The need for a new hospital arose because the existing N&N hospital near the city centre had not been well maintained. In 1986, a formal review by the regional and district health authorities (RHA and DHA) concluded that a twin-site option should be put into practice, based round the existing site and another one at Hellesdon. These early proposals came from networks within the local health community but were opposed by professional hospital consultants. These consultants saw an opportunity to share research expertise and gain prestige by building the new hospital at Colney, near the University of East Anglia. They expanded their own policy networks to include government and university 'movers and shakers'.[9] After this, opposition to the Colney site began to fall away, and permission for the new hospital was granted in 1988. However, at this stage, the Colney site was still considered part of a twin-site project (Greenaway et al., 2007, p. 721).

The appointment of a new pro-Colney DHA chief executive from 1990 to 1992,[10] the national PFI policy of 1992,[11] and the arrival of a new Labour government in 1997 cemented the single site Colney hospital. There was national pressure to ensure the success of what had become a 'flagship' PFI hospital. The DHA was told to facilitate the policy and the newly created Norfolk and Norwich University NHS Trust let a PFI contract to a private sector consortium, Octagon, in 1998. Under this contract, Octagon was to build, maintain, and provide facilities management for the hospital for 30 years (House of Commons, 2006, p. 8). The new hospital was built speedily and let to the NHS Trust in 2001. The negotiation of the new PFI had hence become confined to an exclusive 'policy implementation network' consisting of senior Trust managers, a Treasury civil servant, national civil servants from the Department of Health, and the private sector, largely leaving out the local health community.[12]

Phase 2: The refinancing of the N&N University Hospital   In 2003, only two years after the hospital opened, Octagon refinanced the project (Greenaway et al., 2007, p. 717).[13] Octagon increased its borrowings by 53 per cent and used these funds to accelerate the financial benefits which their investors would receive from the project (House of Commons, 2006). Of the £116 million refinancing gain, £82 million was kept by Octagon. This more than trebled its internal rate of return from 19 per cent (the original contract figure) to 60 per cent (House of Commons, 2006). Octagon was able to reap such enormous benefits largely because the NHS Trust did not have any provision in place to ensure that they received their fair share of the refinancing gains except for a voluntary code (NAO, 2005). In accordance with this code, the Trust received 29 per cent of the refinancing gains (£34 million).

In accepting the terms of the refinancing deal, the Trust was exposed to new risks and costs, whilst Octagon managed to substantially lower its own risk. The length of the PFI contract was extended from 34 to 39 years, and the Trust agreed to receive its 29 per cent share of the refinancing gains over the life of the contract, rather than upfront as Octagon had done. Furthermore, the Trust accepted that the liabilities incurred for terminating the contract early could increase by up to £257 million.

The House of Commons Public Accounts Committee issued a scathing report on the N&N University PFI refinancing project in 2006. They stated that (House of Commons, 2006, p. 1):

The opportunity for large refinancing gains on this early PFI deal does not seem to have been seriously considered as part of the original deal negotiations. Yet, through simply borrowing more, the benefits to Octagon's investors have soared on refinancing to levels which are unacceptable even for an early PFI deal. The Trust further contributed to the inappropriate outcome by accepting that, should it wish to end this contract early, its liabilities could now include all the additional borrowings Octagon used to boost its investors' returns. We would not expect to see another Accounting Officer appearing before this Committee defending what we believe to be the unacceptable face of capitalism in the consortium's dealings with the public sector.

In this statement, the purchaser NHS Trust is made solely responsible for the undesirable outcome. Yet other commentators note that the Department of Health forced the Trust into accepting the terms of the refinancing in order to retain private sector support and interest (Monbiot, 2006). The 29 per cent the Trust did manage to negotiate was only obtained through exposure to potential liabilities. The National Audit Office (NAO) also claimed that the Trust could have brokered a better deal but was constrained by pressure 'to close a pathfinder deal which had already been assessed as value for money' (NAO, 2005, p. 4).[14]

Private finance initiatives: implications for democracy

PFI projects in the UK have major implications for democratic and equitable social policy. In their 2007 report, Hellowell and Pollock concluded that PFI contracts in the NHS are creating unmanageable public financial deficits. This situation has arisen because the cost of PFI contracts is greater than the funds they are provided with through the NHS resource allocation mechanism. The extent of under-funding increases with the size of the PFI.[15] The solution to such under-funding has usually been to cut crucial services, which is detrimental to health provision in the UK.[16] This type of under-funding is far less likely to occur in a state-funded health service because governments generally have access to the cheapest funds and are less likely to be hampered with exorbitant repayments to lenders.

The inflexibility of long-term PFI contracts also impacts negatively on PFI hospitals. Inflexibility creates major constraints to design, service, and financial flexibility, limiting the ability of health care to adapt to changing conditions while exposing hospitals to huge potential risks (Blanken et al., 2009, p. 139). Paradoxically, the purportedly flexible and adaptable organizational character of the private sector appears to introduce 'new rigidities' not present in state provision (Grimshaw et al., 2002, p. 476).

PFI projects also provide a useful illustration of how the new 'governance' paradigm works in practice. Policy networks in this case study were utilized as a means of decision making, and led to more interpersonal and less predictable outcomes, leaving room for more active and innovative forms of leadership (Greenaway et al., 2007, p. 735). However, the outcome was not so positive, and the characteristic volatile features of governance came into play. Decision-making processes and networks often centred on powerful individuals, local and national elites, and experts. Additionally central government was able to manipulate the policy agenda and to dominate local networks through direct pressure, institutional restructuring and setting the policy framework. Private sector involvement only added to the lack of democratic openness through its veil of secrecy and commercial confidentiality (Greenaway et al., 2007, p. 730; Mayston, 1999, p. 251). The terms of the PFI contract were set very much in favour of the private sector consortium, and this consortium was not held publicly accountable for its financial gains as these occurred 'off balance sheet'. As Greenaway et al. (2007, p. 736) conclude: '[j]ust as the PFI has been a convenient way for British governments to provide capital projects off balance sheet, so the networks of sub-central government allow decision making to take place "off the democratic balance sheet"'.

Asset-Based Community Development in the US

Our second case study looks at a development initiative which originated in the US in the 1990s, Asset-Based Community Development (ABCD). According to founders John Kretzmann and John McKnight, major economic shifts in the 1970s and 1980s have caused American cities to become deeply troubled places with devastated communities and a dearth of employment opportunities. There are two possible solutions to this problem. The traditional needs-based approach (Figure 6.1) paints a negative picture of lower income areas as 'needy, problematic and deficient neighbourhoods populated by needy, problematic and deficient people' (Kretzmann and McKnight, 1993, p. 2). Problems are addressed through 'deficiency-oriented policies and programs' which seek to inform people of their problems and of the value of services as the answer to these problems. Kretzmann and McKnight critique this approach, arguing that it fosters an 'environment of service', where people from poor urban areas increasingly see themselves as 'clients' whose wellbeing depends on outsiders. Such an atmosphere is detrimental to community building as it positions people as consumers rather than producers of services. This adds to a cycle of dependence, creates fragmentation, stunts leadership, and fosters a sense of hopelessness (Kretzmann and McKnight, 1993, pp. 4–5).

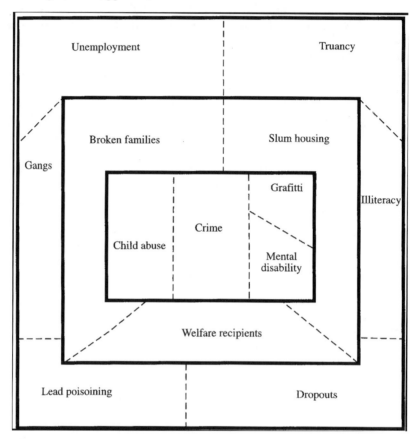

Source: Kretzmann and McKnight, 1993.

Figure 6.1   Neighbourhood needs map

In place of a needs-based approach, which sees the glass as half-empty, Kretzmann and McKnight advocate a 'glass half-full' asset-based approach (Figure 6.2). This approach focuses instead on the 'capacities, skills and assets of lower income people and their neighbourhoods' (Kretzmann and McKnight, 1993).[17] Two reasons are given for utilizing this approach. Firstly, community development depends upon committed local participants and cannot merely be imposed in a top-down manner. Secondly (and this also rings true in the current downturn), federal

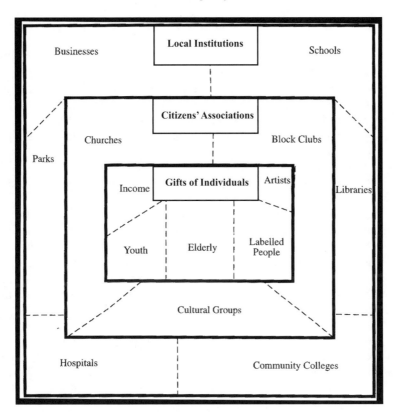

Source: Kretzmann and McKnight, 1993.

Figure 6.2 Community assets map

budget constraints and the inability of lower income areas to attract investment capital mean that 'the prospect for outside help is bleak indeed ... *there is no other choice*' (Kretzmann and McKnight, 1993; emphasis added). In these circumstances, communities need to look to themselves for solutions.

Popularizing ABCD and community participation

The Obama Administration has institutionalized a greater role for the community in the *Serve America Act 2009*. The Act aims to create more opportunities for Americans to serve their country at every stage of their lives through (Kennedy and Hatch, 2009):

- Asking Americans to volunteer a year to solving national challenges
- Increasing opportunities for service for students, working adults, and retirees
- Establishing a 'Volunteer Generation Fund' to help non-profit organizations recruit and manage more volunteers
- Supporting innovation in the non-profit sector through
    - establishing a Commission to study how governments, the non-profit and the private sector can work together to meet national challenges
    - applying effective business strategies to the non-profit sector.

Michelle Obama, who has worked with ABCD organization Public Allies, has actively endorsed ABCD as part of the remedy to the financial crisis and said in a speech that she and President Obama looked forward to working side by side with communities. Her vision sounds much like a 'partnership' type model: 'we hope to be able to provide some of the resources that you need, but we also need you to prepare for the challenge' (ABCD Institute, 2009).

The *Serve America Act 2009* and Michelle and President Obama's support has helped to popularize the ABCD approach in the US, but the ABCD approach is also used globally in the field of community development. Organizations and consultancies that implement an ABCD approach are active in Australia and New Zealand,[18] Ireland and Kenya, South Africa, Namibia, the UK, Canada, and all over the US (ABCD Institute, 2009a).[19] The company ABCD Global Consultancy promotes the approach globally through keynote addresses, seminars, and technical assistance.[20]

International organizations such as the United Nations have aligned themselves with the ABCD approach (Tibaijuka, 2003),[21] and there is potential complementarity between ABCD and the World Banks' 'Community Driven Development' (CDD) approach.[22] The World Bank is currently working towards an 'asset-based' social policy that takes into account multiple actors and interests in a 'polycentric' provision arena (Moser and Dani, 2008).

ABCD: implications for democracy
Kretzmann and McKnight (1993) issue two caveats to the ABCD approach. A focus on assets is not meant to imply that communities do not need outside resources; rather outside resources will be more effectively used if communities are already mobilized. They also acknowledge a history of community organizing, which they seek to build on rather than supplant. However, these caveats have not been adequately

addressed according to critics, who have pointed out a number of issues. ABCD does not clearly delineate a role for external institutions and agencies, and, in pursuing a bottom-up community level approach, it may rule out the value of external support. Peterman notes that in order for neighbourhood development to be effective, contrary to the ABCD criteria it should not be inwardly focused and isolated but must always be thought of in terms of the larger community and society – in other words, links between levels need to be made (Peterman, 2000, p. 174). In addition, ABCD's 'one size fits all' methodology is seen to ignore community and neighbourhood divisions, specificities, and power imbalances, especially related to class and race (Hyatt, 2008; Mansuri and Rao, 2004; Mathie and Cunningham, 2003).

The ABCD approach may also serve to bolster governmental discourses that are utilized to force citizens into accepting responsibility for themselves, their communities, and their families (Cruikshank, 1999; Rose, 1996). In this sense, ABCD easily lends itself to becoming a 'political technology', and an instrument of advanced liberal governmentality. The institutionalization of ABCD principles through legislation makes this possibility even more likely. Critics argue that ABCD, just like US volunteerism (Hyatt, 2008; Lyon-Callo and Hyatt, 2003), embodies much of the neoliberal environment in which it was conceived. External factors such as privatization, the deregulation of banks, and decline in union membership have undermined the authority of citizens (Goode and Maskovsky, 2001; Lyon-Callo and Hyatt, 2003), and in this context ABCD 'acts as a palliative, serving as a rationale for maintaining the status quo, rather than as a genuine catalyst intended to spur social change' (Hyatt, 2008, p. 19). Instead of challenging gross public underfunding of social welfare, ABCD exhibits 'a disdain for public sector entities and a wholesale rejection of the potential of government as a possible agent for redressing the injuries created by structural inequality' (Hyatt, 2008, p. 19). In doing so, ABCD represents a distinct softening of the more confrontational aspects of the traditional 'Alinsky' model of community organizing in the US such as encouraging citizens to demand external resources. Instead, it allows people to passively accept their external circumstances rather than actively confronting them. By removing government from the equation, this approach fosters an attitude of disengagement from politics and the state – which is both depoliticizing and anti-democratic (Hyatt, 2008, p. 25). ABCD thus exemplifies what James Ferguson (1985) has termed an 'anti-politics machine'.

Advocates of ABCD do not see these issues as undermining the approach but as a series of challenges to be met (Mathie and Cunningham, 2003). Some practitioners of ABCD do, however, approach its implementation with a critical eye. Recent ABCD initiatives that utilize national campaigning such as the 2010 KaBoom! Playground project have also illustrated a commitment to engage more directly with politics, which does indicate the potential of the approach if it is applied in a less inwardly focused manner.

The 'New Contractualism' in New Zealand

Our last case study considers the rise of the 'new contractualism' in New Zealand (Davis et al., 1997; Yeatman, 1995). The new contractualism poses a solution to labour market rigidities through fostering the development of more flexibilized employment relations. It is relevant to our topic of inquiry as it diminishes state and union involvement in employment agreements, leaving greater room for non-state actors. The new contractualism is an adaptation of the 'old contractualisms' – the 'social contract' of the 17th and 18th centuries and the 'classical legal contract' of the 19th century – and

> now increasingly underpins the employee-employer relation, some aspects of race relations, and relations between politicians and bureaucrats, spouses, children, and parents, educational institutions and students, as well as between the state and a host of public services. Contractual relations in the world of commerce, which previously were the main realm of contractualism, have spilled over into other domains, constituting an important – though as yet underappreciated – dimension of the neo-liberal phase of societal development. (Ramia, 2002, p. 50)

The new contractualism is one manifestation of the broader NPM reforms which seek to overcome issues of 'government failure' – such as allocative inefficiency, bureaucratic failure, and patterns of wealth transfer that encourage 'rent-seeking' activities – by advocating less state and more market (Wallis and Dollery, 2001, p. 248). This is achieved by incorporating market mechanisms into the public sector or by exposing the public sector to competition (Bredgaard and Larsen, 2007, p. 291; Ramia and Wailes, 2006, p. 56).

In New Zealand, contractualism became institutionalized in the 1980s as part of a cluster of radical NPM reforms which came to be known as 'Rogernomics' or 'the New Zealand Experiment' (Kelsey, 1995). Schick (1998, p. 124) classifies the New Zealand reforms as part of a greater conceptual shift to 'government by contract'. The reforms placed great emphasis on creating formal contract-type relationships specifically focused upon performance and output accountability which were institutionalized through various legislation including the *State Sector Act 1988* and the *Public Finance Act 1989* (Wallis and Dollery, 2001, p. 254). More broadly, reforms advocated privatization, marketization and deregulation in social welfare, health, and employment arenas (Rasmussen and Lamm, 2005, p. 480).

The New Zealand Employment Contracts Act 1991

One of the most radical examples of the new contractualism is the *Employment Contracts Act 1991* (ECA). The ECA advocated direct employee-employer relationships at the workplace level with the aim of encouraging more productive and flexible outcomes (Rasmussen and Lamm, 2005, p. 480). The ECA promoted individual employment agreements over collective agreements and this, coupled with other legislation such as the *Human Rights Act 1993* and the *Privacy Act 1993*, accelerated a climate of individualization in New Zealand. Under the ECA, the abolition of the award system and union membership coverage rights was actively endorsed. Unionization declined from 41.5 per cent of the employed workforce in 1991 to 21.7 per cent in 1995 (Morrison, 1996, p. 7). Barry and Reveley (2002, p. 511) note that a decade after the ECA was implemented, 75 per cent of New Zealanders were on individual employment contracts.[23]

Critics of the ECA argued that its individualized nature encouraged 'take it or leave it' contracts and hard or unfair bargaining by employers (Barry and Reveley, 2002, p. 510). A report on the impacts of the ECA concluded that while it appeared to have a positive effect on economic productivity and growth, employment conditions had worsened (Morrison, 1996, p. 14).

The New Zealand Employment Relations Act 2000

The *Employment Relations Act 2000* (ERA) sought to water down the more radical elements of the ECA and redress the balance of employment relations in favour of collectivism (Ramia and Wailes, 2006, p. 57). The ERA explicitly supports unionism and collective bargaining through enabling unions to have direct access to workplaces; requiring employers to offer the terms and conditions of an applicable collective agreement to new employees in the first 30 days of employment; and formally requiring employees who are part of a collective agreement to be union members (Barry and Reveley, 2002, p. 513; Rasmussen and Lamm, 2005, p. 482). The ERA also promotes good faith in employment relations and acknowledges the inherent inequality of bargaining power in employment relationships (Waldegrave et al., 2003, p. 14).

However, the impact of the ERA on employers has been limited, as a 2003 Department of Labour Report notes (Waldegrave et al., 2003,

p. 12). Unionism in New Zealand faces a number of challenges: the indifference of the majority of workers in non-unionized firms; the lack of union reach, particularly in the private sector; and free-riding, or employees enjoying the benefits of collective agreements without belonging to a union (Haynes et al., 2006, p. 193). The *Employment Relations Law Reform Bill 2004* has attempted to grapple with some of these issues but its effectiveness is as yet unclear.

The 'new contractualism': implications for democracy

As part of a broader economic restructuring in New Zealand, reforms were undertaken in order to foster a higher growth and employment rate. However, these swift and radical NPM reforms had a number of detrimental and dislocating social effects (Dalziel, 2002; Dannin, 1997; Kelsey, 1995). The cuts in social services implemented under the ECA have been described as nothing short of 'overtly socially regressive', particularly unemployment benefits which were cut by up to 30 per cent (Ramia and Wailes, 2006, p. 57). Dalziel (2002) also argues that the supposed positive impact on growth and employment was, in fact, minimal.

Both the ECA and the ERA had paradoxical effects. The ECA, which was introduced in a climate of deregulation, in fact enabled increased regulation in the 1990s. The ERA, which was supposed to strengthen collective bargaining, paradoxically strengthened individual employment relations. This is partly because the move to make collective agreements 'the exclusive domain of unions' has led many employees to opt for individual contracts rather than have third party involvement, as the ERA does not present the option of 'collective contracting' (Rasmussen and Lamm, 2005, p. 482). Rasmussen and Lamm (2005, p. 482) conclude that 'the continuous strong emphasis of individual employee rights [through measures such as personal grievance claims and statutory individual entitlements] cuts across the support for collectivism and, to some degree, it undermines the unions' attempts to create union density'.

The biggest shift wrought by the 'new contractualism' is hence the increased emphasis on individualism. To avoid the potentially negative consequences for democracy, Ramia argues that the new contractualism must be implemented in conjunction with social protection to ensure that social gains such as equal pay, maternity leave, and safe working conditions, are not compromised (Ramia, 2002). By contrast, Yeatman (1995) asserts that individualization creates new possibilities for sociality through the development of 'social contractualism'. However, as noted earlier, the top-down implementation of the new contractualism, the atomistic relations it fosters, and the sometimes opaque nature of governance networks all work to undermine the capacity for solidarity and collective action.

THE STATE OF WELFARE IN EUROPE

The European Social Model and the Welfare Triangle

What lessons can be drawn from these three paradigmatic case studies for European social policy? Firstly, we need to examine the wider context in which member states formulate their welfare regimes. In Europe, the notion of a European social model is central to current debates about welfare regimes. While the concept of 'Social Europe' has its roots in the post-war welfare tradition based on Keynesian and Beveridge-style economics (Preece, 2009, p. 2), it was Jacques Delors who first popularized the term in the mid-1980s. Delors' prime aim was to contrast Europe with the solely market-driven US model of capitalism (Jepsen and Pascual, 2006). Indeed, the distinguishing feature of the otherwise ill-defined European social model is that it presents an alternative to the social model of the USA. In this respect, the European social model is essentially a normative concept used to describe the EU's twin goals of combining sustainable economic growth with social cohesion (Jepsen and Pascual, 2006, p. 231). It thus represents a kind of 'Third Way' between US-style neoliberal deregulation and Keynesian social regulation.

Three conceptualizations of the European social model prevail in mainstream academic and political circles. First, the European social model is presented as an entity with common features (institutions, values, forms of regulation).[24] Second, the European social model is an ideal-typical model, where specific national social models are held up as exemplars for other member states to follow (key exponents of this approach include Esping-Andersen, 1990; Ebbinghaus, 1999; Ferrera et al., 2001; Sapir, 2006).[25] Finally, for many writers (e.g. Amitsis et al., 2003; Lönnroth, 2002; Vaughan-Whitehead, 2003; Wilding, 1997), the idea of a European social model – like that of European citizenship – is part of a wider project for 'building Europe' (Shore, 2000). Instead of emphasizing differences between national models these authors have sought to cultivate a distinctive transnational model and see the social, economic and technological changes wrought by globalization as demanding an EU-level response that will push Europe towards 'modernization' and re-shape future definitions of the European social model.

Academic and political debate on the European social model shares two interconnected features: firstly, the 'reality status' of the concept is taken for granted; and secondly, the very concept of a European social model is ambiguous and polysemic in nature. As Jepsen and Pascual (2006, p. 234) note, this imprecision means the European social model can be used to justify a wide range of different policy positions, not all of them in the interests of the public. For these authors, the European social model is thus a *political* project aimed at legitimizing the EU as a supranational entity and creating a common European identity (Jepsen and Pascual, 2006, p. 239).

Another useful way of categorizing European welfare regimes is the 'welfare triangle' model (Muffels et al., 2002). This provides a straight-forward conceptualization of the key aims of welfare regimes – income, employment, and participation/social integration (see Figure 6.3 which reproduces Figure 2.1). Boeri et al. (2006) similarly see the three objectives of social policies as (1) the reduction of income inequality, (2) protection against insurable labour market risk, and (3) reward to labour market participation (see also Boeri, 2002). The welfare triangle, how-ever, becomes more complex when we add two further axes: the horizontal axis illustrates a continuum of key actors (the state, family, market), and the vertical axis indicates a continuum of responsibility from social partners/community to individual citizen.

The welfare triangle also locates Sapir's four European social models (Nordic, Anglo-Saxon, Mediterranean, Continental) in different parts of the triangle according to how much emphasis they place on (a) the three objectives (income, employment, and social integration) and (b) the actors who implement the objectives. Generally, more emphasis is placed on one particular objective over another or one actor over another – often, especially in the case of objectives such as minimum income versus adequate employment, this is construed as a trade-off.

Barriers to Social Europe

The diversity and complexity that exists both within and between the welfare regimes of the EU member states makes the notion of a singular or common European social model analytically problematic (Mayes and Mustaffa, Chapter 2 this volume; Scharpf, 2002; Schelkle, 2008).

There are also practical as well as epistemological obstacles to promoting a Social Europe. Not least is the weakness of the Open Method of Coordination (OMC) as an instrument for institutionalizing convergence towards a more coherent social model (Scharpf, 2002). Progress towards a more coherent European social model is also compli-cated by the way member states have pursued their agenda for neoliber-alization. Typically, the principle of 'efficiency' has been emphasized

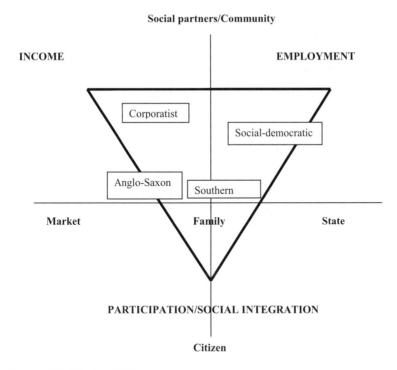

Source: Muffels et al., 2002.

Figure 6.3   Welfare regimes and the welfare triangle

over and above that of equity. For example, Sapir (2006, p. 380) concludes that only the Nordic and Anglo-Saxon social models are sustainable as they exhibit 'high efficiency' whereas the Continental and Mediterranean models are dismissed as unsustainable.

Huffschmid (2005, p. 4) notes that the European social model is inevitably 'embedded into the framework of global competition' as opposed to one of social welfare objectives. The European emphasis on competition is mirrored in the move away from the 'Keynesian National Welfare State' model to the 'Schumpeterian Competition State' (Jessop, 2002). The implications of this are twofold: first, the minimization of the public sector in economic and social re/production through the prioritization of open markets as the only means (or reason) for economic regulation (Huffschmid, 2005, pp. 4–5), and secondly, the inevitable break-up of social structures based on workers' movements and trade unions, which are seen as barriers to economic growth and competitiveness.

This complexity raises the question of whether a singular European social model is feasible and, if so, what kind of model it should be. Here opinion is divided. For some the European social model represents an attempt to reintroduce the failed policies of Keynesian and socialism on a European scale (Cash, 2000). Others take the opposite view, arguing that the European social model could be viable if removed from its neoliberal context and placed in a more democratic framework. This would entail 'strong conceptual changes between means and ends in economic and social policies' (Huffschmid, 2005, pp. 181–2). The issue here is whether the European social model should be a *means* to economic strength and competitiveness or the *end* to which economic and social policy is directed. Proponents of the latter argue that the goals of a renewed European social model should be: full employment, social welfare and security, social equity, ecological sustainability and balanced and co-operative international relations (Huffschmid, 2005, p. 183).

The emphasis on introducing market principles to welfare provision at the national as well as the European level indicates some degree of policy convergence towards marketization or privatization. However, as our previous case studies highlighted, adopting such neoliberal welfare reforms has consequences for the European social model – and for democracy.

COMPETING VISIONS AND CONTRADICTIONS WITHIN EUROPEAN SOCIAL POLICY

The previous section outlined some of the competing visions of the European social model (i.e. as an instrument for promoting growth or a mechanism for achieving the goals of social inclusion and welfare). This section examines how these same tensions between economic and social objectives play out in practice by focusing on the internal contradictions inherent within the EES, the notion of 'flexicurity', and the regulation of increasingly flexible European labour markets.

The EES and Flexicurity

The EES is the most comprehensive attempt to instate a European level social policy, and exemplifies the new OMC. As a form of 'soft law', the OMC encourages convergence in policy at the European level, while leaving responsibility for policy with the member states. Heidenreich and Bischoff (2008, p. 499) describe it as 'the methodical backbone of the Lisbon strategy with which the EU tries to modernize the European employment, economic, educational and social policies'. Member states present annual 'national action plans' which are evaluated by the European Commission against comparative benchmarks and are used to write up annual reports, guidelines, and in some cases recommendations to specific states (Raveaud, 2007, p. 412; Scharpf, 2002, p. 653). Much literature focuses on the beneficial aspects of the OMC such as information exchange, benchmarking, peer review, deliberation, and naming and shaming (Scharpf, 2002, p. 653). However, success depends on the willingness of both member states and partisan political actors to embrace and utilize the EES (Kröger, 2009; López-Santana, 2009; Weishaupt, 2009).

The first guidelines of the EES were approved in December 1997 and formally structured around four pillars: employability, entrepreneurship, adaptability and equal opportunities (Biffl, 2007, p. 4). These ideas were subsequently taken up by the European Council in 2000 which set out the goals of the Lisbon strategy 'to become the most competitive knowledge-based economy in the world, capable of sustainable economic growth with more and better jobs and greater social cohesion'. In 2005, the Lisbon Action Plan listed its three main aims as:

1. Making Europe a more attractive place to invest and work;
2. Knowledge and innovation for growth; and
3. Creating more and better jobs (Schäfer and Leiber, 2009, pp. 6–7).

However, developments such as the Kok Reports of 2003/4, the integration in 2005 of the EES into the Broad Economic Policy Guidelines, the Lisbon Treaty and the 2020 Strategy have led to a greater emphasis on flexibility, competitiveness, growth and employment and the 'dropping out' of social and environmental goals (Raveaud, 2007, pp. 428–9). Taking all this into account, it appears that the EU's response to the challenges of globalization and the financial crisis is to promote growth, efficiency and competition as the means to ensure social protection. These market mechanisms are seen to create a flexible yet stable environment, where competition for funding and contracts ensures the quality of service provision.

Flexicurity is heralded as a possible solution to the detrimental social impacts of flexible labour markets in Europe, and has become central to the 'third way' implementation of the EES. Indeed, Commission President Barroso has described flexicurity as 'essential' for Europe to maintain its competitive edge and its distinctive social model in an age of globalization (Boeri et al., 2006, p. 2).

For Boeri et al. (2006, p. 2) flexicurity is defined as 'flexible contracts' and 'adequate unemployment benefits'; that is, less rigid employment protection legislation and greater prioritization of unemployment benefits. Wilthagen and Tros (2004, p. 169) define it more precisely as:

> A policy strategy that attempts, synchronically and in a deliberate way, to enhance the flexibility of labour markets, work organisation and labour relations on the one hand, and to enhance security – employment security and social security – notably for weaker groups in and outside the labour market, on the other hand.

Flexicurity thus has two components: social inclusion on the one hand, and competitiveness and productivity on the other. In practice, this means creating a flexible environment where activation policies assist jobseekers to find work easily, but which is at the same time highly competitive. Such an environment may lead to high turnover, but also guarantees the assurance of constant (if only short term) employment for workers.

However, this emphasis on creating flexible labour markets tends to impact most negatively on workers with little social capital or bargaining power, which results in a two-tier workforce. This has led Stiglitz (2002) and other critics (e.g. Gray, 2004) of flexicurity to call it 'flexploitation': a thinly disguised attempt to deregulate labour markets and undermine years of trade union bargaining and political activity. The social compensation component of flexicurity is often insufficient to balance the insecurity caused by the flexibilization of labour markets (Seifert and Tangian, 2006). Moreover, an emphasis on part time and temporary jobs shows that job quantity over quality – the *more* without the *better* in the rhetoric of 'more and better jobs' – is being prioritized (Raveaud, 2007).

The success of flexicurity in practice can only be gauged through empirical research, of which there has historically been little. However, recent research has aimed to maximize the positive aspects of flexicurity by moving away from a 'trade-off' mentality (e.g. Schmid, 2009). It would be premature, therefore, to condemn flexicurity as a mere vehicle for flexibilized exploitation. In Denmark and the Netherlands, the model of flexicurity has worked quite well to ensure a low unemployment rate and the protection of unskilled workers, as exemplified in the Danish 'golden triangle' (Madsen, 2002; Jørgensen and Madsen, 2007).[26] However, Gray (2004) counters that the 'golden triangle' only works because it occurs in a climate with a strong degree of unionization. This brings the Nordic welfare systems closest to the goals of a well rounded European social model with a balance of efficiency and equity.[27] Such strong unionization and public services (through taxation) also provide much needed support to the family in caring for children and the elderly. Yet Raveaud (2007, p. 430) claims that the Commission and the EES guidelines are critical of the Swedish and Danish systems, deeming their tax levels too high and their unemployment benefits too generous. Therefore this model of flexicurity may not be exportable elsewhere as it does not fit with the recommendations of the EES. Furthermore, the success of flexicurity depends on the specificities of national welfare regimes.

Labour Disputes and the Posted Workers Directive

One consequence of increased labour market flexibilization in the EU has been the movement of workers from poorer and less stable economies of the new member states to the wealthier, most robust economies of the older member states. Though the European Commission states that the free movement of labour from new member states to other member states should not pose a threat to their labour markets, such labour mobility has led to the destabilization of industrial relations networks and has undermined labour standards in some member states (Woolfson, 2007, p. 209; Woolfson and Sommers, 2006). Problems have taken on a 'Baltic dimension', with several of the more high profile labour disputes featuring Baltic workers.[28]

The Irish Ferries Dispute of 2005 was one of the most prominent cases taken up by the European Court of Justice (ECJ). In this case, Irish Ferries announced they would be replacing over 500 unionized Irish staff on their key Britain–Ireland routes with agency workers from Eastern Europe. These workers would receive half the Irish minimum wage, €7.65 per hour (Krings, 2009, p. 49; Woolfson, 2007, p. 210). The company claimed that this, and other major cost-savings such as re-flagging the vessels to Cyprus, was a necessary move in order to compete with lower-cost airline traffic. However, some of the current staff were not willing to accept the voluntary redundancy package, and the trade unions and the Irish Labour Court ruled that the employers were in breach of their employment agreement. Nevertheless, the company flouted these rulings, and instead sent security guards to accompany its 70 East European workers aboard the *Isle of Inishmore*.

This incident saw original crew members barricade themselves on board for up to nine days, and sparked huge public protests. The biggest of these was a national day of protest organized by the Irish Congress of Trade Unions (ICTU) entitled 'A Threshold of Decency' (Woolfson, 2007, p. 211). An estimated 100,000 people took to the streets to protest against exploitation of migrants, displacement of Irish workers, the threat to labour standards,[29] and a 'race to the bottom'. The dispute was finally resolved, albeit temporarily, by the Irish Labour Relations Commission in December 2005 (Dobbins, 2005). While the unions secured Irish minimum wage standards for the East European contracted personnel (twice the amount that the company was initially seeking), company management secured the right to outsource their labour, and ultimately succeeded in lowering wage costs.

This case demonstrates 'the potential social consequences of the free movement of labour in an enlarged EU' (Krings, 2009, p. 49). The flexibilization of labour erodes hard-won trade union rights and labour standards as well as undermining trade-union solidarity between different member states. Against such threats, some have turned to the 1996 Posted Workers Directive as a potential safeguard. The directive requires that a member states' minimum employment conditions 'must also apply to workers posted temporarily by their employer to work in that member state' with the aim of balancing flexibility and workers' rights (European Commission, 2007). Though the directive attempts to regulate labour standards, it has so far proved largely ineffective due to lack of cooperation between member states (Cremers et al., 2007; Scharpf, 2002). In response to this, the EC has proposed an official recommendation for better implementing the Directive (European Commission, 2008) which focuses on improved administrative cooperation between member states, and better access and exchange of information through an Internal Market Information System and a High-level Committee. However, although the Directive provides a useful legal framework, it is subordinated by the European Commission's emphasis on the free movement of services as enshrined in the EU Treaty and again, its implementation is dependent on cooperation from the member states (Woolfson and Sommers, 2006, p. 65).

Implications for Democracy in Europe

Some scholars contend that the EES and the European social model are incompatible. Raveaud (2007, p. 430) argues that the EES actually undermines the European social model, its emphasis on flexibility jeopardizing other goals such as gender equality and social inclusion. Wilthagen and Tros (2004, p. 167) also criticize 'the flexibility-security nexus' at the heart of the EES which, they say, has become a major challenge to the European social model.

However, other analysts do not pose this nexus as a trade-off and see the EES as a necessary complement to EMU (e.g. Biffl, 2007; Jepsen and Pascual, 2006; Scharpf, 2002; Schmid, 2009). Like the European social model, the EES acts as a 'third way', promoting flexibility and risk-taking for the purposes of innovation and employment whilst simultaneously 'diversifying' social protection to act as a safety net for the individual. Seen in this light, the EES could well be a positive step towards democratic and equitable European social policy. However, in its current form it may be too weak to be effective as there are no formal sanctions if EES aims are not achieved (Heidenreich and Bischoff, 2008, p. 500).

CONCLUSION: RECONSTITUTING DEMOCRACY?

The purpose of this chapter is to examine recent changes in social welfare provision in Europe and to consider their implications for the democratic process. Within that broader context, our study focuses on the role of the voluntary and private sectors in helping to fill gaps in social welfare. Welfare regimes have always relied on the support of non-state actors; yet since the late 1980s a new 'disorganized welfare mix' has emerged, in which reliance on private sector and for-profit providers has deepened and become more visible as governments have withdrawn from direct intervention, or sought to 'roll back' the frontiers of the state. The need to rethink social welfare provision has been driven both by political considerations and by pressures on the financial sustainability of welfare systems. Hence, the emphasis on efficiency, productivity and competitiveness is not purely an ideological agenda of neoliberalization but is also fuelled by very real and pressing questions of affordability which have been magnified by the recent global financial crisis.

How far responsibility for welfare provision lies with the state or non-state sectors is an ongoing debate that reflects fundamental differences between political parties in Europe. Part of the problem for Europe is that no consensus exists within the EU or its member states over what welfare rights and entitlements citizens should be granted in an age of advanced liberalism and globalization. As Eriksen and Fossum (2007) note, it is difficult to have democracy in Europe if there is no agreement on fundamental issues such as the form that democracy – and citizenship – should take.

Following Eriksen and Fossum (2007), we take the goals of a democratic society to be full, meaningful and effective participation of people in the decision-making processes of those organizations that make decisions or take actions that affect their lives. Achieving those goals, and ensuring that those organizations can be held accountable for their decisions, necessarily means having robust systems that enable equality of access and transparency. This concept of democratic society entails a model of social citizenship that is arguably more congruent with the vision of T.H. Marshall and the 'Keynesian post-war Welfare State' than with the current 'Schumpeterian Competition State' (Jessop, 2002). However, we do not wish to romanticize the Keynesian welfare state model, which surely had its own issues to do with accountability and efficiency. Rather, we are suggesting that it may be time to rethink some of the *a priori* assumptions regarding the supposed benefits of opening up welfare provision to increased competition from the private sector – particularly if our goal is a more democratic and socially inclusive society.

Our case studies show that many of the arguments for increased privatization of health and welfare are based on questionable premises. These include the argument that during periods of economic downturn, the best way to save money is to privatize public services (Zurich Municipal, 2009); the claim that the private sector costs less than the public sector and is more efficient in delivering health services (Trades Union Congress (TUC) 2009); or, indeed, the assumption that competition breaks up monopolies. As a report from 2009 by the UK's TUC notes (p. 6):

> The imposition of competition and markets in the public sector means driving a wedge between client and contractor roles and usually results in the restriction of in-house delivery. Local authorities, NHS Trusts and other public sector bodies are required to become 'commissioning' organisations, in effect to be a client and to contract the provision of services to outside organisations. Competition is therefore limited between private firms and consultants and cannot be said to be true competition.

Our criticisms of privatization lie not with the principle of competition *per se* – which we recognize can be a powerful lever of economic innovation and antidote to bureaucratic inertia – but with the commodification that seems to be transforming health and welfare provision into lucrative businesses that benefit in particular large private companies. In this respect, we welcome more debate on the logic of 'for-profit' organizations and the limits of privatization as far as health and welfare provision are concerned.

Moreover, the public sector has a well-established history of service provision and retains some distinctively democratic qualities that are absent in private sector provision. These qualities include an ethos of fairness, antipathy to corruption, and reliability; a producer market oriented to non-paying customers such as pupils and patients and an ethical sense of duty towards the public (Grimshaw et al., 2002, p. 480).

While it is far from perfect, the public sector may thus offer some measure of best practice to the private sector, particularly in areas dealing with democratic accountability and equitable provision.

The lessons from the case studies of what might be termed the Anglo-Saxon and neoliberal approach to welfare reform challenge the dominant view that the private sector necessarily provides a model of best practice to the cumbersome and excessively bureaucratic public sector. Privatization is typically assumed to increase efficiency through alleviating financial pressure from governments, decreasing the need for regulation, and introducing competition with a focus on performance outputs.[30] These principles drive the European Single Market and are continually being enshrined through the rulings of the ECJ. They are also echoed in calls within the EES for greater labour-market flexibilization and competitiveness in the new global knowledge economy. However, considering welfare provision from a democratic standpoint alters these objectives. The key issue here, is not simply whether welfare 'works well' (i.e. delivering efficiency), but whether it works to deliver the goals of a democratic society. This latter discourse positions the recipient of welfare as a citizen with rights, rather than a consumer with entitlements.

All of the case studies that we have presented concerning increased private-sector involvement in welfare provision highlight the potential for significant social and democratic costs. For example, the New Zealand case study of 'new contractualism' promoted a top-down implementation of the Employment Contracts Act which discouraged more democratic local and bottom-up initiatives (Wallis and Dollery, 2001, p. 248). New contractualism was also found to undermine transparency, encouraging softer, more indirect (but correspondingly opaque) governance and regulation (Bredgaard and Larsen, 2007, p. 291). The New Public Management reforms that introduce private sector principles into the public sector can thus lead, paradoxically, to new forms of regulation. They also do not necessarily imply reduced public expenditure (Ascoli and Ranci, 2002; Dalziel, 2002; Rasmussen and Lamm, 2005). Public-spending reductions can also disguise off-balance sheet costs. The UK PFI case study illustrates how little of the efficiency gain from the refinancing went to the public sector hospital and local health authority that it was supposed to benefit.

With their characteristic focus on social participation through charitable work and bottom-up community initiatives, voluntary sector organizations provide an alternative to both state and private sector provision. Greater voluntary sector involvement thus addresses the concern voiced by many that welfare provision should be 'not-for-profit'. The more fluid and participatory structures of accountability that apply to voluntary sector organizations enable them to be more creative, dynamic and less constrained by the dictates of profit margins or government bureaucracy. However, the down side of that dynamism and fluidity is increased volatility and variability in the quality of service provision, not to mention lack of organizational transparency.

Furthermore, the voluntary sector is increasingly subject to the same constraints as government and private-sector providers. The introduction of more formalized partnerships with state and market bodies has led to greater stakeholder demands for increased performance and 'value for money'. Finally, there is also the danger of voluntary sector co-optation by government. This has two negative aspects: first, the blurring of the boundaries between government and the voluntary sector as the former increasingly steers and appropriates the latter for delivery of its services (what Wolch (1990) termed the 'shadow state'); and second, as noted in the US ABCD case study, an increasing tendency to delegate the costs as well as the responsibilities of welfare provision onto those communities, neighbourhoods and families that are least able to bear them. The blurring of boundaries between different actors is a result of the new 'disorganized welfare mix' and can be a cause for concern when the interests of vulnerable actors are coopted by more powerful sectors.

This brings us back to the fundamental dilemma of the welfare mix: the tension between efficiency and democratic accountability. Who can be held accountable in a diffuse, multi-actor social welfare arena? Private providers, while deemed efficient, are not accountable to the *demos*, but to their shareholders and investors, and as Mörth (2008) observes, this has significant implications for public involvement and democracy. In the case studies cited above, this raises the question of private-sector motivation for engaging in welfare provision. Do private providers 'fill the gaps' in welfare provision or do they maintain and exacerbate those gaps? Given that private providers owe their existence to gaps in state-funded provision, and given their mandate to return profits to their shareholders and investors, some conflicts of interest between the goals of welfare and commerce appear almost inevitable.

We are left with the unresolved question of how far the state or government should assume responsibility for the health, welfare and well-being of its citizens in an advanced liberal democracy. Our findings also highlight the contradictions between the EES and European social model and the goals of the EMU and the Single Market. While some argue that the primary aim of the EES should be to provide a social safety net, others see it as a vehicle for driving economic growth and achieving the goals set out in the Lisbon agenda. Within this Janus-faced policy, environment narratives of 'growth, competitiveness, innovation and flexibilization' compete with discourses of 'social inclusion', 'equal opportunities' and 'social security'. The corollary of this is a bipolar EU agenda. Yet despite attempts to resolve the tensions within this schizophrenic policy environment, discourses of economy and efficiency invariably trump competing discourses of social welfare and democracy.

NOTES

1. Under the 'organized welfare mix' model civil society and the welfare state were in close collaboration, coordinated through negotiated public-private partnerships. Voluntary agencies sustained long-term volunteering, and coordination was based on trust rather than output accountability, while state representatives facilitated rather than enforced coordination between themselves and non-state organizations (Bode, 2006, p. 349).
2. We do not use 'disorganized' as a pejorative term or in opposition to 'efficient' but rather as a way to characterize the increasing heterogeneity of contemporary welfare regimes, and to highlight their relationship to the conditions of post modernity prevalent in most advanced liberal economies. As Wolch (1990, pp. 4 and 41) notes, this new West European 'disorganized welfare mix' shares characteristics with the Anglo-Saxon welfare regime that underwent neoliberal restructuring in the 1980s.
3. For a useful discussion of how the terms 'public' and 'private' developed in the history of Western thought see Mörth (2008).
4. Indeed, Kendall and Knapp (1996) have characterized the voluntary sector in the UK a 'loose and baggy monster'.
5. The rationale for PFI schemes is both microeconomic and fiscal, though these rationales have been critiqued. The fiscal argument states that as PFI occurs off-budget, a tight fiscal policy can be maintained. The micro-economic stance claims that PFI is better value for money and more cost efficient. However, critics argue that these off-budget costs are transferred to future generations and that PFI schemes increase financial deficits and force higher risks on the public sector.
6. New Labour's commitment to its PPP policy was also a response to Chancellor Gordon Brown's desire to keep the UK within the public sector borrowing requirement set out as a condition for EMU membership.
7. In 2005/6 there were 53 PFI projects in the NHS arena. By April 2007, this figure had increased to 85 PFI contracts with the NHS, with plans for a further 41 schemes. 21 PFIs with a total capital value of £3.14 billion were at the planning stage or in procurement in April 2008, in comparison with one publicly financed scheme, valued at £243 million (Hellowell and Pollock, 2007, pp. 5 and 13).
8. Usually, hospitals built under PFI contracts are leased to NHS Trusts by the private sector owners for periods ranging from 30 to 60 years. The NHS Trust pays for clinical services, staff, supplies, and also an annual fee to the contractor, from the Trust budget (Hellowell and Pollock, 2007, p. 9).
9. These included the University Vice Chancellor, the chairs of the RHA and DHA, and an influential local MP (Greenaway et al., 2007).
10. Opposition from the local health community and local green campaigners was muted. This was largely because the former did not want to jeopardize the new investment and facilities, and the latter was preoccupied with other causes (Greenaway et al., 2007, p. 723).

11. Under this model, a purchaser-provider split was introduced between the (purchaser) DHA and the newly created (provider) NHS Trusts. Tensions existed between these two new groups because the DHA was concerned with health provision while the NHS Trust was preoccupied with getting the new investment off the ground as quickly as possible (Greenaway et al., 2007, p. 724).

12. However an alternative policy network did form around a campaign group, Keep Our Hospital in Norwich (KOHIN) (Greenaway et al., 2007).

13. Octagon was in a strong position to do so because the construction phase had been successfully completed, the PFI market had stabilized, and commercial interest rates had fallen (Asenova et al., 2007, p. 20).

14. However, the VFM assessment was strongly compromised by the refinancing (Blanken et al., 2009, p. 138).

15. According to estimates based on data from the Department of Health and a Freedom of Information survey, 40 Trusts paying PFI unitary charges in 2005/6 were under-funded by approximately 2.5% of their income. Trusts with PFI schemes with values over £50 million had a shortfall in income averaging 4.4% (Hellowell and Pollock, 2007, p. 6).

16. The significantly under-funded PFI hospitals in Worcestershire and South-East London are an example (Hellowell and Pollock, 2009, p. 18).

17. The ABCD approach emphasizes the assets present in a community, rather than dwelling on what is absent; it is internally focused, encourages 'local definition, investment, creativity, hope and control'; and it is relationship driven, recognizing the importance of relationship building (Kretzmann and McKnight, 1993, pp. 9–10).

18. Inspiring Communities; Bank of I.D.E.A.S. Also in Australia an ABCD Resource Kit has been developed through LaTrobe and Monash Universities (ABCD Institute, 2009b).

19. The ABCD Institute; Partners for Livable Communities; Public Allies: New Leadership for New Times; The Greater Rochester Health Foundation; Grassroots Grantmakers.

20. ABCD Global Consulting (2010).

21. UN-HABITAT views the ABCD as complementary with 'the enabling approach' that they have pursued for over 15 years and advocates its use in developing countries (Tibaijuka, 2003).

22. However, a key difference is that the former is concerned with community mobilization and the latter with institutional reform (Mathie and Cunningham, 2003).

23. However, this was partly due to a 'rollover' effect caused by Section 19(4) of the ERA, which stated that if parties failed to re-negotiate a collective contract, all workers would be deemed to be employed on individual contracts with identical terms and conditions as the expired collective agreement (Barry and Reveley, 2002, p. 511).

24. I.e. it embodies the European goals of full employment, adequate social protection, and equality. For examples of this approach see: Hay et al. (1999); Scharpf (2002); Vaughan-Whitehead (2003).

25. Sapir (2006) builds on the four European social models (Continental, Mediterranean, Nordic, and Anglo-Saxon) and holds up the Nordic and Anglo-Saxon models as exemplars.

26. The triangle consists of three components – flexible labour markets, generous welfare systems and active labour market programmes – which work together to ensure that workers either return to employment after only a short spell of unemployment, or they are assisted by active labour market programmes to find employment (Madsen, 2002, p. 2).

27. Indeed, some argue that the social democratic welfare regime is uniquely suited to realizing both social and economic objectives (Goodin et al., 1999).

28. These include the Laval (or Vaxholm) case involving Latvian construction workers in Sweden, the Viking Rosella dispute involving Estonian workers on Finnish Ferries, and the Irish Ferries Dispute involving Latvian and Lithuanian workers on Irish Ferries.
29. For example, Woolfson (2007, p. 211) notes that work-related deaths went up in Ireland from 50 in 2004 to 73 in 2005.
30. For the argument that post-industrial societies are being fundamentally reshaped by a 'cult of efficiency', see Stein (2001).

7. The rise of the unelected. The UK health system and the rise and fall of arm's length bodies

David G. Mayes and Zaidah Mustaffa

INTRODUCTION

Over recent years there has been a rapid increase in the number of agencies run by people who are appointed rather than elected, which help provide the major services of the welfare state. While these agencies may be working for the public sector, they are not necessarily staffed by public sector employees and may be purely private concerns. This could be a growing and insidious threat to democracy, as not only are elected ministers responsible directly for a diminishing share of activities in the field but it may be very difficult to affect their behaviour by democratic means. Frank Vibert (2007), however, argues that this view may be incorrect and that the creation of these bodies may lead to a better balance of democratic monitoring.

While agencies for the delivery of welfare services may be more efficient than government departments, this is not necessarily the case.[1] Moreover, some agencies are deliberately designed to make sure that the new enterprises are highly accountable in a way which was not the case beforehand. Monitoring agencies, ombudsmen and independent assessors may all help ensure that the agencies behave fairly, respond to customer interests and more generally conform closely to their objectives. Properly implemented, such a system of agencies may enable democratic accountability to be exercised more effectively. It is not just that they can ensure that individual justice is done in standing up for the rights of the individual against powerful organizations but that the wishes of government are carried out efficiently and the objectives followed. If this is the case then governments may be able to achieve an ideal balance between the efficient provision of the services they seek and accountability for their actions.

In this chapter, we seek to clarify the role of these agencies and the part they play in augmenting or diminishing the democratic process. To make the analysis more tangible we consider the example of health services, drawing mainly on the UK, where the issue has been widely studied and debated.[2] The principles involved are extendable to other jurisdictions even where the balance is different. We follow Vibert's (2007, note 70) classification in considering:

1. service providers
2. risk assessors
3. boundary watchers
4. auditors and inspectors
5. umpires and whistle-blowers.

This is by no means the only classification available and Gash et al. (2010) offer a different taxonomy, distinguishing between function, form and governance as set out in Figure 7.1. This effectively adds two further dimensions to Vibert's functional classification. The key feature that their analysis emphasizes is that bodies can be of varying distance from the control of departments and hence more or less able to exercise independent professional judgement, and at the same time they can be more or less democratically accountable. Thus whether such a system simultaneously adheres to efficient delivery, democratic accountability and the other desirable features of such arrangements depends on the detail of their form, function and governance.

To obtain a balanced system where democratic principles are followed, a network of these independent agencies is required. Thus independent observatories and assessors are required to demonstrate for governments and parliaments that service providers are undertaking the tasks that have been assigned to them efficiently and fully. This is not simply a matter of a financial audit to make sure the funds have been spent subject to rigorous internal controls but that procedures and services have been as desired and are benchmarked against the best domestic and foreign examples.

Of course, it can also be argued that having such a network of balancing agencies in itself increases the administrative cost of the provision of services and hence increases the deadweight cost. This latter has certainly been a widespread perception of the health service in the UK. But health services round the world face the same problems of containing costs, setting priorities and trying to enable limited resources to provide the best services they can for people irrespective of their incomes and wealth. This cannot be done without the administrative overhead if one wishes to be fair across patients and ensure adequate standards of care and professionalism.

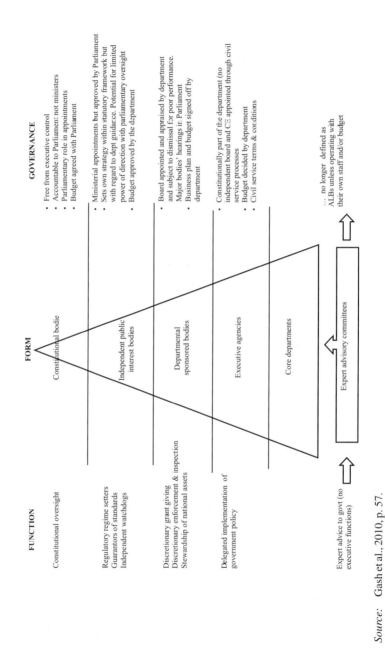

Source: Gash et al., 2010, p. 57.

Figure 7.1   New taxonomy for ALBs proposed by the Institute for Government

It is therefore a political decision as to what services should be provided, the structure that should be used to provide them and the methods used to ensure quality of behaviour and accountability. It is then a professional or business matter to decide how to provide those services, given the objectives and constraints, in a manner that will provide the best value for the 'customer' and the taxpayer. It is similarly a technical or judicial decision over whether the provider has performed as well as it could and whether each individual has been treated properly. If there are general objections to the structure and behaviour then it is up to the democratic process to do something about it. But the implication is that detailed political intervention in the process of delivery or assessment is likely to be counterproductive as it will impede fairness and longer-term efficiency. There is also a danger that the assessment method will be somewhat arbitrary and it will be difficult for the performance of the provider to be objectively assessed. The first recourse for the individual who feels they have been unfairly treated should be the provider, failing that there should be an appeal to an independent arbiter or tribunal. Similarly the assessment of the performance of the organization as a whole should be open, objective and observable. Only if these procedures do not result in rectification of individual or system-wide deficiencies should political intervention be necessary, unless of course the political view on the objectives or the best medium of delivery has changed.

It is noticeable that Vibert's framework does not single out regulators as a significant and separately identifiable category of independent bodies. Yet it is this category that has caused most concern in the European environment. Although this concern is expressed primarily at the European level it applies within the nation states as well. In this environment, considerable ability to set the rules that govern behaviour is delegated to a non-elected body. This is most obvious in areas outside the health service, say in the rules for the operation of financial markets laid down by financial supervisory authorities or central banks. In a national environment parliament can readily claw back any such authority if it objects to how it is being exercised and indeed, as Majone (2011) points out, those running such regulatory bodies will tend to hold back if they detect widespread objections that would threaten their independence. Nevertheless, curbing the independence of a body that has been set up because independence was a key ingredient for establishing its credibility and maintaining longer term stability in the system, is a step that would only be undertaken with some reluctance because of the damage it would also cause.

The success of many of these independent bodies therefore occurs through their ability to respond to the wider views of society, whether directly expressed by the government or parliament or indirectly detected from society at large. This is one of the reasons why such regulatory bodies spend much effort before acting in putting out proposals for consultation and conducting impact studies. They must be seen to be taking views into account as well as actually taking them into account. As is discussed below in the case of the UK health service, while there have been problems, there is no significant democratic deficit in the sense applying at the EU level, not least because there is no indirectly appointed equivalent of the European Commission that has the sole right to initiate policy.

THE UK HEALTH SERVICE

The network of agencies involved in the provision of health services in the UK is complex to say the least and framed in its own particular use of terms, which differ from those used by other countries, not just in Europe but in the English-speaking world. Agencies within the health care system in the UK such as the now defunct Health Protection Agency and the Genetics and Insurance Committee are called arm's length bodies (ALBs) within the Department of Health. The government refers to such agencies as non-departmental public bodies (NDPBs), which include executive bodies, advisory committees and tribunals, but the more popular and often-used term is quangos, originally an acronym for quasi-autonomous non-governmental organizations, but also defined as quasi-autonomous national organizations. The official definition of NDPBs is agencies that 'are not government departments, or even sub-sections of government departments' but rather 'agencies of government that operate to a greater or lesser extent at arm's-length from Ministers' (MacLeavy and Gay, 2005, p. 7). NDPBs have also been called quasi-autonomous organizations (QAOs), para-government organizations (Hood and Schuppert, 1988), extra-governmental organizations (EGOs) and unelected agencies (Weir and Hall, 1994). It would be pointless to develop our own categorization, so we use these terminologies largely interchangeably to refer to arm's length bodies, reflecting the phraseology common in the field.

Types and Categories of Quangos

Within the extensive quango literature, several categorizations and types of quangos have been developed. As discussed above, Vibert (2007) listed five broad categories of unelected agencies – service providers, risk assessors, boundary watchers, auditors and inspectors, and umpires and whistle-blowers. Service providers provide services to the public. Risk assessors are mainly concerned with assessing, measuring and managing risks, and provide advice to the public based on their assessment. Such risks have a number of dimensions, relating on the one hand to the individual and whether any particular treatment will achieve the outcome desired and to the system as a whole as costs and technologies change. Boundary watchers scrutinize activities in the market for issues relating to the environment, ethics, and social wellbeing. A simple boundary is human rights. While eventually an invasion of such rights could be challenged in the courts, it is much better if it can be headed off early on in the process. Inquisitor agencies (auditors and inspectors) monitor the services and activities of government departments for compliance to standards, policies and practices and in a manner that should be devoid of political bias. Umpires and whistle-blowers are agencies that act as channels for complaints and independent dispute resolution.[3]

There are other ways of categorizing agencies depending upon one's point of interest. Maggetti (2010) lists three broad categories of non-elected agencies – (1) supranational bodies such as the EU and other international organization committees, (2) non-majoritarian national authorities such as central banks, and (3) independent regulatory agencies such as pharmaceutical regulators, financial market regulators and environmental commissions. This is clearly helpful in the current context of arrangements within the EU. By looking largely just at the UK we might accidentally downplay the role of EU-level agencies.

The UK government offers its own definitions of NDPBs and distinguishes between four categories:

1. executive NDPBs, which are agencies with statutory establishment delivering administrative, regulatory, and commercial functions for the government and are responsible for their own staffing needs and budgets
2. advisory NDPBs, which are agencies that provide independent and expert advice to the government on particular issues, and whose staffs and costs come from the related department
3. tribunal NDPBs, which have jurisdiction over specific legal areas, and whose staffs and costs come from the related department, and
4. independent monitoring boards, previously known as boards of visitors, which are agencies that monitor for example the management and administration of the prison system, and the treatment of prisoners (see MacLeavy and Gay, 2005; Gash et al., 2010).

Other definitions of NDPBs and quangos, such as that provided by Weir and Hall (1994), have also included local and regional agencies, grant-maintained schools and the police. However, Hogwood (1995) argued that NDPBs are mainly labels put by government on agencies that it appoints but are applied inconsistently (p. 208). Quangos and appointed agencies are known to exist in varying legal forms (Vibert, 2007), and have several characteristics in terms of government funding, existence of board or committee and staff status (Hogwood, 1995).

These facets should also be scrutinized carefully along five conditions of agencies' existence and operations, namely finances (where they get funding from), ministerial responsibility (to what extent the minister is held accountable for the agency's policy implementation and service provision), control mechanisms (the mechanisms in place available to the minister to intervene in the agency's operations in cases such as non or poor performance), public task (whether the agency is established to carry out tasks that the government should be providing, or to secure a budget for a quango to carry them out), and public domain (that the agency is perceived to be government-related, rather than market-driven) to distinguish clearly between the genuine quangos and those agencies that are performing functions for the government under market or contractual relationships (Greve et al., 1999). However, quangos have consistently been loosely defined to be any agency that is funded by public money, perceivably exists independently from government departments and elected representatives, and performs services or functions to the public that would otherwise be carried out by the government (see Flinders, 1999). The lack of consensus on the definition of quangos has resulted in controversial claims on the actual number, costs and extent of existence of quangos in Britain.

A Brief History of Quangos in the UK, their (Original) Roles and Functions

As a constitutional monarchy, the UK functions somewhat differently from some other countries in Europe. The royal prerogative has allowed elected officials to delegate the state's activities, and responsibilities are to appointed agencies, boards or commissions (see MacLeavy and Gay, 2005).[4] The use of appointed agencies in the UK dates back to the sixteenth century, when the oldest quango, the Trinity House Lighthouse Service, was set up in 1514 (Lewis, 2005). Generally, governments establish NDPBs and quangos to develop, manage and deliver public policies and services effectively and efficiently, independent of the political influence and ideologies of the incumbent government. By making such agencies in some sense above politics, in that they have general support in parliament whatever the particular hue of the government of the day, they can take a longer term view than just the life of a single parliament. However, in the UK it is not possible to make it especially difficult to close or influence such agencies as they cannot be written into the constitution, as there is no written constitution, and there cannot be requirements in parliament for more than a simple majority. They are thus clearly subject to democratic control.[5] Quangos and arm's length bodies are thus legitimate in a technical sense and usually have some grounding in advancing social welfare for their specific form.

Quangos are often created to address and act on sensitive issues such as equality and discrimination, where their ability to be at arm's length from ministerial powers and political influence helps them achieve their objective (Skelcher et al., 2000). In the era of scientific, technological and medical advances, these specially set up agencies are staffed by scientists, doctors, experts and specialists who are involved in making decisions and design policies that they would not otherwise be able to contribute within the traditional government structure. Quangos provide opportunities for people otherwise disadvantaged in the workforce under traditional government appointments such as women, minorities and people with disabilities. Quangos also take the heat off civil servants and politicians who may not be trained in the practicalities and technicalities of specialized service provision and delivery. Also, quangos can introduce private sector management techniques into the government and take advantage of the private market, for cheaper, competitive and efficient service provision and delivery (Flinders, 1999).

These are of course all characteristics that well designed NDPBs may have. Poorly designed bodies will not have these characteristics. Designers may be fallible and of course some may be seeking to create these institutions for less objective reasons. Thus these structures may or may not work successfully. As we note later, some have gone badly wrong.

The modern use of quangos within the British government is long-standing, dating primarily from the period of Conservative government from 1979 to 1997. The changes in this period introduced significant structural and organizational changes to the public sector. The government introduced market-type mechanisms by including some element of competition within the public sector (such as competitive sourcing, internal contracting and internal market for the NHS), and new public management in an effort to try to get greater efficiency and offer an element of choice (at least to people in urban areas). Over previous years the cost of the NHS had been increasing sharply and its relative quality falling, with rising waiting lists for operations in hospitals and increasing public dissatisfaction. Some functions previously performed by the local government were either abolished because they were perceived as threats to the national government, or assumed by the central government or shifted to unelected quangos in an effort to gain control of activities and costs (Davis, 1993; Elcock, 1994).

These changes were partly politically motivated where local government was run by other political parties – Labour and Liberal Democrats – and partly motivated by the desire to reduce public spending (Hogwood, 1995; Talbot, 2001). The new public management (NPM) introduced during this era also focused on downsizing and decentralization, breaking down large hierarchical and bureaucratic forms of administration and organization into smaller, autonomous management units. This 'new' form of administration created mechanisms outside the normal democratic process to audit, inspect, review, advise and set standards for the government (Hogwood, 1995; Talbot, 2001). Smaller units not only permitted an element of competition and the opportunity to provide relative assessments of providers, but they also offered the possibility of being more responsive to local interests and more flexible.

However, it is the more recent modernization agenda promulgated under the Labour government between 1997 and 2010 that has received widespread blame for the rapid increase in the number and costs of running quangos in the UK. One of the main foci of the new approach, which has been labelled 'the third way' is the emphasis on public-private sector partnership, or the 'joined-up government' of public service provision (Falconer, 2005). This has escalated delegated governance within the public sector. This approach is also labelled 'institutionalitis,' or having 'the tendency to respond to every problem by setting up another organization' (Flinders, 2004, p. 775).

Shortly after winning the election in 1997, the new government published a consultation paper *Opening Up Quangos*. While acknowledging that they had inherited a large number of quangos from the previous government, the paper also set out the needs and the benefits of using appointed agencies to respond to sensitive issues, make independent decisions, provide flexible and quick services to the public and include groups of minorities within the workforce (Greenwood et al., 2002). The consultation paper also advocated the need to expose these quangos to public scrutiny and accountability. In 1998, the government published *Quangos: Opening the Doors* and offered guidelines on the appointment and administration of such appointed agencies. These guidelines include that the agencies should hold open public meetings, release summary reports of the meetings, invite evidence from the public to discuss public concerns, make annual reports publicly available, among others. However, the agencies were still allowed the flexibility and discretion to abide by the framework, given the phrase 'where practicable and appropriate' (Flinders and Cole, 1999) and the paper was received with scepticism.

During his election campaign in 2009, the present prime minister, David Cameron (2009), pledged to reduce the number of quangos in the government and address the issues of accountability and public expenditure. The current coalition government is closely scrutinized in its follow up on the pledge and primarily to provide efficient services to the public and reduce government administrative costs. The Cabinet Office maintained that it had 790 NDPBs in 2008, a 10 per cent decrease since 1997, employed 111,000 people and spent £38.4 billion of public money (Gay, 2010). However the TaxPayers' Alliance listed 1,148 quangos in the same year, 2008 (a marginal decrease from 1,162 in 2007), which employed 733,000 people and cost the public £90 billion (so much for commonly agreed definitions) (Farrugia and O'Connell, 2008). Generally, quangos in the UK have had a poor public reputation (see Flinders, 1999).[6] Their existence has been criticized for being outside the democratic process, and they have been criticized for putting too much emphasis on efficiency and effectiveness to the detriment of accountability, legitimacy and democratic practice. The argument runs that they duplicate functions and result in waste.

Agencies within the UK Department of Health

Within the Department of Health (DH), three types of arm's length bodies (ALBs) exist:

1. executive agencies, which are part of and accountable to the Department of Health
2. executive NDPBs, which are outside the Department of Health but whose roles and functions form the processes of the government, and
3. special health authorities, which are independent of the Department and provide national service to the public or other NHS agencies, and may be required to comply with obligations and directions from the ministry. They operate mainly at the national level.

The Medicines and Healthcare Products Regulatory Agency (MHRA) is the Department's executive agency responsible for regulating medicines and medical devices. The Care Quality Commission (CQC), the independent regulator for quality health care and social care provided by the NHS, and other health care and social care providers, is an executive NDPB, while the National Institute for Health and Clinical Excellence (NICE) and the NHS Litigation Authority are special health authorities under the Department of Health.

Within the health care system, the TaxPayers' Alliance listed 59 quangos (Farrugia and O'Connell, 2008) (Table 7.1) while the official number from the DH is 20 (2010). The NHS's arm's length bodies (ALB) cost taxpayers more than £1.6 billion and employed approximately 18,000 in 2010. Following the election of the Conservative–Liberal Democrat coalition government, the structure of the UK health system has been undergoing yet another rapid restructuring exercise. The changes are due to be fully completed in 2012/2013. The current structure is depicted in Figure 7.2.

Table 7.1   List of 59 health care quangos

Auditing agencies

| 1 | Healthcare Commission (Commission for Health Care Audit and Inspection) |
| 2 | Independent Regulator for NHS Foundation Trusts |

Equipment, medicines & resources

3	NICE
4	NHS Blood and Transplant Authority
5	Medicines and Healthcare Products Regulatory Agency
6	NHS Purchasing and Supply Agency
7	Plasma Resources UK Ltd

Expert advisory

8	Administration of Radioactive Substances (Advisory Committee)
9	Registration of Homeopathic Medicines (Advisory Board on)
10	Borderline Substances (Advisory Committee on)
11	Clinical Excellence Awards (Advisory Committee on)
12	Dangerous Pathogens (Advisory Committee on)
13	Hepatitis (Advisory Group on)
14	British Pharmacopoeia Commission
15	Human Medicines, Commission on
16	Carcinogenicity of Chemicals in Food, Consumer Products and the Environment (Committee on)
17	Medical Aspects of Radiation in the Environment (Committee on)
18	Mutagenicity of Chemicals in Food, Consumer Products and the Environment (Committee on)
19	Medical Effects of Air Pollutants (Committee on)
20	Safety of Devices (Committee on the)
21	AIDS (Expert Advisory Group on)
22	Gene Therapy Advisory Committee
23	Genetics and Insurance Committee
24	Herbal Medicines Advisory Committee
25	Human Genetics Commission

26   Sexual Health and HIV (Independent Advisory Group on)
27   Independent Reconfiguration Panel
28   Borderline Products (Independent Review Panel for)
29   Advertising of Medicines (Independent Review Panel for)
30   Vaccination and Immunisation (Joint Committee on)
31   National Joint Registry Steering Committee
32   Nutrition (Scientific Advisory Committee on)
33   Antimicrobial Resistance (Specialist Advisory Committee on)
34   Standing Dental Advisory Committee
35   Alcohol Education and Research Council
36   Human Fertilisation and Embryology Authority
37   Human Tissue Authority
38   National Biological Board

NHS personnel
39   Doctors and Dentists Review Body
40   Nurses and Other Health Professions Review Body
41   Pharmacy Postgraduate Education (Steering Committee on)
42   Appointments Commission
43   Postgraduate Medical Education and Training Board
44   NHS Litigation Authority
45   NHS Professionals

Patient welfare
46   Patient Information Advisory Group
47   Patient and Public Involvement in Health (Commission for)
48   Social Care Inspection (Commission for)
49   Healthcare Regulatory Excellence (Council for)
50   General Social Care Council
51   Health Protection Agency
52   Health and Social Care Information Centre
53   Mental Health Act Commission
54   National Patient Safety Agency
55   The Information Centre

Other
56   National Treatment Agency for Substance Misuse
57   NHS Business Services Authority
58   NHS Institute for Innovation and Improvement
59   Social Care Institute for Excellence

Source: TaxPayers' Alliance (www.taxpayersalliance.com).

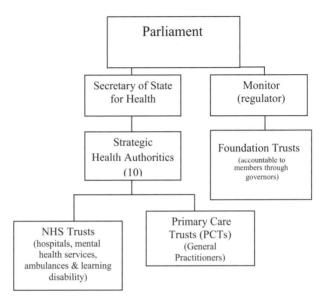

Source: Rivett, 2011.

Figure 7.2   Current (2011) organizational structure of the NHS

The restructuring exercise of the UK's health system will see the establishment of a new commission, board and health watchdog, while also cutting the number of arm's length bodies (ALBs) (Figure 7.3). The Department of Health (DH) is led by the Secretary of State for Health, a cabinet minister. The DH and the secretary of state for health are responsible for overseeing the entire health care system from planning, policy-designing, funding and delivering of health care to the public. Under the previous Labour Government, the DH is responsible for commissioning and purchasing health care for the public. The current Coalition government proposes a distinction of responsibility between commissioning and providing health care roles of the NHS, with the setup of the NHS commissioning board and the GP Commissioning Consortia. The NHS commissioning board's primary role is to lead the way towards commissioning high and improved quality health care (Department of Health, 2010). The NHS commissioning board will also consolidate the functions and roles previously undertaken by ALBs to ensure health care delivery efficiency and cost-cutting action.

The GP Commissioning Consortia will take over the role of the primary care trusts (PCTs) under the previous Labour Government, of commissioning health care for the public. This commissioning role

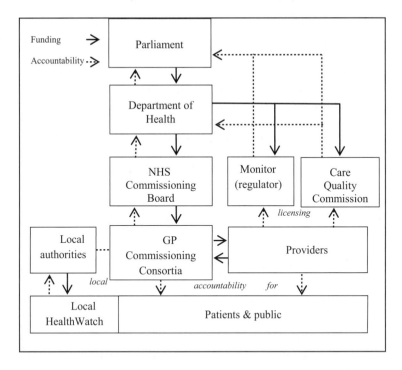

Figure 7.3   Proposed structure of the health care system in the UK (2012/2013)

includes identifying the health needs of the public and working (purchasing) with hospitals, dentists, optometrists, and voluntary services to deliver health care to satisfy the needs of the public. The Consortia are funded by the DH, and are thus accountable to the DH and the Secretary of State for Health. Under the previous government, PCTs commission and provide health care to the public, but the current Coalition Government distinguishes between the commissioning and the providing roles.

The Care Quality Commission was established in 2009, to replace its equivalent under the previous health care structure – the Healthcare Commission. The CQC, an ALB (executive NDPB), retained in the recent review of health care ALBs, acts as an independent registration and inspection authority for the NHS. Among its roles are registering all health care providers, assessing and publishing reports of the performance of health care providers, investigating serious health care services failure, scrutinizing patients' complaints, and reporting to Parliament on national health care delivery, funding and implementation.

The reforms of public bodies in 2010 saw the shift of quangos' functions back to government departments and are argued to improve accountability of these quangos.

In certain situations and times, the use of appointed bodies is crucial, especially within the health care system, particularly when specialized technical knowledge and expertise, which the elected politicians/ministers do not possess, are crucial to making decisions, and when there is a need for transparency, independence and impartiality in policy-designing and decision-making. Decisions and policies related to health care are made at arm's length from the elected person/minister, by persons who have the required technical knowledge and expertise, and independent from political influence and bias. The fear is that they develop a life of their own and do not respond to the overall democratic wishes.

PROBLEMS WITH QUANGOS

Public Spending

Perhaps the biggest concern regarding the existence and running of quangos in the UK relates to their cost. The New Labour government was accused of building a quangocracy, with annual spending of £170 billion, more than twice the budget for the Ministry of Defence (Watts, 2007). Popular media has also published the very high costs of maintaining 'quangocrats'. NHS quango bosses were reported to be highly paid and received double digit increases between 2006 and 2008. For example, the salary of Andrew Dillon, chief executive of the National Institute for Health and Clinical Excellence (NICE), was reported to be £202,000 with a salary increase of 44 per cent in 2008. Kent Woods, the head of the Medicines and Healthcare Products Regulatory Agency, was paid £218,000 with a 36 per cent salary increase (Donelly, 2009). The chief executive of the Olympic Delivery Authority (a public agency set up for delivering the infrastructure for the London 2012 Olympics) is being paid more than £390,000, while Tony Fountain, chief executive of the Nuclear Decommissioning Authority (an NDPB responsible for civil nuclear liabilities and assets) was paid between £365,000 and £369,999 a year (McKinstry, 2011). The Prime Minister receives a salary of only £142,500 a year, and this has been made the benchmark for the Civil Service since it made public the salaries of British civil servants as part of the effort to 'open up the corridors of power.' There has been massive public outcry regarding the costs of maintaining the quangocrats, not just because they are expensive, but because the public have not perceived an increase in the quality of service provision, and could see little impact of these agencies on the wider society (McKinstry, 2011).

The Conservative Party's manifesto in 2009 pledged to reduce spending on quangos and public bodies to save £1 billion annually by reducing quangocracy. David Cameron (2009) similarly remarked that 'we will never get control of public spending unless we get control of quangos'. The Government's commitment to reduce the NHS's administrative costs was visible through its review of the arm's length bodies of the NHS in 2010 (Department of Health, 2010) (Table 7.2). The report announced that cutting down on the number of health care quangos could reduce the NHS's administrative costs by 45 per cent. The Secretary of Health also announced that the reduction in the number of health care quangos would save the Department an estimated £180 million by 2014–15 (O'Dowd, 2010). However, the Public Administration Select Committee (2010–11) in its report *Smaller Government: Shrinking The Quango State* argued that massive cost savings through quango reforms were 'exaggerated' and that the government was creating the false impression that it would save more public money than it actually could. The National Audit Office (NAO) recorded that 80 per cent of expenditures by NDPBs are concentrated in only 15 NDPBs, while 75 per cent of NDPBs' expenditure came from grants, funding universities, legal aid and other government functions (Gash et al., 2010).

Accountability

The quangos have been criticized as franchised democracy, with little or no accountability to elected officials for their actions. The power to design policies, provide public services or give public advice is transferred from the publicly elected representative to appointed individuals, weakening the structure of democracy and public involvement (Stott, 2000). Downward accountability or accountability to the public of these quangos has also been sidelined. Quangos are oftentimes not required to publicize their work, or to consult and inform the public (Weir and Hall, 1994) and therefore the public is devoid of opportunities to scrutinize their work and service. Public perceptions and suspicion of patronage within quangos also contribute to the lack of perceived accountability of the quangos (Gash et al., 2010). Lack of accountability of the current quangos is further aggravated by high profile quango executives who are perceived to be associated with the members of the elected parties. The public mistrust of quangos is argued to be due to lack of transparency over the appointment of chiefs of staff and funding and budget responsibilities, unclear, complex and confusing arrangements, and relationships between quangos and sponsoring government departments (Gash et al., 2010).

Table 7.2   List of health care quangos, UK, 2010: DHS proposals for retention, abolition or transfer

1	National Institute for Health and Clinical Excellence (NICE)	Retain
2	Health Protection Agency	Abolish
3	National Treatment Agency for Substance Misuse	Abolish
4	Alcohol Education and Research Council	Abolish
5	Care Quality Commission	Retain
6	Medicines and Healthcare Products Regulatory Agency	Retain
7	General Social Care Council	Transfer
8	Human Fertilisation and Embryology Authority	Retain
9	Human Tissue Authority	Retain
10	Monitor	Retain
11	Council for Healthcare and Regulatory Excellence	Remove
12	NHS Blood and Transplant	Retain
13	NHS Business Services Authority	Retain
14	National Patient Safety Agency	Abolish
15	NHS Institute for Innovation and Improvement	Remove
16	NHS Litigation Authority	Retain
17	Health and Social Care Information Centre	Retain
18	NHS Appointments Commission	Abolish

Source: DHS, 2010.

Discussion

Quangos in the UK have been debated and discussed since their inception without much resolution. Margaret Thatcher aimed to reduce the number of quangos in 1979, but agencies and departments performing at arm's length from the government and ministers still thrive. Tony Blair promised to cut the number of arm's length agencies and bodies when he came to power in 1997, but was only able to abolish the smaller players, while establishing more powerful quangos to serve his own government's policies and objectives. The Labour government showed some commitment to reduce or alleviate quangocracy by publishing reports on quangos in 1998 (*Quangos: Opening the Doors* and *Opening up the Quangos*). The Conservative Party pledged in its election manifesto to reduce quangocrats and in its Green paper *Better Regulation*, pledged to 'tame' the quangos by restricting them to those making administrative and technical decisions requiring experts and specialists, those that should be independent of political meddling, and those requiring a high level of transparency. To do this the government proposed (1) a sunset clause so that quangos' roles, responsibilities and performance are reviewed and assessed every seven years so that they may either be downscaled or merged in the future, and (2) to modernize governance structures to become 'non-ministerial departments' (NMDs), which are directly accountable to Parliament, but have a sponsoring government department to assist in budgets and appointments of senior positions (*Better Regulation*). The Coalition government elected in 2010 published its public bodies reforms report on October 14, 2010, promising to abolish 192 agencies or arm's length bodies, merge 118, retain 380, and retain and reform 171. Forty more quangos are under review by the government, and debates are still on-going on the future of quangos within government. The current Coalition government has demonstrated commitment towards shrinking quangocracy, but according to the Public Administration Select Committee, its efforts have been poorly managed, with little to no consultation, and the tests conducted to justify each quango's existence have been applied inconsistently (Public Administration Select Committee, 2010–11). In light of the current debates on quangocracy, Gash et al. (2010) from the Institute for Government outlined two fundamental problems of the quango state in the UK – unclear roles and responsibilities of the agencies, and the challenge of balancing independence or freedom and control of these agencies. A 'bonfire of the quangos' may be required but deeper policy revisions and decisions are urgently needed to address the problems of quangos in the UK.

It appears that quangos will stay – the public do not trust politicians to make decisions for them, while politicians have another agency to blame, in cases of bad decision-making. They are needed as well to ensure that decisions for the public are made independently of political and ideological interventions. The Institute for Government recommends three core suggestions in order to curb the issues and problems related to quangocracy:

1. establishment of new quangos must be approved by the central government, and should be inspected and analysed by Select Committees;[7]

2.   guidelines for their establishment should have a 'sunset clause' to disclose to the public the timeframe in which the agencies' perform-ance should be reviewed, or the agencies disbanded; and

3.   the introduction and implementation of Governance and Perform-ance (GAP) Reviews, recommended to be conducted every third year of their existence, to ensure the agencies deliver and perform, or that their existence is still relevant in light of current situations.

QUANGOS IN THE NETHERLANDS

In the Netherlands, quangos or ZBOs (*zelfstandige bestuursorganen*) increased dramatically in the 1980s and 1990s, though their existence has been known to exist for decades (Leeuw and van Thiel, 1999). The number of quangos in the Dutch government remains controversial due to disagreement over their definition. Figures in 2000 reported 18 per cent of the state department's budget spent on 431 quangos that employed 130,000 people (van Thiel, 2004a). ZBOs in the Netherlands exist at the national and local levels, and are governmental reform instruments, particularly those created in the 1980s. As in the UK, they are perceived to do a better job at policy implementation compared to traditional government bureaucracy (van Gestel et al., 2007), though empirical evidence suggested that the quangocratization in the Netherlands is a trend, rather than an informed decision by politicians and government bureaucrats (van Thiel, 2004b). Dutch quangos exist either by 'hiving off a division of a ministry' or 'hiving a private organization into the public sector' (van Thiel, 2004a). The motives for setting up ZBOs in the Netherlands do not differ too much from those in the UK – greater efficiency within public service provision and policy implementation, and the involvement of experts in technical decision-making.

The debates surrounding quangocratization in the Netherlands have shifted from the pragmatic issues of quangos as effective instruments for policy implementation and service provision that is independent of political meddling, to the issues of the ministerial accountability of quangos with their own executive and regulatory powers (van Gestel et al., 2007). Similar issues of high maintenance and transition costs of quangos, persistent political interference within the bodies, problems with performance measures and indicators, the growing strength of the bodies' powers, and public accountability and legitimacy persist within the Dutch context (van Thiel, 2004a, 2004b), although the public outcry in the Netherlands is not as loud as in the UK. Predictions emerge that Dutch ZBOs will shift even further from political and ministerial influence given the recent developments of European legislation (see van Gestel et al., 2007).

QUANGOS IN DENMARK

In Denmark, quangos exist in several forms – special public agencies (e.g., Post Denmark), state-owned enterprises with public ownership or influence (e.g., Copenhagen Airport), public foundations, self-governing institutions, voluntary organizations, and private firms on long-term contract with the state (e.g., Falck fire and ambulance service). Although quangos are not an entirely new phenomenon in the country, institutional reform within the government sector was not met with high enthusiasm (Greve, 1999).

Special public agencies perform special functions within the government (e.g., the National Bank) and are placed outside the normal classification. They are independent, and politicians do not intervene in their functions, although the current trend is that they are shifting to other forms of governance and will see their number diminish. State owned enterprises are viewed as the Danish government's privatization exercise. The current trend within the Danish public administration is public-private partnerships or cooperation (Greve, 2000), an extension to private firms' gaining long-term contracts with the state. This administrative structure was advocated as the future governance structure in Denmark's public administration by the then Minister of Finance Morgen Lykketoft, and increasingly used as a public service provision tool (Greve, 1999).

The public-private cooperation structure within the Danish government corresponded with the government's 'shared power' concept, and the government also published reports and initiatives to encourage such partnerships. In 1993, the Ministry of Finance published *A New View of the Public Sector (Nyt syn på den offentlige sector)* as broad guidelines to the development of public-private cooperation in public sector delivery (Greve, 2000). Four types of public-private cooperation exist within the Danish government – contracting out, strategic contracting out, development contracts, and joint-stock companies covered by investor agreement.

Unlike the UK, the Danish government supported public-private cooperation within public service provision, and published reports, guidelines and a legal framework for such cooperation to exist. For example, law L 383 was introduced to allow Danish local government opportunities to engage in market-based projects, while L 384 was initiated 'for a more wide framework for cooperation on business-policy

between private companies, state, local government and county government with regard to business development projects, export of welfare
services, regional development projects and the finance of EU-initiated
programmes' (Greve, 2000, p. 58). The Ministry of Finance, Ministry of
Business and Industry and Ministry of the Interior are responsible for
administering and managing the public-private engagement in the
public service sector in Denmark. The Ministry of Finance established
Økonomistyrelsen or the Council for Contracting Out to act as consultants for companies and organizations interested in engaging in such
cooperative projects. The *Erhvervsfremmestyrelsen*, an agency within the
Ministry of Business and Industry, specifically looks after development
contracts within the public-private cooperative engagements. The presence of such guidelines and bodies ensures to a limited extent that public
service policy and provision in Denmark do not fall too deep into the
'grey zone' of typical quangos, though democratic accountability and
blame shifting by politicians still remain as governance problems (Greve,
1999).

REFLECTIONS

Quangos in the UK health service appear to be both necessary and
controversial. Despite promises to reduce their number and their cost
they have proved to be very resilient. They are thus likely to remain part
of the landscape. The UK is not alone in pursuing this organizational
form but in the Netherlands and more particularly Denmark the arrangement has been less controversial. It appears clear that such bodies can
help in the delivery of services and in particular provide a framework
where independent technical decisions can be taken within guidelines
laid down by parliament, in a way that will avoid short run political
influence. Such influence could result in the objectivity of decisions
being questioned, and introduce short run uncertainty into areas where a
longer term approach is needed and continuity is necessary, for building
up confidence among the public and other stakeholders.

For such bodies to perform their role without a serious threat to
democracy, they must have clear objectives that transcend short run
political expediency and are shared widely across political parties and
across time. (Of course some such bodies will be introduced for specific
problems, such as the body charged with organizing the rebuilding of
Christchurch in New Zealand following the recent earthquakes.[8])
Independent assessment is also required if there is to be a balance of
power, and the findings must be reported to parliament if the process is to

be democratically accountable. In many ways this form of accountability is preferable to the traditional route for accountability of government departments. Although such departments may be subject to audit by an independent government auditor, whose reports then go to parliament, there is no guarantee that the oversight will be as thorough as that provided by an independent body with careful analysis and expert evaluation. Thus in many respects, where the subject matter is appropriate, a network of independent agencies can make government more, rather than less, accountable than provision by traditional departments.

However, there is no magic recipe. Attempts to get greater efficiency through independence are not guaranteed nor are attempts to keep costs down. Expanding the number of organizations and attracting suitable independent leaders from private practice can prove expensive. Debate on the issue will continue, but despite 'the rise of the unelected' the use of such agencies may be beneficial rather than harmful for democracy. The conclusion depends on the agencies, the terms under which they are set up and their governance. In some countries this could be a recipe for corruption. The evidence from the UK Health Service is mixed but it appears that the execution has been at fault rather than the design of the quango system itself.

NOTES

1. In a study of the relative efficiencies of various public sector corporate forms with private companies delivering similar services, Wong (1990) shows that, provided public sector organizations have the incentives which apply in the private sector, with responsible boards, raising their own debt and competition for their services, they can be just as efficient as the private sector.
2. We also refer briefly to the Netherlands and Denmark which we have covered in more detail in our research.
3. Some consider that whistle-blowing is no longer the politically correct phraseology and that one should refer to covert human information sources.
4. In New Zealand, which shares the same traditions, it is normal to refer to the state as 'the crown' in this regard and set up crown agencies.
5. Some agencies are directly created by the crown. Universities for example are created by royal charter and therefore require the monarch to withdraw the charter personally. However, since universities rely on public funding they are still effectively subject to government control, although no recent government has attempted to limit academic freedom outside wartime.
6. However, others such as the National Economic Development Office developed an enviable reputation for objectivity and hence were instrumental in facilitating agreement between the government, employers and trade unions, as the argument could then be about the appropriate policy and not about the facts of the situation.
7. Parliamentary committees in the particular policy area.
8. CERA, Canterbury Earthquake Recovery Authority.

8. Democratic governance and policy coordination in the EU

Anna Michalski

INTRODUCTION

In the last 20 years, European integration has had a growing impact on national policies and political and administrative structures as a result of EU legislation and the rulings of the European Court of Justice. In parallel with the traditional perspective on European integration by law, other alternative modes of governance have emerged. These new forms of governance are noticeable also in the field of economic and social policy where increasingly elaborate policy coordination processes have been set up as a response to the complex public policy problems caused by contemporary social phenomena and deepened European integration. Policy coordination was brought in as an alternative form of EU governance to address implications of deep economic interdependence but one which did not necessitate formal transfer of competences to the EU.

The introduction of the euro brought the issue of convergence of national economic policy and welfare regimes to the forefront. The common monetary policy carried a risk to economic competitiveness which differed significantly among European economies and exposed the euro area countries to the challenges of deep economic interdependence. At the time, however, the 'constitutional asymmetry' was extended into the framework of the EMU as the European monetary regime could not, for political reasons, be matched by an integrated framework of economic policy on the European level.

Facing a number of similar challenges to economic competitiveness and sustainability of national welfare systems, the European political leaders, meeting in the European Council in March 2000, decided to launch the Lisbon Strategy. The Lisbon Strategy incorporated the goal of creating the world's most competitive knowledge-based economy built on sustainable economic development with full employment and a high degree of social cohesion among the EU member states (European Council, 2000). Behind these bold objectives lay a willingness to address a number of challenges to European welfare regimes caused by global- ization, the ageing of the populations and deteriorating public finances. The rationale behind the efforts to achieve a greater convergence of social policy reform trajectories in the EU member states was in part grounded in the awareness of deep economic interdependence, partly in the perception of the European welfare state as a distinct societal paradigm with implications for democracy which sets Europe apart from other regions in the world. Since social and welfare policies are at the heart of national sovereignty, policy convergence was to be achieved through voluntary coordination of national policy firmly anchored in a procedural governance framework based on an innovative form of governance, the 'open method of coordination' (OMC) and political leadership from the European Council.

This chapter is divided into the following sections. The first section discusses the theoretical foundations of policy coordination, and the second looks at different approaches to legitimacy and democratic policy-making associated with soft governance. A discussion on forms of legitimacy of the OMC follows. The next section evaluates the experi- ences of policy convergence in the EU in the 10 years of the Lisbon Strategy by reviewing its impact in terms of policy outcomes, institu- tional structures, prevailing ideas and discourses, followed by a section examining the impact of the OMC on national actors. The chapter then investigates the consequences for democratic policy-making of the setting-up of a framework economic governance of the European semes- ter in the wake of the economic crisis, and argues for the necessity to improve the conditions for democratic policy-making on national and European levels. A concluding discussion follows.

POLICY COORDINATION IN A THEORETICAL PERSPECTIVE

The Lisbon Strategy has been interpreted as a novel kind of political governance framework of the EU (Radaelli, 2003). Borrás and Radaelli (2011, p. 464) defined this kind of long-term, strategic initiative as 'specific forms of institutional arrangements' which 'address complex problems in a strategic, holistic, long-term perspective … set substantive output-oriented goals' and are 'implemented through combinations of old and new organizational structures'. As the Lisbon Strategy came to encompass areas where the EU had not acquired policy competence or where integration was deemed politically undesirable a specific form of structured policy coordination, the OMC, was construed. In the beginning of 2000, the OMC was not an entirely new mode of governance as it had already been practised in the EU in the areas of employment, macro-economic coordination and to coordinate national public administrative practices where it had resulted in a highly procedural form of policy learning. What was new, however, was the political dimension of the Lisbon Strategy and the emphasis on political endorsement at the highest level by the national political leaders in the European Council (Radaelli, 2003). As a governance framework, the Lisbon Strategy had the additional advantages of combining a number of substantial policy goals but leaving vague the exact form of implementation concerning the sequencing of goal-fulfillment as well as connections to other policy goals. It also created a link between the national (one may argue the regional and local levels) and European levels through a structured framework but without recourse to the legislative hierarchy of the Community method. Policy coordination through the OMC carried political undertones but the result-oriented discourse of the Lisbon Strategy prevented discussion on policy choice based on ideology.

OMC as a distinct form of policy coordination has been perfected by the EU since the late 1990s. Policy coordination as a means of integration did not rise to prominence before the launch of the European Employment Strategy (EES) which was subsequently written into the employment chapter of the Amsterdam Treaty in 1997. The OMC is today practised in a number of policy areas where the member states have wanted to retain formal policy competence but where a gradual convergence of national policy has been deemed desirable. In the area of socio-economic policy, the most prominent areas include the EES, the OMC Social Inclusion and Social Protection, and the Broad Economic Policy Guidelines.

Before reviewing the experiences to date of the OMC, it is important to analyse the different conceptual lenses used by scholars to understand the implications of policy coordination. These lenses are grounded in different theoretical approaches and analytical starting points, and, as shown later, have strong implications for the conclusions that are drawn concerning the significance of the OMC as a governance tool and its effects on the legitimacy of the EU. For instance, when analysing policy coordination, Borrás and Radaelli (2010) use 'proceduralization' as an organizing concept emphasizing the importance of agency, while Heidenreich (2009) uses 'effectiveness' emphasizing instead the impact of OMC on national policy. Here, I organize conceptual understandings of the

OMC according to their consequences for EU governance in a wide sense which enables an analysis also of the developments since 2010.

The literature on OMC contains a number of theoretical perspectives. From a social constructivist perspective, the OMC is seen as a form of experimental governance where the emphasis lies on reiterative deliberations among policy experts in stable networks forming epistemic communities (Sabel and Zeitlin, 2007). Mutual learning through a continuous process of assessment of policy outcomes and joint evaluation of individual experiences constitutes the backbone of the OMC processes and anchors them in the national policy environment. In terms of efficiency, the OMC is seen as a method that is appropriate for a policy environment in flux characterized by a high degree of uncertainty and where policy choices are in need of continuous revision and up-dating. Networks make the collection of relevant experiences, data and other informational input possible and enhance the quality of policy appraisal. These networks composed by national and European civil servants, experts and stakeholders are tied together through socialization mechanisms and the diffusion of ideas and norms results in ideational convergence. Their democratic legitimacy rests on the 'openness, transparency and broad participation in public problem-solving activities' as the OMC is seen as constituting a necessary complement to representative democracy (Zeitlin, 2005). As experimental governance treats OMC as an ideal case of policy coordination, it is convinced of a beneficial impact on national policy output and administration and tends to regard expert networks as inherently good.

The perspective of rational institutionalism treats the OMC as part of a multi-level governance framework where policy outcomes depend on the interaction between a principal (the member states) and an agent (the Commission). This simple model based on rational choice theory is less well placed to explain the impact of mutual learning, exchange of experiences and practices. It is also at a disadvantage to account for the mechanisms behind voluntary policy coordination and convergence to European solutions. On the other hand, the subsidiarity argument is convincing from a rational choice theory as it explains de-politicization as a strategy of the executive to circumvent democratic procedures of monitoring and therefore rests on a rational calculation of transaction costs. Approaches resting on assumptions of rational agency such as the diffusion theory (Börzel and Risse, 2012), policy transfer (Dolowitz and Marsh, 1996) or Europeanization (Graziano, 2011) provide persuasive explanations for the mechanisms of policy change on a substantial and ideational level as well as institutional adaptation. Expanding on the

Europeanization theory the up-loading, or projection, of national solutions sheds light on member states' pursuit of interests on the European level and points towards the two-level game in which member states engage in order to offset the tension emanating from the pressure to fall in line behind European policy solutions and safeguard national preferences. Europeanization also provides a workable hypothesis for differentiated outcomes of policy coordination on the national level by pointing to the misfit thesis which explains why member states adopt different strategies when implementing shared goals.

The perspective of normative political theory sees the OMC as a form of deliberative democracy on the supranational level within a multi-level polity of democratic policy-making (Joerges, 2007). This theoretical perspective builds on a Habermasian take on deliberative democracy where the central questions concern the quality of the deliberations, the representativeness of the participants, the transparency of the deliberative networks and ultimately the consequences and policy outcome of consensus-building processes. The deliberative perspective has with time become more critical towards the OMC due to its perceived lack in democratic legitimacy chiefly because it 're-casts vast areas of (redistributive) policy as essentially technical or organizational matters to be decided on the basis of scientific and technical expertise rather than public debate' (Offe, 2008, quoted in Kröger, 2009). It also leaves out 'political conflicts and political alternatives' that are taking place outside the processes and therefore 'works contrary to the standards of public deliberation'. Scholars have taken issue with the consequences of governance through networks by pointing at depoliticization and 'policies without politics' as outcomes of technocratic policy-making as well as the erosion of the deliberative content and agonistic qualities of representative democracy (Scharpf and Schmidt, 2000). The development of policy coordination on the EU level without ensuring accountability and constitutional checks and balances constitutes a 'constitutional asymmetry' which even the positive outcomes in terms of output legitimacy may not be able to counterbalance (Scharpf, 2002).

IMPLICATIONS FOR DEMOCRACY OF SOFT GOVERNANCE IN SOCIAL POLICY

The governance literature often enters into a discussion of OMC's democratic legitimacy by reminding the reader that when soft governance was introduced it was widely assumed to improve the democratic deficit of the EU by involving a wide range of actors in open and transparent policy-making (Kröger, 2009, p. 5; Zeitlin, 2005, p. 12). The relationship between OMC and legitimacy is not straightforward and, in order to evaluate it, it is necessary to consider whether a process built on voluntary policy diffusion and non-binding rules is in need of democratic legitimacy in the first place. From a legal perspective the argument that OMC lacks democratic legitimacy appears problematic in that the OMC rests on voluntary coordination of national policy and therefore no formal transfer of competence has taken place between the national and European levels. Member states decide of their own accord whether or not to reform national policies in agreement with the best practices established in policy networks of experts, civil servants and stakeholders. This is often referred to as the OMC's respect of the principle of subsidiarity.

Subsidiarity as a legitimizing principle is based on the argument that policy coordination on the European level protects national prerogatives and therefore does not need to undergo the same stringent criteria of democratic legitimacy as European legislation. Studies, however, have established that although the OMC is 'unlikely to affect national policy making *directly*', it has a 'long-term effect upon member states' social policy through the framing of the perception and definition of problems, as well as related policy responses' (Büchs, 2008, p. 767). It has also been established that OMC impacts on member states' institutional and procedural arrangements (Zeitlin, 2005). In the literature on soft governance, scholars argue that the weakness of democratic legitimacy of the OMC is due to the lack of systematic and qualitative involvement of subnational authorities and national parliaments in the coordination processes and their unsatisfactory embeddedness in the framework of multi-level governance but not to an inherent lack of legitimacy of soft coordination *per se*. This argument overlooks a related problem, namely, that in order to be fully in line with subsidiarity, subnational authorities and national parliaments which all, albeit to varying degrees, hold competences in this field, must be involved in providing input and evaluating the effects of policy reform, or else the purported protection of national sovereignty is not respecting national constitutional prerogatives (Dawson, 2009). From a subsidiarity perspective important questions as to 'which mechanisms coordinating decentralized policies are set in force' have been left unanswered and therefore, because the impact of OMC on actors on the national and subnational levels is generally underestimated, serious concerns should be raised about how accountability is exercised (Benz, 2007, p. 510). The OMC's claim to respect national sovereignty may be considered democratically legitimate but only 'from a narrowly intergovernmentalist perspective' (Zeitlin, 2005, p. 12).

FORMS OF LEGITIMACY OF THE OMC

Legitimacy is a concept with many meanings. Beyond the constitutional dimension concerning the division of competences discussed before, different perspectives condition the assessment of the nature and function of the OMC in the EU policy-making structures. Here three sources of legitimacy will be considered: output legitimacy which is based on legislative outcomes resulting from the procedural interactions among EU institutions; the expert-oriented experimentalist legitimacy that focuses on the dynamic problem-solving activities of officials and technocratic experts; and deliberative legitimacy that emphasizes participation, public debate and communicative exchange.

Output legitimacy in the context of soft governance and the OMC highlights the 'looseness' of the method and deplores the lack of legislative power on the European level which in the case of social policy constitutes a constitutional bias in favour of the market (Scharpf, 2002). Predictably, the 'asymmetry' school is not surprised by the meagre results of the policy coordination processes, which are regarded as too weak to redress the dominance of market liberalism on the European level or to persuade reluctant national governments to let national policy converge towards European policy solutions. The 'asymmetry' school emphasizes diversity among national welfare systems as the reason for the lopsidedness of European economic integration, not only by stressing different structures, provisions and funding but also by pointing to deeper factors such as norms and traditions which are translated into political preferences and popular expectations on the state. The liberal bias of European economic integration can only be redressed if 'the "good Europeans" in Continental and Scandinavian social market economies realize that integration through law is a mode that is structurally biased against their interests and normative preferences' (Scharpf, 2009, p. 34). The 'asymmetry' school does not consider democratic legitimacy of the OMC as the crucial issue as long as national governments are able to produce the social policy output that their citizens demand. For the proponents of this school, it is the constitutional asymmetry between economic integration and social policy which is at the heart of the EU's democratic deficit and public malaise.

The experimentalist school looks at accountability and peer review on the one side and subsidiarity on the other as the essential ingredients of legitimacy of the OMC. This school emphasizes the novel character of non-uniform, de-centralized law-making of the OMC as befitting the sui generis character of the EU where new sources of legitimacy and accountability must be found. On a deeper level this school derives legitimacy from the OMC's inherent 'respect for subsidiarity' in that it conforms to the member states' constitutional choice of not transferring competences to the European level in the realm of welfare policy. As long as the coordination processes are open, transparent and broad-based 'public-solving activities aimed at promoting mutual learning through coordinated monitoring of decentralized experimentation in pursuit of common goals', the OMC is inherently legitimate and 'could transform the EU into a new form of pragmatist democracy' (Zeitlin, 2005, pp. 13–14).

The classical deliberative school emphasizes democratic policy-making focusing on the representativeness of actors, transparency of the proceedings, quality of the public debate, and judicial review and is ultimately grounded in the notion of rule of law. The deliberative school was initially favourably disposed to soft governance and the OMC as loci for authoritative and transparent discourse on matters pertaining to the national welfare state but, as the process has evolved, the proponents of this school are increasingly questioning the legitimacy of the OMC. The source of their disquiet relates to the trade-off between legitimacy and efficiency as the OMC is increasingly favouring the latter through a weakening of the representativeness of the actors by not involving social partners, national parliaments and subnational stakeholders to the extent necessary. The processes are also becoming less transparent, favouring executive power on the European and national levels and reducing the possibility for stakeholders and concerned citizens having a say (Dawson, 2009). Concerns for the democratic qualities of soft governance are also put forward, in particular the lack of judicial review processes and the weak supervision on behalf of democratically elected bodies. The deliberative school refutes the experimentalist school's claim of peer review acting as a source of accountability and in general deplores the severance of the traditional links between political and legal accountability which it considers a threat to the nature of the EU as a law-bound polity (Dawson, 2009; Joerges, 2007).

Although it is now over ten years since soft governance was introduced, scholars have still not come to a conclusion whether the OMC is part of the problem or the solution to the EU's democratic deficit. Empirical studies into the functioning of the OMC increasingly question the input legitimacy of the OMC by demonstrating that the processes have not fulfilled the original pledge of involving a broad range of stakeholders in open and transparent deliberative processes where the participants are held accountable for the outcomes to elected bodies. In fact, scholars have shown that the functioning of soft governance tends to work against those principles (Kröger, 2009; Dawson, 2009, p. 11; Hartlapp, 2009): learning and authoritative deliberation favour exclusive committees of like-minded officials and experts, not frank debate among stakeholders representing different interests; peer review does not function since the committee participants have an interest in supporting each other's national solutions instead of questioning them; and the de-politicization of the OMC has resulted in a dominance of European and national executives who act as gatekeepers regulating and restricting the access to the deliberative processes and have contributed to the dominance of the national ministries of finance in the Council and in national inter-ministerial coordination bodies (Michalski, 2004). Overall, the de-politicization is seen as major problem inherent to the OMC (Kröger, 2009) as deliberation among non-political experts masks the real nature of the process where government representatives make normative assessments of public policy 'to formulate and define problems, goals and strategies' which are normally incumbent upon elected officials (Pfister, 2009). Furthermore, as soft policy outcomes influence the 'framing of general EU policy or single decisions of EU public bodies' and 'decisions at the national level', they have influence over national policy choices although exactly how much, when and where may be hard to ascertain (Borrás and Conzelmann, 2007, p. 534). Soft governance policy outcomes may in fact be regarded as 'quasi-law' but the OMC foregoes legislation on the European level thereby avoiding the cumbersome checks and balances and judicial review (Borrás and Conzelmann, 2007).

POLICY COORDINATION AND SOCIAL POLICY

There are several distinct social models in Europe. Heterogeneity in a union of 27 member states is not surprising and various political and constitutional measures have been devised to safeguard the positive sides of diversity. In general terms, the EU has treated the question of homogeneity among member states carefully. Only in the context of enlargement of the EU and the introduction of the euro was aspiring countries' readiness for membership assessed although in the latter case the stringency of the evaluation has been doubted. Once a country is part of the EU, compliance to EU rules and regulations is monitored and if necessary enforced by the Court but the underlying question of the 'fit' of national economic and social regimes is seldom posed. Nevertheless, there is an underlying ambition of convergence of member states' economic performance. This is particularly salient for the EMU whose initially strict formal fiscal regime was introduced with an implicit ambition of policy convergence in economic policy. In social policy, the EU has trodden carefully and soft governance has been preferred to legislation, even when the contemplated regulations would have concerned only minimum standards. Because the OMC is based on a voluntaristic approach to policy convergence through the diffusion of best practices, scholarly attention has largely centered on the efficiency of the method and its impact on national policy regimes. To date, most scholarly accounts conclude that soft governance in the framework of the OMC has not influenced the content of member states' social policy to a significant degree (Kröger, 2009): partly, because influence of this kind is inherently difficult to disentangle from that emanating from the domestic setting or the global environment and partly because the OMC's soft instruments, designed to correspond to a context of diversity, actually work at cross-purposes by encouraging the emergence of 'optimal' policy models which are then transcribed into policy prescriptions directed at the member states (Hartlapp, 2009).

A widespread perception of the soft governance approach of the Lisbon Strategy therefore is that it has failed to coax member states to live up to their commitments taken on the European level thereby causing the EU to fail to achieve the strategy's overall objectives. The image of political leaders gladly signing up to 'unrealistic goals' (Hartlapp, 2009, p. 9) on the European level without making a real commitment to carry out the necessary reforms on the national level has reflected negatively on the efficiency of the OMC. However, research into the OMC shows a more nuanced albeit complex picture of the influence that policy convergence processes exert on national policy regimes and institutions. Scholars have found that policy coordination processes have contributed to 'shifts in governance and policy-making arrangements, including administrative reorganization and institutional capacity building' (Zeitlin, 2005, p. 22). The OMC has also encouraged convergence at the ideational level, shaping the formulation of reform agendas and the diagnosis of problems (Radaelli, 2003). Whether the convergence is genuine, changing perceptions and understandings, or instrumental either by conforming to the language promoted by European institutions or by using the Lisbon guidelines as an external justification, the OMC processes have contributed to convergence towards a shared ideational basis for social policy reforms in Europe. On balance, therefore, it may be concluded that the OMC's impact is fairly strong on the ideational dimensions of national governance, in particular in respect of administrative arrangements for policy coordination, but large variations exist among member states in the way that they have allowed the objectives and recommendations to influence the elaboration of National Reform Programmes (Zeitlin, 2007, p. 3). The overall impression of evidence collected in the member states is that their stake in the OMC 'may be described as formal participation' and that 'there is little evidence of real influence of the OMC on national social policies', although some member state governments use the Lisbon Strategy instrumentally 'to press for structural changes in social and economic policy' (Golinowska and Żukowski, 2009, p. 368).

Learning through Comparison and Exchange of Experience

Underlying the EES and OMC Social Inclusion and Social Protection lies a shared 'conviction that member states should learn from one another through iterative reporting, benchmarking and peer review in the pursuit of common policy goals' (Hartlapp, 2009, p. 2). An overall assessment of the efficiency of learning in the EES and the OMC Social Protection and Social Inclusion concludes that the representatives in these committees 'have been rather successful in identifying common challenges and promising policy approaches, which have in turn contributed to broad shifts in national policy thinking' although the effects are 'not always recognized as "learning"' (Zeitlin, 2005, p. 23). The learning dimension has been particularly strong in new member states where civil servants, experts and stakeholders have adapted to prevailing ideas, norms and administrative structures of European policy coordination (Potůček, 2009).

Moreover, observations regarding the effectiveness of the EES in a context of national diversity are positive: the 'European employment guidelines have proved highly adaptable to the wide variety of employment systems across the Union, encouraging convergence to objectives, performance, and broad policy approaches through contextualized benchmarking, self-assessment, peer review and exchange of good practices' (Zeitlin, 2007, p. 5). An assessment of these mechanisms and the contexts in which they are deployed concludes, however, that 'indicators seem to be the [instrument] best suited to stimulate learning processes through reflexive self-evaluation' as there is clear evidence that member states 'introduce or improve national structures for supervising the labour market' and track national and European policy targets (Hartlapp, 2009, p. 10).

This rather positive overall assessment of the learning environment of the OMC, in particular the EES, is, however, qualified in a number of empirical analyses. Regarding the quality of the deliberations, empirical studies have found that peer review has not exercised the function of 'dynamic accountability' which it was initially intended to do, but has instead been geared towards identifying common approaches among different national contexts that can be generalized at the EU level, or exported to other countries. Civil servants have refrained from engaging in true debate about the pros and cons of national policy approaches and have certainly not criticized or held individual member states to account (Dawson, 2009). In regard to learning through establishing guidelines and recommendations, some studies show that 'consultations on formulating guidelines have increasingly taken the character of "interest-driven bargaining" rather than "result in open deliberation"' (Jobelius, 2003, p. 25; Radulova, 2007, pp. 374–5 quoted in Hartlapp, 2009, p. 6). In fact, several studies stress the 'political dimension' of the OMC which 'may be used by national actors for their "leverage effect" or as "selective amplifiers" for advancing national interests' (Erhel et al., 2005; Visser, 2005 quoted in Hartlapp, 2009).

Surveys have been conducted into the functioning of the OMC processes after the accession of countries in Central and Eastern Europe. Here, it has been noted that the increased number of participants has lowered the quality of the committees' deliberations and in general new member states' representatives have been less resourceful in terms of knowledge, language skills, and back-up from ministries in the capitals, and generally have a lower seniority than those from the old member states. In the case of the Social Protection Committee the large number of committee members was perceived to be a problem for the quality of the deliberation and enlargement was seen as 'making the reaching of consensus opinion within committees, and the pace of the deliberative exchanges within peer reviews more difficult' (Horvath, 2009). Participants in the OMC Social Protection have been quoted as considering enlargement making 'the present process "unsustainable ... it is more difficult to go into depth when so many countries meet at one time"' (Dawson, 2009, p. 8).

Another important aspect of OMC governance is the role of social partners, NGOs, national parliaments and subnational authorities in the OMC structures. The reasons for enlarging the groups of civil servants and experts to include stakeholders on the European level in the OMC learning processes are found in the wish to legitimize the processes by making them more transparent and representative, as well as to increase the efficiency of the policy guidelines and recommendations by including a wider range of interests. On the national level, stakeholders' involvement is seen as important in connecting the European and national levels for reasons of efficiency in uploading content in the deliberations onto the European level and downloading recommendations and guidelines to be implemented in the member states through the National Reform

Programmes of the Lisbon Strategy. When national 'ownership' was singled out by the Commission in 2006 as a prerequisite for democratic legitimacy critical remarks were raised about the efforts to involve stakeholders in meaningful interaction at national and European levels (European Commission, 2006). Much of the criticism is directed at national executives' attempts to act as gatekeepers of the OMC on the European level, a tendency that grew stronger after the re-launch of the Lisbon Strategy in 2005 when the Commission's Secretariat General streamlined the negotiations with individual member states on the National Reform Programmes. This development has been interpreted as an intergovernmental drift in the relations between the Commission and member states' executive offices which have centralized competences on the national level. Informal and voluntaristic processes have rendered national parliaments and social partners more vulnerable to executive dominance and 'the lack of extensive local and regional participation is one of the primary obstacles to both the method's [the OMC] effectiveness and its legitimacy' (Dawson, 2009, pp. 9–11; Hartlapp, 2009). However, the OMC literature also includes examples from the EES where subnational authorities have been involved effectively in the national-level processes (drawing up and implementing the National Action Plans) empowering them vis-à-vis the national executive (López-Santana, 2009).

IMPACT ON POLICY-MAKING AT THE NATIONAL LEVEL

The initial optimism that the OMC would broaden participation, improve transparency and cross-sectoral learning and increase the potential for experimental governance (Sabel and Zeitlin, 2007) has turned into concerns about the democratic legitimacy of the OMC. This concern stems from the observation of a 'de-politicization' of the OMC as the processes have become dominated by national governments, civil servants and experts who effectively manage the questions of who, how and to what extent stakeholders are allowed to take part (Kröger, 2009). Also in official evaluations of the Lisbon Strategy and the OMC, the lack of national stakeholders' involvement is identified as a major weakness, chiefly out of efficiency concerns (implementation), but also out of concern over a faltering 'national ownership' and weak 'empowerment' of stakeholders (European Commission, 2010a). Subsequently, a more effective and systematic involvement of national stakeholders, in particular regional and local authorities and national parliaments, has been identified as key to the success of Europe 2020, the successor to the Lisbon Strategy (European Commission, 2010b).

Subnational Authorities' Participation in National Policy Coordination

National state structures determine the responsibilities of subnational authorities in terms of implementation of policy but also their regulatory, fiscal and administrative autonomy. The high degree of heterogeneity in constitutional structures among member states is a central aspect in understanding the involvement of subnational authorities in the OMC and in general the stronger the competences of regional and local authorities, the more significant is their role in national policy processes connected to OMC. Above and beyond the diversity of national constitutional arrangements, member states are affected by challenges to the role of the state in devising, funding, delivering and evaluating policy. In the wake of challenges from economic globalization and the emergence of new social phenomena, most European states have undergone processes of regionalization, decentralization and devolution. Some countries, such as Belgium, Spain and Italy, have experienced very strong transformations whereas others have devolved policy competence to lower levels of government as a way of off-loading the central government's responsibilities. The scaling back of the central state has resulted in regional and local authorities having to take on more responsibilities for the funding and implementation of public policy. This is particularly pronounced in areas such as welfare, which are provided by local authorities in the large majority of member states.

Most previous research on the OMC has assumed that subnational authorities have an important role to play as regards the input, implementation, and feedback mechanisms of the measures that national governments have committed themselves to (Zeitlin, 2005; Dawson, 2009; Büchs, 2008; López-Santana, 2009). The high degree of heterogeneity in constitutional structures among member states is a central aspect in understanding the involvement of subnational authorities in the OMC and in general the stronger the competences of regional and local authorities, the more significant their role in national policy processes. Following from extensive regional and local autonomy is the necessity to put measures in place for effective coordination between levels of government which are likely to benefit European-level policy processes. López-Santana (2009, p. 4) has argued that in order to understand how 'lower levels can have a say at the national level and to interpret cross-national findings, scholars must capture the nature of intra-governmental relations in a state'. However, these general remarks should not hide the fact that even among countries with similar constitutional structures significant variations exist. For instance, Austria, a federal country where strong corporate traditions co-exist alongside extensive regional autonomy, coordination of various stakeholders, including regions, municipalities and NGOs is less extensive than in Ireland, a unitary state with strong traditions of organized consultative frameworks which has facilitated coordination and allowed for effective input of stakeholders both in policy formulation and evaluation.

The nature and intensity of the involvement of subnational authorities in the OMC therefore vary from one country to the other. However, vertical policy cooperation mechanisms exist in a majority of the member states. These may be of a formal nature (e.g. representation on a committee), informal (for example circulation of draft reports or ad hoc meetings) or through specific projects, often with EU funding (INBAS GmbH/ENGENDER, 2010). In Belgium, Germany, Spain and the UK, the involvement of regions is particularly important and based on extensive legislative and administrative (implementation) competences (Michalski, 2012). At the other end of the spectrum, Cyprus, the Czech Republic, Greece, Hungary, Lithuania, Poland, Romania and Slovakia have low or otherwise unsatisfactory levels of involvement of subnational authorities.

As the OMC relies on learning and peer review as its principal instruments, the Lisbon Strategy's national progress reports were to become instances of learning on the basis of policy evaluation and feedback from actors on the ground. Hartlapp (2009) however points at the weaknesses of the feedback loops and the failure to involve the regional and local levels as the circle of actors involved is small and often dominated by central government. In some countries, such as the Czech Republic, Denmark and Greece, there are no, or very unsatisfactory, mechanisms of policy evaluation. In Denmark the process is characterized as extremely top-down based on interaction between central government and NGOs whereas 'the local and regional level of the public sector has been almost invisible in the whole process' and characterized as 'an attempt to be open and inclusive that did not succeed' (INBAS GmbH/ENGENDER, 2009, p. 28). In the Czech Republic, 'monitoring and evaluation is an underdeveloped part of the OMC process in the area of social inclusion' dominated by ministries which control the data and do not make an effort to make them easily available to stakeholders (INBAS GmbH/ENGENDER, 2009, p. 23). Among the countries with the most elaborated feedback mechanisms we find to a large measure those member states which also have well-developed structures for the involvement of subnational authorities, primarily Ireland, Finland, Germany, the Netherlands, Spain and the UK (Michalski, 2012). In these countries, stakeholders' involvement is strong in all phases including monitoring and evaluation. These findings corroborate López-Santana's (2009) study of the EES's impact on intra-governmental relations of Spain, Belgium and Sweden. In all three countries, despite different constitutional structures, decentralization of competence in the social area is extensive. In Belgium, open coordination has provided 'a new opportunity for federal and federated policymakers to cooperate and coordinate with each other … informally shifting the nature of intra-governmental collaboration from reporting/weak consultation in the direction of bargaining' (2009, p. 8). In Spain, 'the process of drafting and implementing the EES' has been the opportunity to create 'national coordinating spaces … where subnational entities have had a "say"' (2009, p. 10). Whereas in Sweden, 'this centralized country, where subnational levels are (mainly) implementers and managers of LMPs [labour market policies], these entities did not have as much of a "say" as in the other two member states' (2009, p. 12). López-Santana contends that the de jure (formal) institutional set-up shapes and filters the nature of involvement of subnational actors which is an important factor in understanding 'why stakeholder participation on the OMC remains uneven' (2009, p. 13).

Regions and local authorities have sought to gain representation and have a 'say' on the European level ever since European legislation began to have a decisive impact on their areas of competence. In the area of open coordination the Brussels-based activities of regional and local interest organizations have been stepped up progressively. Contrary to the social partners and the European Parliament (EP), regional and local actors have no mechanism to address the European Council's spring summit directly. Just as in other policy areas of concern, subnational authorities have better access and interact more with the Commission than with the national representatives in the European Council or the Council of Ministers, a state of affairs which further underlines the member states' inclination to keep infra-national actors' involvement in European level policy-making at a minimum.

Constitutional diversity and differences in regard to competences and resources of subnational actors have prevented a unified representation of regional interests on the European level. The subnational authorities are represented in multiple fora. In the Committee of the Regions (CoR) large, powerful regions tend to dominate. The CoR emphasizes increasingly the importance of regional interests in the Lisbon Strategy with its growing emphasis on economic growth and the use of the regional and cohesion funds for the financing of various growth and employment objectives. In 2009, the CoR published a White Paper to launch a debate on multi-level governance with the aim of strengthening the role of regions by reforming the OMC 'to make it more inclusive by developing participatory governance indicators and territorial indicators' (CoR, 2009, p. 1).

Finally, EU financing has helped in implementing the objectives elaborated in the EES and the OMC Social Protection and Social Inclusion on the ground by introducing new best practices and carrying out pilot studies and projects. Through the regional policy, subnational actors come in direct contact with officials from the Commission and representatives from other regional and local authorities. The European level interaction through the partnership principle has changed the national political dynamics in the favour of subnational actors which explains the member states' insistence on reinforcing their role as 'gatekeepers' between the regions and European institutions. EU funding has also been directed at the governance side of the OMC by financing networks and consultative practices which have improved participation, learning and exchange of best practices at European and national levels.

National Parliaments' Involvement in National Policy Coordination

The question of democratic legitimacy on grounds of parliamentary (representative) democracy is increasingly raised in the context of soft coordination. A number of shortcomings with the ideal-type governance model of OMC has prompted scholars to argue that 'the current model of participation not only marginalizes parliaments at the EU and national levels but is also detrimental to *national* parliamentary democracy more generally as it strengthens executives whilst weakening parliamentary power in national policy-making processes' (Büchs, 2008, p. 781). Particularly troublesome from the perspective of parliamentary democracy is the difficulty for citizens to gain insight into their and other national governments' positions in the OMC. This lack of transparency 'weakens the accountability of national governments to their parliaments and electorates' (Büchs, 2008, p. 778).

A study into national parliaments' involvement in the national progress reports concludes that the countries found to have the most extensive and systematic parliamentary input are also those where the subnational authorities' involvement is far-reaching, such as Belgium and Germany followed by Finland, Ireland, the UK and Spain (Michalski, 2012). In a few other countries, Estonia, Luxembourg, Malta, the Netherlands and Sweden, parliaments are considered to have some influence, while in the remaining countries which represent more than half of all the member states, parliaments are little or not at all involved. Often national reform programmes are made available to parliament, but are not debated in parliamentary organs. In a few other member states, MPs debate national reform programmes in plenary or in committee where they also have the opportunity to put questions to relevant ministers, but only in some member states are MPs called upon to give their formal approval to national reports.

In relation to the EES, the social partners, interest-based organizations and civil society groups have far better access to committees, hearings and other consultative mechanisms than national parliaments which remain largely marginalized in the national OMC processes in a majority of the member states (Michalski, 2012). In those member states where subnational authorities are not systematically included in national coordination process, national parliaments are also far less involved. These observations are supported by scholars who note that 'so far national parliaments have remained uninterested and marginalized in OMC' and 'have failed to make an impact in OMC' (Raunio, 2007, pp. 5–6). Visser (2005, p. 208) summed up the involvement of most national parliaments by noting that 'the process has remained rather bureaucratic and isolated from parliamentary influence … the audience for learning [being] almost entirely limited to the Ministry of Social Affairs and a handful of local, national and European civil servants'.

In countries where national parliaments are actively involved in contributing to the drawing up of national progress reports, they also have a role in the monitoring of the national executive and evaluation of national policies in the framework of the Lisbon Strategy (Michalski, 2012). On a general level, however, there is little evidence of parliamentary involvement in monitoring the national executive's action on either the national or European level. Even more worryingly, there is a lack of debate on the content and orientation of national executives' input into the OMC process on the European level as national parliaments tend to rubber stamp national contributions and implementation reports in plenum or committee without a thorough debate. The reasons for the limited involvement of national parliaments in the OMC was summarized by Duina and Raunio (2007, pp. 498–9) as belonging to one of three different categories:

- first, the intergovernmental nature of the OMC involving primarily national civil servants presenting national reports and initiatives in Brussels contributes to circumventing national parliaments which are informed too late about the executive's action to make a meaningful contribution;

- second, the lack of transparency and the pronounced informality of the OMC make it harder for national parliamentarians to follow the processes. The characteristics of the OMC do not sit well with established formal rules and mechanisms of national parliaments and contribute to the difficulty for national parliaments of exercising effective scrutiny;
- third, as the impact of OMC on policy in the member states is still regarded as fairly modest and as the OMC does not, contrary to the Community model, produce binding rules, MPs take the scrutiny of soft coordination outcomes less seriously than supranational law.

In most member states, there is a lack of debate on the OMC guidelines, indicators and national progress reports. Neither parliaments nor the media have demonstrated interest in debating potential outcomes of policy coordination of welfare policies on the European level, despite the fact that welfare belongs to the core of national policy and is hotly contested in national elections. There simply seems to be no cognitive link between European-level soft coordination and national welfare policy outcomes among opinion-makers in the national political setting. Tsakatika (2007, pp. 554–5) has referred to the lack of involvement of national parliaments as a problem of accountability on two levels: on the one hand the lack of 'authoritative democratic check on rule-making where authorization derives from direct election of parliamentarians'; on the other, 'the public deliberative side of policy-making that addresses questions of values and principles involved in policy choice, simplifies dilemmas and brings the questions at stake closer to citizens'. In the context of OMC, national parliamentary involvement in sanctioning, monitoring the executive and assessing policy outcome does not satisfy either criterion of accountability. Given the influence of OMC on national policy orientation and governance structures, the dismal parliamentary input cannot be considered satisfactory on grounds of democratic legitimacy and constitutes a lacuna in national models of representative democracy.

Scholars have referred to the common interests of European and national parliaments to oversee the activities of the executive as a 'multi-level' scrutiny (Maurer and Wessels, 2001). There are examples of cooperation between functional committees of the EP and national parliaments as well as vertical political cooperation through party groups (Neunreither, 2005, quoted in Tsakatika, 2007, p. 560). The EP has taken the initiative to bring together members of the European and national parliaments in an annual meeting ahead of the spring European summit. The Joint Parliamentary Meeting discusses questions of common concern linked to the up-coming summit. It does not issue a final resolution but releases an account of the orientation of the debates where European and national parliaments share common views and where they do not (Tsakatika, 2007). Neunreither notes that functional cooperation may be most useful in parliamentary monitoring and scrutiny while political cooperation is more useful from a deliberative perspective. He points, however, to a number of difficulties in the cooperation between committees. National members of parliament often feel 'overwhelmed by their counterparts at the EP and point out that procedures are to the latter's advantage' (Neunreither, 2005, quoted in Tsakatika, 2007, p. 560). Members of the EP on their side feel that 'the role of national parliamentarians is primarily to hold their own governments to account rather than spend time in Brussels overstretching the EP's busy work schedule'. MEPs feel that while from 'the EP's side information flows towards the national parliaments are unhindered and growing', there is 'no equivalent' on behalf of national parliamentary committees, which are 'accused of being reluctant to provide much desired input in a timely fashion'. These findings point to the difficulty of setting up workable multi-level governance scrutiny mechanisms. One interesting observation in this regard is that COSAC (the EU's Conference of Committees of National Parliaments) has never debated parliamentary scrutiny of OMC issues despite having discussed policy questions related to the Lisbon Strategy (Duina and Raunio, 2007, footnote no. 3).

In conclusion, a pattern of extensive variation among member states emerges, explained by the stickiness of existing constitutional structures, political practices and traditions. A few countries have developed quite extensive and effective consultation and coordination mechanisms along with systematic evaluation and feedback on policy implementation. These member states involve a wide range of stakeholders, including national parliaments and subnational authorities, in national policy-making connected to the OMC. In federations and regionalized states more elaborate domestic coordination processes have been put in place. In these member states, OMC has contributed to the development of more cooperative practices between subnational and national authorities, and representatives of constitutional regions are extensively involved in European level policy-making. National practices of good governance also explain why certain centralized member states have put extensive mechanisms of involvement of sub-national authorities in place, and in these countries participation in the OMC has become part of the already ongoing interaction between levels of government. A large majority of EU member states, however, has not developed structures that involve subnational authorities to a significant extent. One explanation is that subnational authorities lack the resources to exert their interests vis-à-vis the central government; another that existing patterns of interaction do not lend themselves easily to the kind of governance practices on which the OMC depends. In some countries, consultation with stakeholders is dominated by civil society groups as they have proven to be more readily mobilized and fit more easily into the OMC governance framework. These findings point to a reappraisal of the argument that the OMC has a unifying impact on national structures and procedural arrangements in the case of subnational authorities whose involvement is dependent on resources, interests and existing patterns of interaction between levels of government. It confirms the argument that the OMC is to a large extent dominated by the executive as only subnational authorities primarily in federal and regionalized member states have a say in policy-making, while national parliaments throughout the EU member states do not influence the content and execution of policy in the OMC despite a strong role in the elaboration of welfare policies in the national setting. Far from preserving national sovereignty, the voluntary character of the OMC has rendered the participation of subnational authorities and national parliaments in European multi-level governance more precarious as the national procedures are adapting to conform to European governance. From this perspective, the OMC appears to be challenging democratic policy-making rather than alleviating the problem of legitimacy of the EU.

POLICY COORDINATION IN THE WAKE OF THE ECONOMIC CRISIS

As a result of the economic crisis of 2010 and the ensuing sovereign debt crisis, the EU has taken a number of measures to strengthen the framework of social and economic policy coordination (Michalski, 2013). Not surprisingly, political leaders in the European Council saw much stronger governance of economic policy as a prerequisite for saving the euro, and as a result the decision-making structures of the Stability and Growth Pact were reformed to become considerably stricter. The majority of the member states also adhered to the Treaty on Stability, Coordination and Governance (the Fiscal Compact) of 2012 which was concluded outside the framework of the EU due to the opposition of the UK and the hesitancy of a few other member states not part of the euro. The Treaty aims at further strengthening the fiscal discipline on the national level and the European institutions' monitoring of national budgets.

Since the economic crisis has exposed substantial differences in competitiveness of national economies resulting in sizeable macro-economic imbalances, most acutely in the countries in the euro area, diverging national economic and social conditions, uneven administrative capabilities and underperforming welfare institutions have come into focus. The diversity of economic and social performance among member states in the euro area is perceived as an aggravating background factor, and the dismal record of the Lisbon Strategy, whose aim was to coax member states into adopting competitiveness enhancing policies, was recognized as a governance failure. The crisis coincided with the relaunch of the Lisbon Strategy, and as a result of the difficulties of coordinating national policy, the Commission proposed a reorientation of policy priorities and a strengthening of policy coordination as part of an upgrading of the EU's economic governance.

The European Semester: the EU's Framework for Economic Governance

The Commission launched the Europe 2020 Strategy in March 2010 arguing that in order to exit from the crisis the EU needed economic growth more than anything else (European Commission, 2010b). According to the Commission, the EU should direct its efforts into creating smart growth in order to boost competitiveness; sustainable growth in order to fulfill its ambitious climate change objectives and avoid a further deterioration of member states' future financial liabilities; and inclusive growth in order to fight social exclusion and widening income differentials in Europe.

The most significant change lies arguably in the integration of Europe 2020 into a new strengthened framework for economic governance, the European semester. The European semester represents an integrated framework of recurrent assessment of national social and economic policies aimed at ensuring macroeconomic stability, fiscal prudence and financial discipline. It was introduced through the legislative measures adopted in November 2011, the so-called six-pack (five regulations and one directive), and the 'distinct mechanisms for issuing recommendations under the economic and employment policy provisions' in the treaties (Armstrong, 2011, no page numbers). The yearly policy cycle starts with the Commission's Annual Growth Survey which provides overall guidance and priorities for economic policy. On this basis the European Council discusses the overall economic orientation of the EU at the spring summit, announces policy guidelines and invites member states to fulfill general economic measures in line with the commitments of the Stability and Growth Pact and the Europe 2020 Strategy. In April, the member states submit the national reform programmes in view of their commitments under Europe 2020, stability and convergence reports of the Stability and Growth Pact and reports on macroeconomic imbalances. On the basis of member states' performance in regard to these policy processes the Commission draws up individual country reports which are subsequently adopted by the Council of Ministers along with recommendations addressed to individual member states. At the end of June, the European Council is called upon to endorse the country-specific reports and recommendations in order to lend further weight to the procedure. During the autumn, the member states draw up national budget proposals according to their national rules and procedures and as prime ministers and finance ministers have endorsed the guidelines on the economic priorities for all member states along with country-specific recommendations directed at individual member states, it is expected that these find their way into the national budgets.

In order to further enhance the surveillance of national draft budgets, the Commission put forward another two regulations in November 2011, the so-called two-pack (European Commission, 2011). These regulations which are directed at the countries in the euro area aim at strengthening the role of the Commission in monitoring national draft budgets by introducing a common budgetary time-line and making it mandatory upon member states to submit national draft budgets to the Commission and the Eurogroup by mid-October each year. In the event that the draft budget does not conform to the budgetary policy obligations of the Stability and Growth Pact the Commission may ask the member state to revise the budget. Furthermore, the Commission may draw up an opinion on individual member states' draft budgets which will be made public. If requested by the parliament of the member states concerned the Commission will present its opinion in the national parliament. Interestingly, as the two-pack became the object of intense negotiations between the Council and the EP in 2012, a division opened up between the parties to the left and right of the political spectrum where the former expressed strong concern over the intrusive role of the Commission managing the European semester and its enhanced powers of budgetary surveillance within the European framework of economic governance, while the latter emphasized the case for fiscal discipline and economic growth as necessary components in a crisis exit strategy.

The European Semester and Democratic Policy-making

The enhanced framework for economic governance for which the European semester constitutes both the pinnacle and umbrella completed its first policy cycle in 2012. For this reason, any assessments as to its impact on policy coordination and different forms of legitimacy can only be provisional. However, the following remarks seem pertinent:

First, there is no doubt that with the European semester, the EU has endowed itself with a framework for economic governance which is more comprehensive, centralized and coercive than before and therefore carries the potential of a strong influence on national economic and social policy. It is more comprehensive in that differences in competitiveness of national economies are monitored in a new process on macroeconomic imbalances. The framework of economic governance is now comprised of three processes: the Stability and Growth Pact, the macroeconomic imbalances procedure and Europe 2020 which together constitute the input of the evaluation of national economic performance. It is more centralized because on the one hand policy coordination has come to rely even more strongly on the work of the Commission and national civil servants meeting in working groups and committees, and on the other is the role played by the European Council in solving the financial crisis and staking out the political priorities of Europe 2020. And it is more coercive in that the decisions to sanction member states in breach of the rules of the Stability and Growth Pact can only be stopped by a majority of the member states voting against the decision.

Second, although the European semester primarily relies on policy coordination, it has taken on a radically different character to the loose coordination of the Lisbon Strategy. A new aspect of policy coordination is found in the introduction of hard law through the six- and two-packs which regulate the functioning of the Stability and Growth Pact, national administrative structures and statistical requirements concerning budgets, surveillance of excessive deficits and macroeconomic imbalances. The EU institutions, in particular, the Commission, have made clear that these measures are drawn up in respect of the principles of subsidiarity and proportionality but certain member states and certain party groups in the EP have made their reservations known on grounds of democratic accountability. As yet it is too early to know exactly where the remit of the obligations contained in the new legislative acts stop and where the sphere of national independent action starts. Another aspect of policy coordination which has changed with the new framework for economic governance is the nature of the policy coordination which has been made considerably stricter. The stricter form of policy coordination is found not only in the Stability and Growth Pact's new decision-making rules, but also in the application of peer review which has become ubiquitous. As a result of the economic crisis, member states' earlier reluctance to name-and-shame each other into action has dissipated and today official publication and publicly disclosed assessments of national performance are widely used, near-coercive instruments. The OMC processes in the social sphere of the Europe 2020 Strategy have remained largely untouched but with the added political clout that the reporting into the over-arching economic governance framework entails.

Third, although the strengthened framework for economic governance in the EU has for the most part been seen as a measure to come to grips with the crisis, which incidentally explains the relative expedience with which the legislative acts of the six-pack were passed, strong concerns of centralized economic governance by the EU and the impact on national democracy are raised. Critical voices are heard in respect to the diminishing role of national parliaments in the adoption of national budgets as MPs' opinions risk being overshadowed by evaluations and recommendations from the EU institutions. However, the rising awareness of the importance of the European semester has prompted the EP into taking a more active stance as it has argued for a stronger role for itself as well as for national parliaments in holding national and European executives accountable to their decisions. Moreover, the sovereign debt crisis has involved national parliaments in the granting of financial rescue packages which have increased the awareness and knowledge of national MPs of European policy-making. By way of conclusion, it is possible to argue at this stage of a rapid policy development that the European semester represents a strengthening of economic governance on the European level which holds a distinct risk of undermining the ability of national parliaments to influence national economic policy-making and maintain an effective voice in framing the national budget. At the same time, it opens a possibility for national parliaments to argue for a more active role in the policy processes underlying the European semester, and for improved cooperation between national parliaments and the EP in monitoring the executive and influencing the debate as to the orientation of economic policy.

CONCLUDING DISCUSSION

The rationale of the Lisbon Strategy and its successor the Europe 2020 Strategy with all their ambiguities and governance flaws must be understood against a background of a deepening of economic integration that did not equip the EU, or the member states, with instruments for managing the differences in economic and welfare performance. The emphasis of the chapter has therefore come to lie on explaining the rationale behind the choice of policy coordination in the guise of the OMC in view of other possible approaches and the setting up of an integrated governance framework which relies on voluntary integration, strong proceduralization and a certain vagueness in policy orientation. The analysis of the experience of the OMC in welfare policy and employment points to a number of developments that require further research as a form of enhanced soft governance is set to dominate the EU's socio-economic regime. Firstly this concerns a tendency to de-politicization and centralization in the policy networks on the European level which has strengthened during the efforts to find solutions to the financial crisis, binding civil servants in the Commission, the European Central Bank and national finance ministries increasingly closer together. Secondly, the weak participation of subnational authorities and national parliaments has further strengthened the ability of national executives to steer policy developments without first anchoring decisions on options and direction with national actors. Thirdly, the OMC, seen as a governance tool of policy coordination, in a paradoxical manner fulfills neither the requirements for output legitimacy (as outcomes in terms of policy reform on the national level have been modest), nor the requirements for input legitimacy, as the processes where OMC is applied have become increasingly closed-off from contributions and participation from actors carrying representative qualities and expertise.

The chapter concludes by highlighting the potentially important changes that the enhanced economic governance framework, the European semester, entails. This framework has been set up as a response to the consequences of the financial and economic crisis with the aim of improving the efficiency and expedience of national policy convergence in order to sustain the euro, but without considering the effects on democratic policy-making on either the European or the national level.

References

ABCD Global Consulting (2010), 'Home', available at http://www.abcdglobal.org/index.html (accessed 25 February 2010).

ABCD Institute (2009), 'Michelle Obama', available at http://www.abcdinstitute.org/faculty/obama/ (accessed 20 February 2010).

ABCD Institute (2009a), 'Partners', available at http://www.abcdinstitute.org/partners/ (accessed 25 February 2010).

ABCD Institute (2009b), 'Resources', available at http://www.abcdinstitute.org/resources/ (accessed 20 February 2010).

Aidukaite, J. (2009), 'The Estonian model of the welfare state: tradition and changes', in S. Golinowska, P. Hengstenberg and M. Żukowski (eds), *Diversity and Commonality in European Social Policies: The Forging of a European Social Model*, Warsaw: Friedrich Ebert Stiftung and Wydawnictwo Nauwkowe Scholar, pp. 110–36.

Alesina, A. and E. Spolaore (1997), 'On the number and size of nations', *Quarterly Journal of Economics*, **112** (4), 1027–56.

Alesina, A., R. Bacquir and C. Hoxby (2004), 'Political jurisdictions in heterogeneous communities', *Journal of Political Economy*, **11** (2), 348–96.

Ambler, J.S. (1994), 'Who benefits from educational choice? Some evidence from Europe', *Journal of Policy Analysis and Management*, **13** (3), 454–76.

Amin, A. (1994), *Post-Fordism: A Reader*, Oxford: Wiley-Blackwell.

Amitsis, G., J. Berghans, A. Hemerijck, T. Sakellaropoulos, A. Stergiou and Y. Stevens (2003), 'Connecting welfare diversity within the European Social Model', Background report for the International Conference of the Hellenic Presidency of the European Union on the Modernisation of the European Social Model (May), Ioannina, Greece.

Andersen, J.G. and J.J. Pedersen (2007), 'Continuity and change in Danish active labour market policy, 1990–2007: the battlefield between activation and workfare', *CCWS Working Paper No. 2007-54*, Aalborg: Centre for Comparative Welfare Studies (CCWS), Aalborg University, Denmark.

Anheier, H.K. (2001), 'Third sector economy', in J. Michie (ed.), *Reader's Guide to the Social Sciences*, Chicago: Fitzroy Dearborn, pp. 1648–49.

Antolín, P. and F. Stewart (2009), 'Private pensions and policy responses to the financial and economic crisis', OECD Working Papers on Insurance and Private Pensions, No. 36, available at http://www.oecd.org/insurance/private–pensions/42601323.pdf (accessed 27 January 2013).

Armstrong, K.A. (2011), *The Lisbon Agenda and Europe 2020: From the Governance of Coordination to the Coordination of Governance*, School of Law Legal Studies Research Papers, No. 89/2011, London: Queen Mary University of London.

Arnesen, A.L. and L. Lundahl (2006), 'Still social and democratic? Inclusive education policies in the Nordic welfare states', *Scandinavian Journal of Educational Research*, **50** (3), 285–300.

Arts, W. and J. Gelissen (2002), 'Three worlds of welfare capitalism or more? A state-of-the-art report', *Journal of European Social Policy*, **12** (2), 137–58.

Ascoli, U. and C. Ranci (2002), *Dilemmas of the Welfare Mix: the New Structure of Welfare in an Era of Privatization*, New York: Kluwer Academic/Plenum Publishers.

Asenova, D., M. Beck and S. Toms (2007), 'The limits of market-based governance and accountability – PFI refinancing and the resurgence of the regulatory state', *White Rose Research Online*, **35**, 1–28.

Aspalter, C., J. Kim and S. Park (2009), 'Analysing the welfare state in Poland, the Czech Republic, Hungary and Slovenia: an ideal typical perspective', *Social Policy and Administration*, **43** (2), 170–85.

Astiz, M.F., A.W. Wiseman and D.P. Baker (2002), 'Slouching towards decentralization: consequences of globalization for curricular control in national education systems', *Comparative Education Review*, **46** (1), 66–88.

Austrian Museum for Social and Economic Affairs (2009), *Well Insured: Social Security in Austria*, Vienna: Austrian Museum for Social and Economic Affairs.

Baetz, J. (2012), 'Germans float direct EU control over Greek budget', Associated Press, 29 January, available at http://www.google.com/hostednews/ap/article/ALeqM5j2ko8XmNnDdfLpPq8-yzHfOJW7qw?docId=403f48e97cc24ef798851866b62da067 (accessed May 2013).

Bahle, T. (2003), 'The changing institutionalization of social services in England and Wales, France and Germany: is the welfare state on the retreat?', *Journal of European Social Policy*, **13** (1), 5–20.

Bannink, D. and M. Hoogenboom (2007), 'Hidden change: disaggregation of welfare regimes for greater insight into welfare state change', *Journal of European Social Policy*, **17** (1), 19–32.

Barnes, H., P. Sissons and H. Stevens (2010), 'Employment and support allowance: findings from a face-to-face survey of customers', *Research Report No. 707*, London: Department for Work and Pensions.

Barro, R.J. (1991), 'Small is beautiful', *Wall Street Journal*, October 11.

Barry, M. and J. Reveley (2002), 'Contradictory rights and unintended consequences: the early impact of the Employment Relations Act on the New Zealand waterfront', *The Journal of Industrial Relations*, **44** (4), 508–24.

Begg, I. and D. Mayes (1991), 'Social and economic cohesion among the regions of Europe in the 1990s', *National Institute Economic Review*, **138**, 63–74.

Bellis, A., M. Sigala and S. Dewson (2011), 'Employer engagement and Jobcentre Plus', *Research Report No. 742*, London: Department for Work and Pensions.

Benarrosh, Y. (2000), 'Tri des chômeurs: le nécessaire consensus des acteurs de l'emploi: acteurs locaux de l'emploi', *Travail et Emploi*, **81**, 9–26.

Benz, A. (2007), 'Accountable multilevel governance by the open method of coordination?', *European Law Journal*, **13** (4), 505–22.

Berman, P. (1998), 'National Health Insurance in Poland: a coach without horses?', *Harvard School of Public Health Publications*, available at http://www.hsph.harvard.edu/ihsg/publications/pdf/No–63.pdf (accessed 14 October 2009).

Berman, P.A. and T.J. Bossert (2000), 'A decade of health sector reform in developing countries: what have we learned?', *Harvard School of Public Health Publications*, available at http://www.hsph.harvard.edu/ihsg/publications/pdf/closeout.PDF (accessed 14 October 2009).

Besley, T. and S. Coate (2003), 'Centralized versus decentralized provision of local public goods: a political economy approach', *Journal of Public Economics*, **87** (12), 2611–37.

Biffl, G. (2007), 'The European employment strategy: a new form of governance of labour markets in the European Union', *WIFO Working Papers*, **301**, 1–14.

Bjorvatn, K. and A.W. Cappelen (2003), 'Inequality, segregation, and redistribution', *Journal of Public Economics*, **87** (7–8), 1657–79.

Blanken, A., G. Dewulf and M. Bult-Spiering (2009), 'The private finance initiative in the English health sector', in B. Rechel, J. Erskine, B. Dowdeswell, S. Wright and N. McKee (eds), *Capital Investment for Health: Case Studies from Europe*, Copenhagen, World Health Organisation on behalf of the European Observatory on Health Systems and Policies, pp. 123–42.

Bode, I. (2006), 'Disorganized welfare mixes: voluntary agencies and new governance regimes in Western Europe', *Journal of European Social Policy*, **16** (4), 346–59.

Boeri, T. (2002), 'Let social policy models compete and Europe will win', paper presented at a Conference hosted by the Kennedy School of Government, Harvard University, 11–12 April.

Boeri, T., J.I. Conde-Ruiz and V. Galasso (2006), 'The political economy of flexicurity', *FEDEA Working Paper*, **15**, 1–46.

Boltanski, L. and E. Chiapello (1999), *Le nouvel esprit du capitalisme*, Paris: Gallimard.

Bonoli, G. (1997), 'Classfying welfare states: a two-dimension approach', *Journal of Social Policy*, **26** (3), 351–72.

Bonoli, G. and Natali, D. (2012), *The Politics of the New Welfare State*, Oxford: Oxford University Press.

Bonvin, J.–M. and M. Orton (2009), 'Activation policies and organisational innovation: the added value of the capability approach', *International Journal of Sociology and Social Policy*, **29** (11–12), 565–74.

Borck, R. (2007), 'Voting, inequality and redistribution', *Journal of Economic Surveys*, **21** (1), 90–109.

Borrás, S. and T. Conzelmann (2007), 'Democracy, legitimacy and soft modes of governance in the EU: the empirical turn', *Journal of European Integration*, **29** (5), 531–48.

Borrás, S. and C. Radaelli (2010), *Recalibrating the Open Method of Coordination*, Stockholm, Swedish Institute of European Policy Studies.

Borrás, S. and C. Radaelli (2011), 'The politics of governance architectures: creation, change and effects of the EU Lisbon Strategy', *Journal of European Public Policy*, **18** (4), 463–84.

Börzel, T. and T. Risse (2012), 'When Europeanisation meets diffusion: exploring new territory', *West European Politics*, **35** (1), 192–207.

Bossert, T. and C. Wlodarczyk (2000), 'Unpredictable politics: policy process and health reform in Poland', *Harvard School of Public Health Publications*, available at http://www.hsph.harvard.edu/ihsg/publications/pdf/No–74.PDF (accessed 14 October 2009).

Boudreau, J.A. (2003), 'Questioning the use of "local democracy" as a discursive strategy for political mobilization in Los Angeles, Montreal and Toronto', *International Journal of Urban and Regional Research*, **27** (4), 793–810.

Bourdieu, P. and J. Passeron (1977), *Reproduction in Education, Society and Culture*, London, Beverly Hills: Sage Publications.

Bray, M. (1999), 'Control of education: issues and tensions in centralization and decentralization', in R.F. Arnove and C.A. Torres (eds),

Comparative Education: The Dialectic of the Global and the Local, Boston, Oxford: Roman and Littlefield, pp. 207–33.

Bredgaard, T. and F. Larsen (2007), 'Implementing public employment policy: what happens when non-public agencies take over?', *International Journal of Sociology and Social Policy*, **27** (7–8), 287–300.

Bredgaard, T. and F. Larsen (2008), 'Redesigning the governance of employment policies: decentralised centralisation in municipal job-centres', paper presented at CARMA's 25th Annual Conference, Aalborg University, Denmark, 10 October.

Briffault, R. (1999), 'Government for our time: business improvement districts and urban governance', *Columbia Law Review*, **99**, 365.

Broadbent, J. and R. Laughlin (2005), 'The role of PFI in the UK's modernisation agenda', *Financial Accountability and Management*, **21** (1), 75–97.

Brodie, J. (2000), 'Imagining democratic urban citizenship', in E.F. Ishin (ed.), *Democracy, Citizenship and the Global City*, London: Routledge, pp. 110–28.

Brooks, L. (2008), 'Volunteering to be taxed: business improvement districts and the extra-governmental provision of public safety', *Journal of Public Economics*, **92** (1–2), 388–406.

Büchs, M. (2008), 'How legitimate is the open method of co-ordination?', *Journal of Common Market Studies*, **46** (4), pp. 765–86.

Cameron, D. (2009), *David Cameron: People Power – Reforming Quangos*, available at http://www.conservatives.com/ News/Speeches/2009/ 07/David_Cameron_People_Power_–_Reforming_Quangos.aspx (accessed 12 October 2011).

Carmel, E. and T. Papadopoulos (2009), 'Governing social security: from protection to markets', in J. Millar (ed.), *Understanding Social Security: Issues for Social Policy and Practice*, Bristol: Policy Press, pp. 93–110.

Caruso, G. and R. Weber (2008), 'Getting the max for tax: an examination of BID performance measures', in G. Morçöl, L. Hoyt, J. Meek and U. Zimmermann (eds), *Business Improvement Districts: Research, Theories, and Controversies*, Florida: CRC Press, pp. 319–49.

Casey, B.H. (2004), 'Pension reform in the Baltic States: convergence with "Europe" or with "the world"', *International Social Security Review*, **57** (1), 19–45.

Cash, B. (2000), 'European integration and government: dangers for the United States', *Chicago Journal of International Law*, **1** (2), 315–22.

Castells, M. (1996), *The Rise of the Network Society, the Information Age: Economy, Society and Culture*, **1**, Cambridge: Polity Press.

Castles, F.G. (1998), *Comparative Public Policy: Patterns of Post-war Transformation*, Cheltenham, UK and Northampton, MA, USA: Edgar Elgar.

Castles, F.G. and D. Mitchell (1993), 'Worlds of welfare and families of nations', in F.G. Castles (ed.), *Families of Nations: Patterns of Public Policy in Western Democracies*, Aldershot: Dartmouth, pp. 93–128.

Castra, D. and A. Pascual (2003), 'L'insertion professionnelle des publics précaires: une alternative au recrutement concurrentiel', *Revue Européenne de Psychologie Appliquée*, **53** (3–4), 167–78.

Cerami, A. (2011), 'Social mechanisms in the establishment of the European economic and monetary union', *Politics & Policy*, **39** (3), 345–72.

CESifo (2012), *CESifo Forum 13*, Special Issue (January), Munich: CESifo.

Chassard, Y. (2001), 'European integration and social protection: from the Spaak report to the open method of co-ordination', in D. Mayes, J. Berghman and R. Salais (eds), *Social Exclusion and European Policy*, Cheltenham, UK and Northampton, MA, USA: Edward Elgar, pp. 227–305.

Chawla, M., P. Berman and D. Kawiorska (1998), 'Financing health services in Poland: new evidence on private expenditures', *Health Economics*, **7**, 337–46.

Christensen, T. and P. Laegried (2001), 'New public management: the effects of contractualism and devolution on political control', *Public Management Review*, **3** (1), 73–94.

Coca-Stefaniak, J.A., R. Rinaldi, C. Parker and S. Quinn (2009), 'Evolution of town centre and place management models: a European perspective', *Cities*, **26** (2), 74–80.

Collins, J.L. (2008), 'The specter of slavery: workfare and the economic citizenship of poor women', in J.L. Collins, M. di Leonardo and B. Williams (eds), *New Landscapes of Inequality: Neoliberalism and the Erosion of Democracy in America*, Santa Fe: School for Advanced Research Press, pp. 131–51.

Congleton, R.D. (2007), 'On the feasibility of a liberal welfare state: agency and exit costs in income security clubs', *Constitutional Political Economy*, **18** (3), 145–59.

Cook, I.R. (2008), 'Mobilising urban policies: the policy transfer of US business improvement districts to England and Wales', *Urban Studies*, **45** (4), 773–95.

CoR (Committee of the Regions) (2009), *White Paper on Multi-level Governance*, CONST–IV–020, Brussels.

Coulter, F., C. Heady, C. Lawson and S. Smith (1997), 'Social security reform for economic transition: the case of the Czech Republic', *Journal of Public Economics*, **66** (2), 313–26.

Craig, P. (2010), *The Lisbon Treaty: Law, Politics, and Treaty Reform*, Oxford: Oxford University Press.

Cremers, J., J.E. Dolvik and G. Bosch (2007), 'Posting of workers in the single market: attempts to prevent social dumping and regime competition in the EU', *Industrial Relations Journal*, **38** (6), 524–41.

Cruikshank, B. (1999), *The Will to Empower: Democratic Citizens and Other Subjects*, Ithaca: Cornell University Press.

Cummings, W.K. and A. Riddell (1994), 'Alternative policies for the finance, control, and delivery of basic education', *International Journal of Educational Research*, **21** (8), 751–76.

Cutright, P. (1965), 'Political structure, economic development, and national social security programs', *American Journal of Sociology*, **70** (5), 537–50.

Daguerre, A. (2004), 'Importing workfare: policy transfer of social and labour market policies from the USA to Britain under New Labour', *Social Policy and Administration*, **38** (1), 41–56.

Dalziel, P. (2002), 'New Zealand's economic reforms: an assessment', *Review of Political Economy*, **14** (1), 31–46.

Damgaard, B. and J. Torfing (2010), 'Network governance of active employment policy: the Danish experience', *Journal of European Social Policy*, **20** (3), 248–62.

Dannin, E. (1997), *Working Free: The Origins and Impact of New Zealand's Employment Contracts Act*, Auckland: Auckland University Press.

Daun, H. (2006), 'Privatisation, decentralisation and governance in education in the Czech Republic, England, France, Germany, and Sweden', in J. Zajda (ed.), *Decentralisation and Privatisation in Education: The Role of the State*, Dordrecht: Springer, pp. 75–97.

Davies, S. and L. Quirke (2007), 'The impact of sector on school organizations: institutional and market logics', *Sociology of Education*, **80** (1), 66.

Davis, G., B. Sullivan and A. Yeatman (1997), *The New Contractualism?*, Nathan: Centre for Australian Public Sector Management, Griffith University.

Davis, H.S.J. (1993), *The Growth of Government by Appointment – Implications for Local Democracy*, Luton: LGMB.

Dawson, W.H. (1973 [1890]), *Bismarck and State Socialism: An Exposition of the Social and Economic Legislation of Germany since 1870*, London: Swan Sonnenschein.

Dawson, M. (2009), 'EU law "transformed"? Evaluating accountability and subsidiarity in the "streamlined" OMC for social inclusion and social protection', in S. Kröger (ed.), *What We Have Learnt: Advances, Pitfalls and Remaining Questions in OMC Research*, European Integration online Papers (EIoP), **13** (8), 1–15, available at http://eiop.or.at/eiop/texte/2009–008a.htm (accessed 15 March 2010).

De Grauwe, P. (2011), 'What kind of governance for the eurozone?', in W. Meeusen (ed.), *The Economic Crisis and European Integrationi*, Cheltenham, UK and Northampton, MA, USA: Edward Elgar, pp. 7–16.

De Rougemont, D. (1966), *The Idea of Europe*, New York: Macmillan.

De Vries, M.S. (2000), 'The rise and fall of decentralization: a comparative analysis of arguments and practices in European countries', *European Journal of Political Research*, **38** (2), 193–224.

Deacon, B. (2000), 'Eastern European welfare states: the impact of the politics of globalization', *Journal of European Social Policy*, **10** (2), 146–61.

Deakin, N. (2002), 'Public-private partnerships: a UK case study', *Public Management Review*, **4** (2), 133–47.

Dean, H., J.-M. Bonvin, P. Vielle and N. Farvaque (2005), 'Developing capabilities and rights in welfare-to-work policies', *European Societies*, **7** (1), 3–26.

Department of Health (2010), *Liberating the NHS: Report of the Arm's Length Bodies Review*, available at http://www.dh.gov.uk/prod_consum_dh/groups/dh_digitalassets/@dh/@en/@ps/documents/digitalasset/dh_118053.pdf (accessed May 2013).

Diamond, P. (2006), 'Optimal tax treatment of private contributions for public goods with and without warm glow preferences', *Journal of Public Economics*, **90** (4–5), 897–919.

Directorate-General for Economic and Financial Affairs (2011a), 'The economic adjustment programme for Greece: Fifth review – October 2011', *European Economy Occasional Papers 87*, available at http://ec.europa.eu/economy_finance/publications/occasional_paper/2011/pdf/ocp87_en.pdf: European Commission (accessed May 2013).

Directorate-General for Economic and Financial Affairs (2011b), 'The economic adjustment programme for Portugal: Second review – Autumn 2011', *European Economy Occasional Papers 89*, available at http://ec.europa.eu/economy_finance/publications/occasional_paper/2011/pdf/ocp89_en.pdf: European Commission (accessed May 2013).

Dobbins, T. (2005), 'Irish ferries dispute finally resolved after bitter standoff', *Industrial Relations News*, available at http://www.eurofound.europa.eu/eiro/2005/12/feature/ie0512203f.htm (accessed 30 September 2010).

Dolowitz, D. and D. Marsh (1996), 'Who learns what from whom: a review of the policy transfer literature', *Political Studies*, **44**, 343–57.

Donelly, L. (2009), 'NHS quango bosses have seen their salaries increase by up to 77 per cent', *The Telegraph*, available at http://www.telegraph.co.uk/health/ healthnews/4333813/NHS-quango-bosses-enjoy-pay-boosts-of-up-to-77-per-cent.html (accessed August 2011).

Dostal, J.M. (2008), 'The workfare illusion: re-examining the concept and the British case', *Social Policy & Administration*, **42** (1), 19–42.

Drøpping, J.A., B. Hvinden and K. Vik (1999), 'Activation policies in the Nordic countries', in M. Kautto (ed.), *Nordic Social Policy: Changing Welfare States*, London: Routledge, pp. 133–58.

Duina, F. and T. Raunio (2007), 'The open method of coordination and national parliaments: further marginalization or new opportunities?', *Journal of European Public Policy*, **14** (4), 489–506.

Dulmus, C.N., L. Paglicci, S. Rapp, J. Dennis, J.S. Wodarski and M.D. Feit (2000), 'Workfare programs', *Journal of Human Behavior in the Social Environment*, **3** (2), pp. 1–12.

Dworkin, A.G. (2005), 'The No Child Left Behind Act: accountability, high-stakes testing, and roles for sociologists', *Sociology of Education*, **78** (2), 170.

Ebbinghaus, B. (1999), 'Does a European social model exist and can it survive?', in G. Huemer, M. Mesch and F. Traxler (eds), *The Role of Employer Associations and Labour Unions in the EU*, Aldershot: Ashgate, pp. 1–26.

Ebbinghaus, B. (2011), 'The varieties of pension governance. Pension privatization in Europe', in B. Ebbinghaus (ed.), *The Varieties of Pension Governance. Pension Privatization in Europe*, Oxford: Oxford University Press, pp. 3–22.

Edquist, K. (2006), 'EU social-policy governance: advocating activism or servicing states?', *Journal of European Public Policy*, **13** (4), 500–18.

Edwards, J. and M. Keen (1996), 'Tax competition and Leviathan', *European Economic Review*, **40**, 113–34.

Elcock, H. (1994), *Local Government*, 3rd Edition, London: Routledge.

Enjolras, B., J.L. Laville, L. Fraisse and H. Trickey (2001), 'Between subsidiarity and social assistance – the French republican route to activation', in I. Lødemel and H. Trickey (eds), *'An Offer You Can't Refuse': Workfare in International Perspective*, Bristol: Policy Press, pp. 41–70.

Epple, D. and H. Sieg (1999), 'Estimating equilibrium models of local jurisdictions', *Journal of Political Economy*, **107** (4), 645–81.

Epple, D., A. Zelenitz and M. Visscher (1978), 'A search for testable implications of the Tiebout Hypothesis', *Journal of Political Economy*, **86** (3), 405–25.

Erdmann, Y. (1998), 'The development of social benefits and social policy in Poland, Hungary and the Slovak Republic since the system transformation', *East European Quarterly*, **32** (3), 301–14.

Erhel, C., L. Mandin, and B. Pallier (2005), 'The leverage effect. The open method of coordination in France', in J. Zeitlin, P. Pochet and L. Magnusson (eds), *The Open Method of Coordination in Action: The European Employment and Social Inclusion Strategies*, Brussels: Peter Lang, pp. 217–47.

Eriksen, E.O. and J.E. Fossum (2007), 'A done deal? The EU's legitimacy conundrum revisited', *RECON Online Working Paper*, **16**, 1–21.

Esping-Andersen, G. (1990), *The Three Worlds of Welfare Capitalism*, Cambridge: Polity Press.

Esping-Andersen, G. (1996), *Welfare States in Transition*, London: Sage.

Esping-Andersen, G. (1997), 'Hybrid or unique? The Japanese welfare state between Europe and America', *Journal of European Social Policy*, **7** (3), 179–89.

Esping-Andersen, G. (1999), *Social Foundations of Post-industrial Economies*, Oxford: Oxford University Press.

European Commission (n.d.-a), 'Bulgaria: operational programme "transport"', *Regional Policy – Inforegio*, available at http://ec.europa.eu/regional_policy/country/prordn/details_new.cfm?gv_PAY=BG&gv_reg=ALL&gv_PGM=1005&LAN=7&gv_per=2&gv_defL=7 (accessed 13 April 2010).

European Commission (n.d.-b), 'Economic, social and territorial cohesion', *Glossary*, available at http://europa.eu/scadplus/glossary/economic_social_cohesion_en.htm (accessed 16 March 2010).

European Commission (n.d.-c), 'The European structural funds: a solidarity policy', *Regional Policy – Inforegio*, available at http://ec.europa.eu/regional_policy/atlas/factsheets/pdf/fact_eu25_en.pdf (accessed 15 March 2009).

European Commission (n.d.-d), 'Structural funds and cohesion fund', *Glossary*, available at http://europa.eu/scadplus/glossary/structural_cohesion_fund_en.htm (accessed 15 March 2010).

European Commission (2000), *Comparative Social Inclusion Policies and Citizenship in Europe: Towards a New European Social Model*, Directorate General for Research, Brussels, May.

European Commission (2006), *Time to Move Up a Gear. Annual Progress Report on Growth and Jobs*, Brussels, available at http://europa.eu.int/growthandjobs/annual-report_en.htm (accessed 15 March 2010).

European Commission (2007), 'Communication on the posting of workers in the framework of the provision of services – maximising its benefits and potential while guaranteeing the protection of workers', available at http://europa.eu/rapid/pressReleasesAction.do?reference= MEMO/07/239&format=HTML&aged=0&language=EN&guiLanguage =en (accessed 13 February 2010).

European Commission (2008), 'EU calls for urgent action to improve working conditions for 1 million posted workers', available at: http:// europa.eu/rapid/pressReleasesAction.do?reference=IP/08/514&format= HTML&aged=0&language=EN&guiLanguage=en (accessed 15 February 2010).

European Commission (2010), 'News and Events', *European Social Fund*, available at http://ec.europa.eu/employment_social/esf/news/ (accessed 1 March 2010).

European Commission (2010a), *Lisbon Strategy Evaluation Document*, SEC(2010) 114 final, Brussels, February 2.

European Commission (2010b), *Europe 2020: A Strategy for Smart, Sustainable and Inclusive Growth*, COM(2010)2020, Brussels, March 3.

European Commission (2011), *Proposal for a Regulation on Common Provisions for Monitoring and Assessing Draft Budgetary Plans and Ensuring the Correction of Excessive Deficit of the Member States in the Euro Area*, COM(2011)821 final, Brussels, 23 November.

European Commission (2011a), 'Your social security rights in Greece', available at http://ec.europa.eu/employment_social/empl_portal/SSRin EU/Your%20social%20security%20rights%20in%20Greece_en.pdf

European Council (2000), *Conclusions*, summit at Lisbon, March 22–23.

Falconer, P. (2005), 'New Labour and the modernisation of public services', *Public Policy and Administration*, **20**, 81–5.

Falkner, G. (2007), 'The EU's Social Dimension', in M. Cini and N.P.-S. Borragan (eds), *European Union Politics* (2nd ed.), Oxford: Oxford University Press, pp. 268–80.

Falkner, G. (2009), 'European integration and the welfare state(s) in Europe', Working Paper, **3**, Vienna: Institute for European Integration Research, Austrian Academy of Sciences, pp. 1–27.

Farrugia, B. and J. O'Connell (2008), *ACA to YJB: A Guide to the UK's Semi-Autonomous Public Bodies: 2007–08*, TaxPayers' Alliance, available at http://www.taxpayersalliance.com/sapb.pdf (accessed 7 April 2013).

Ferguson, J. (1985), *The Anti-politics Machine: 'Development', Depoliticization, and Bureaucratic Power in Lesotho*, Minneapolis: University of Minnesota Press.

Ferreira, S. (2003), 'The past in the present Portuguese social security reform', paper for the inaugural ESPAnet conference 'Changing European societies – the role for social policy', organised by the Danish National Institute of Social Research, Copenhagen, 13–15 November.

Ferrera, M. (1996), 'The "southern" model of welfare in social Europe', *Journal of European Social Policy*, **6** (1), 17–37.

Ferrera, M., A. Hemerijck and M. Rhodes (2001), 'The future of the European "social model" in the global economy', *Journal of Comparative Analysis: Research and Practice*, **3**, 163–90.

Finn, D. (2008), 'The British "welfare market": lessons from contracting out welfare to work programmes in Australia and the Netherlands', Joseph Rowntree Foundation, available at www.jrf.org.uk/publications/lessons-contracting-out-welfare-work-programmes-australia-and-netherlands (accessed 16 January 2013).

Fischer, T. and A.S. Hoffmann (2012), 'European economic governance: what about the social dimension?', in K. Nicolaïdis, S. Hare, G. Bajnai, V. Rossi, S. Hoffmann, A. Watt, J. Viehoff and T. Fischer (eds), *Solidarity: For Sale? The Social Dimension of the New European Economic Governance*, Gütersloh: Bertelsmann Stiftung, pp. 9–22.

Flear, M. (2009), 'The open method of coordination on health care after the Lisbon Strategy II: towards a neoliberal framing?', in S. Kröger (ed.), *What We Have Learnt: Advances, Pitfalls and Remaining Questions in OMC Research*, European Integration online Papers (EIoP), **13** (12), 1–16, available at http://eiop.or.at/eiop/texte/2009012a.htm (accessed 15 March 2010).

Flinders, M. (1999), 'Setting the scene: quangos in context', in M. Flinders and M.J. Smith (eds), *Quangos: Accountability and Reform*, Hampshire: Macmillan, pp. 3–16.

Flinders, M. (2004), 'MPs and icebergs: parliament and delegated governance', *Parliamentary Affairs*, **57** (4), pp. 767–84.

Flinders, M. and M. Cole (1999), 'Opening or closing Pandora's box? New Labour and the quango state', *Talking Politics*, **12** (1), 234–39.

Frediani, A.A. (n.d.), 'Participatory methods and the capability approach', HDCA – Human Development and Capability Association, available at: www.capabilityapproach.com/pubs/Briefing_on_PM_and_CA2.pdf (accessed 16 January 2013).

Fyfe, N.R. and C. Milligan (2003), 'Out of the shadows: exploring contemporary geographies of voluntarism', *Progress in Human Geography*, **27** (4), 397–413.

Garfinkel, I., L. Rainwater and T.M. Smeeding (2006), 'A re-examination of welfare states and inequality in rich nations: how in-kind transfers and indirect taxes change the story', *Journal of Policy Analysis and Management*, **25** (4), 897–919.

Gash, T., I. Magee, J. Rutter and N. Smith (2010), *Read Before Burning*, Institute for Government, available at http://www.institutefor government.org.uk/publications/6/ (accessed May 2013).

Gay, O. (2010), 'Quangos', *Key Issues for the New Parliament 2010*, available at http://www.parliament.uk/documents/commons/lib/research/ key_issues/Key%20Issues%20Quangos.pdf (accessed May 2013).

Giddens, A. (1996), 'T.H. Marshall, the state and democracy', in M. Bulmer and A.M. Rees (eds), *Citizenship Today: the Contemporary Relevance of T.H. Marshall*, London: UCL Press, pp. 65–80.

Giddens, A. (1998), *The Third Way: The Renewal of Social Democracy*, Cambridge: Polity Press.

Goetschy, J. (2009), 'The Lisbon Strategy and social Europe: two closely linked destinies', in M.J. Rodrigues (ed.), *Europe, Globalization and the Lisbon Agenda*, Cheltenham, UK and Northampton, MA, USA: Edward Elgar.

Golinowska, S. (2009), 'The national model of the welfare state in Poland. Tradition and changes', in S. Golinowska, P. Hengstenberg and M. Żukowski (eds), *Diversity and Commonality in European Social Policies: The Forging of a European Social Model*, Warsaw: Friedrich Ebert Stiftung and Wydawnictwo Nauwkowe Scholar, pp. 213–60.

Golinowska, S. and M. Żukowski (2009), 'Diversity, similarity and commonality', in S. Golinowska, P. Hengstenberg and M. Żukowski (eds), *Diversity and Commonality in European Social Policies: The Forging of a European Social Model*, Warsaw: Friedrich Ebert Stiftung and Wydawnictwo Nauwkowe Scholar, pp. 323–78.

Golinowska, S., P. Hengstenberg and M. Żukowski (eds) (2009), *Diversity and Commonality in European Social Policies: The Forging of a European Social Model*, Warsaw: Friedrich Ebert Stiftung and Wydawnictwo Nauwkowe Scholar.

Goode, J. and J. Maskovsky (2001), *The New Poverty Studies: The Ethnography of Power, Politics, and Impoverished People in the United States*, New York and London: New York University Press.

Goodin, R.E., B. Headey, R.J.A. Muffels and H. Dirven (1999), *The Real Worlds of Welfare Capitalism*, New York: Cambridge University Press.

Gough, I. (2000), 'Welfare regimes in East Asia and Europe: comparisons and lessons', *Annual World Bank Conference on Development Economics*, Paris.

Goul Andersen, J. and M.B. Carstensen (2009), 'The Welfare State and welfare reforms in Denmark', in S. Golinowska, P. Hengstenberg and M. Żukowski (eds), *Diversity and Commonality in European Social Politics: The Forging of a European Social Model*, Warszawa: Friedrich Ebert Stiftung, pp. 70–109.

Government of the Republic of Lithuania (2011), Convergence programme of Lithuania of 2011: Official translation, available at http://ec.europa.eu/europe2020/pdf/cp_lithuania_en.pdf (accessed May 2013).

Gray, A. (2004), *Unsocial Europe: Social Protection or Flexploitation?*, London: Pluto Press.

Graziano, P.R. (2011), 'Europeanization and domestic employment policy change: conceptual and methodological background', *Governance: An International Journal of Policy, Administration, and Institutions*, **24** (3), 583–605.

Graziano, P., S. Jacquot and B. Palier (2011), *The EU and the Domestic Politics of the Welfare State Reforms*, Basingstoke: Palgrave Macmillan.

Greenaway, J., B. Salter and S. Hart (2007), 'How policy networks can damage democratic health: a case study in the government of governance', *Public Administration*, **85** (3), 717–38.

Greenwood, J.R., R. Pyper and D.J. Wilson (2002), *New Public Administration in Britain*, Oxford: Routledge.

Greve, C. (1999), 'Quangos in Denmark and Scandinavia: trends, problems and perspectives', in M. Flinders and M.J. Smith (eds), *Quangos: Accountability and Reform*, London: Macmillan, pp. 93–108.

Greve, C. (2000), 'Governance by contract: creating public-private partnerships in Denmark', in Y. Fortin and H. van Hassel (eds), *Contracting in the New Public Management: From Economics to Law and Citizenship*, Amsterdam: IOS Press, pp. 49–66.

Greve, C., M. Flinders and S. van Thiel (1999), 'Quangos – What's in a name? Defining quangos from a comparative perspective', *Governance: An International Journal of Policy and Administration*, **12** (2), 129–46.

Grimshaw, D., S. Vincent and H. Willmott (2002), 'Going privately: partnership and outsourcing in UK public services', *Public Administration*, **80** (3), 475–502.

Gross, J.S. (2008), 'Business improvement districts in New York City's low- and high-income neighbourhoods', in G. Morçöl, L. Hoyt, J. Meek and U. Zimmermann (eds), *Business Improvement Districts: Research, Theories and Controversies*, Florida: CRC Press, pp. 221–49.

Habicht, J. and A.E. Kunst (2005), 'Social inequalities in health care services utilisation after eight years of health care reforms: a cross-sectional study of Estonia, 1999', *Social Science & Medicine*, **60** (4), 777–87.

Hamilton, G. (2002), *Moving People from Welfare to Work: Lessons from the National Evaluation of Welfare-to-Work Strategies*, Final Report to the U.S. Department of Health and Human Services, Washington, DC.

Handler, J.F. (2003), 'Social citizenship and workfare in the US and Western Europe: from status to contract', *Journal of European Social Policy*, **13** (3), 229–43.

Handler, J.F. (2004), *Social Citizenship and Workfare in the United States and Western Europe: the Paradox of Inclusion*, Cambridge and New York: Cambridge University Press.

Handler, J.F. (2009), 'Welfare, workfare, and citizenship in the developed world', *Annual Review of Law and Social Science*, **5**, 71–90.

Haney, L.H. (1911), *History of Economic Thought: A Critical Account of the Origin and Development of the Economic Theories of the Leading Thinkers in the Leading Nations*, New York: The Macmillan Company.

Hantrais, L. (2000), *Social Policy in the European Union*, Basingstoke: Macmillan.

Hartlapp, M. (2009), 'Learning about policy learning. Reflections on the European employment strategy', in S. Kröger (ed.), *What We Have Learnt: Advances, Pitfalls and Remaining Questions in OMC Research*, European Integration online Papers (EIoP), **13** (7), 1–16, available at http://eiop.or.at/eiop/texte/2009-007a.htm (accessed 15 March 2010).

Hartman, L. (2011), *Konkurrensens konsekvenser: vad hander med svneks välfärd*, Stockholm: SNS Förlag.

Hasenfeld, Y. and D. Weaver (1996), 'Enforcement, compliance, and disputes in welfare-to-work programs', *The Social Service Review*, **70** (2), 235–56.

Häusermann, S. (2012), 'The politics of old and new social policies', in G. Bonoli and D. Natali, *The Politics of the New Welfare State*, Oxford: Oxford University Press, pp. 111–34.

Hay, C. (2007), 'What doesn't kill you can only make you stronger: the Doha development round, the Services Directive and the EU's conception of competitiveness', *Journal of Common Market Studies*, **45** (Annual Review), 25–43.

Hay, C. and D. Richards (2000), 'The tangled webs of Westminster and Whitehall: the discourse, strategy and practice of networking with the British core executive', *Public Administration*, **78**, 1–28.

Hay, C., M. Watson and D. Wincott (1999), 'Globalisation, European integration and the persistence of European social models', *POLSIS*, Birmingham: University of Birmingham.

Hayek, F. von (1944), *The Road to Serfdom*, London: Routledge.

Haynes, P., P. Boxall and K. Macky (2006), 'Union reach, the "representation gap" and the prospects for unionism in New Zealand', *Journal of Industrial Relations*, **48** (2), 193–216.

Heidenreich, M. (2009), 'The open method of coordination: a pathway to the gradual transformation of national employment and welfare regimes', in M. Heidenreich and J. Zeitlin (eds), *Changing European Employment and Welfare Regimes*, Abingdon: Routledge, pp. 10–36.

Heidenreich, M. and G. Bischoff (2008), 'The open method of co-ordination: a way to the Europeanization of social and employment policies?', *Journal of Common Market Studies*, **46** (3), 497–532.

Heinelt, H., D. Sweeting and P. Getimis (eds) (2006), *Legitimacy and Urban Governance: A Cross-National Comparative Study*, London and New York: Routledge.

Hellowell, M. and A. Pollock (2007), *Private Finance, Public Deficits: A Report on the Cost of PFI and its Impact on Health Services in England*, Centre for International Public Health Policy, University of Edinburgh, Edinburgh, pp. 1–40.

Hellowell, M. and A. Pollock (2009), 'The private financing of NHS hospitals: politics, policy and practice', *Institute of Economic Affairs*, 13–19.

Hemerijck, A. (2012), *Changing Welfare States*, Oxford: Oxford University Press.

Hengstenberg, P. (2009), 'Foreword', in S. Golinowska, P. Hengstenberg and M. Żukowski (eds), *Diversity and Commonality in European Social Policies: The Forging of a European Social Model*, Warsaw: Friedrich-Ebert-Stiftung and Wydawnictwo Nauwkowe Scholar, pp. 9–12.

Hepburn, E. (2008), 'The rise and fall of a "Europe of the Regions"', *Regional & Federal Studies*, **18** (5), 537–55.

Hettne, J. (2010), 'Kan Lissabonfördraget minska EU:s sociala underskott?', *European Policy Analysis*, **4**, The Swedish Institute for European Studies, Stockholm, pp. 1–15.

Hodson, D. and I. Maher (2001), 'The open method as a new mode of governance: the case of soft economic policy co-ordination', *Journal of Common Market Studies*, **39** (4), 719–46.

Hogwood, B.W. (1995), 'The "growth" of quangos: evidence and explanations', *Parliamentary Affairs: A Journal of Comparative Politics*, **48** (2), 207–25.

Holle, P. (2010), 'What New Zealand might learn from local government amalgamation in Canada', Law and Economics Association of New Zealand, Auckland, 24 February.

Holzmann, R. (2013), 'Global pension systems and their reform: world-wide drivers, trends and challenges', *International Social Security Review*, **66** (2), 1–29.

Hood, C. and G.F. Schuppert (1988), 'The study of para-government organisations', in C. Hood and G.F. Schuppert (eds), *Delivering Public Services in Western Europe: Sharing Western European Experience of Para-government Organisation*, London: Sage, pp. 1–26.

Horstmann, I.J. and K.A. Scharf (2008), 'A theory of distributional conflict, voluntarism and segregation', *Economic Journal*, **118** (527), 427–53.

Horvath, A. (2009), 'What kind of consensus? Conflicting notions of effectiveness within the Social Protection Committee', in S. Kröger (ed.), *What We Have Learnt: Advances, Pitfalls and Remaining Questions in OMC research*, European Integration online Papers (EIoP), **13** (12), 1–16, available at http://eiop.or.at/eiop/index.php/eiop/article/view/2009_017a/125 (accessed 15 March 2010).

House of Commons (2006), *The Refinancing of the Norfolk and Norwich PFI Hospital*, London: House of Commons Committee of Public Accounts.

Hudson, M., J. Phillips, K. Ray, S. Vegeris and R. Davidson (2010), 'The influence of outcome-based contracting on Provider-led Pathways to Work', *Research Report No. 638*, London: Department for Work and Pensions.

Huffschmid, J. (2005), *Economic Policy for a Social Europe: A Critique of Neo-liberalism and Proposals for Alternatives*, Basingstoke and New York: Palgrave Macmillan.

Hyatt, S. (2008), 'The Obama victory, asset-based community development and the re-politicization of community organizing', *North American Dialogue*, **11** (2), 17–26.

INBAS GmbH/ENGENDER asbl. (2009), Country reports, in *Study on Stakeholders' Involvement in the Implementation of the Open Method of Coordination (OMC) in Social Protection and Social Inclusion*, Vienna, available at http://www.stakeholders-socialinclusion.eu/site/en (accessed 6 May 2010).

INBAS GmbH/ENGENDER asbl. (2010), *Discussion Paper for the Working Seminar on Stakeholder Involvement in the Implementation of the Social Inclusion Strand of the Open Method of Coordination*, Vienna, available at http://www.stakeholders-socialinclusion.eu/site/en (accessed 6 May 2010).

Irwin, N. (2010), 'The contagion effect: Greece's debt crisis could spread across Europe', *Washington Post*, 7 May, available at http://www.washingtonpost.com/wp-dyn/content/article/2010/05/07/AR2010050700642.html (accessed 10 May 2010).

Jepsen, M. and A. Serrano Pascual (2006), *Unwrapping the European Social Model*, Bristol: Policy Press.

Jessop, B. (1999), 'The changing governance of welfare: recent trends in its primary functions, scale, and modes of coordination', *Social Policy and Administration*, **33** (4), 348–59.

Jessop, B. (2002), *The Future of the Capitalist State*, Cambridge: Polity Press.

Jobelius, S. (2003), *Who Formulates European Employment Guidelines?*, Paper presented at the ESPAnet *Changing European Societies – The Role of Social Policy* conference, Copenhagen, Denmark, 13–15 November.

Joerges, C. (2007), 'Democracy and European integration: a legacy of tensions, a reconceptualization and recent true conflicts', *EUI Working Paper Law*, **25**, 1–28, European University Institute, San Domenico di Fiesole.

Jones, K., C. Cunchillos, J. Klausenitzer, N. Hirth, R. Hatcher, R. Innes and S. Johsua (2008), *Schooling in Western Europe: The New Order and its Adversaries*, Houndmills: Palgrave Macmillan.

Jørgensen, H. and P. Kongshøj Madsen (2007), *Flexicurity and Beyond: Finding a New Agenda for the European Social Model*, Copenhagen: DJØF Publishing.

Kaestner, R., N. Kaushal and G. Van Ryzin (2003), 'Migration consequences of welfare reform', *Journal of Urban Economics*, **53**, 357–76.

Karamessini, M. (2008), 'Continuity and change in the southern European social model', *International Labour Review*, **147** (1), 43–70.

Karsten, S. (1999), 'Neoliberal education reform in the Netherlands', *Comparative Education*, **35** (3), 303–17.

Kaufmann, D., A. Kraay and P. Zoido (1999), 'Governance matters', World Bank Policy Research Department Working Paper No. 2196.

Kelsey, J. (1995), *The New Zealand Experiment: A World Model for Structural Adjustment*, Auckland: Auckland University Press.

Kendall, J. and M. Knapp (1995), 'A loose and baggy monster: boundaries, definitions and typologies', in R. Hedley, C. Rochester and J. Smith (eds), *An Introduction to the Voluntary Sector*, London: Routledge, pp. 66–95.

Kendall, J. and M. Knapp (1996), *The Voluntary Sector in the United Kingdom*, Manchester: Manchester University Press.

Kennedy, E.M. and O. Hatch (2009), 'The Serve America Act: a legislative initiative to expand and improve domestic and international service opportunities for all', US Government, available at http://s3.amazonaws.com/btcreal/855/Kennedy_Hatch_Serve_America_Act_Summary.pdf (accessed 20 February 2010).

Kenway, P. (2008), 'Addressing in-work poverty', Joseph Rowntree Foundation, available at www.jrf.org.uk/sites/files/jrf/2269-poverty-employment-income.pdf (accessed 16 January 2013).

Kim, J.S. and G.L. Sunderman (2005), 'Measuring academic proficiency under the No Child Left Behind Act: implications for educational equity', *Educational Researcher*, **34** (8), 3.

Komorovsky, C. (2006), 'Poland: health care crisis provokes strikes and protests', *World Socialist website*, 13 June 2006, available at http://www.wsws.org/articles/2006/jun2006/pola-j13.shtml (accessed 14 January 2009).

Koppel, A., K. Meiesaa, H. Valtonen, A. Metsa and M. Lember (2003), 'Evaluation of primary health care reform in Estonia', *Social Science & Medicine*, **56** (12), 2461–66.

Korpi, W. and J. Palme (1998), *The Paradox of Redistribution and Strategies of Equality: Welfare State Institutions, Inequality, and Poverty in the Western Countries*, Stockholm: Swedish Institute for Social Research.

Korpi, W. and J. Palme (2008), 'The paradox of redistribution and strategies of equality: welfare state institutions, inequality and poverty in the Western countries', *American Sociological Review*, **63** (5), 661–87.

Kozierkiewicz, A., W. Trąbka, A. Romaszewski, K. Gajda and D. Gilewski (2005), 'Definition of the "Health Benefit Basket" in Poland', *European Journal of Health Economics*, **6** (1), 58–65.

Krajewski-Siuda, K. and P. Romaniuk (2008), 'Poland – an "Experimental Range" for health care system changes. Two reforms: decentralization and centralization and their consequences', *Journal of Public Health/Zeitschrift für Gesundheitswissenschaften*, **16** (1), 61–70.

Kretzmann, J.P. and J.L. McKnight (1993), *Building Communities from the Inside: a Path Towards Finding a Community's Assets*, Evanston, IL: Centre for Urban Affairs and Policy Research.

Kreutz, S. (2009), 'Urban improvement districts in Germany: new legal instruments for joint proprietor activities in area development', *Journal of Urban Regeneration and Renewal*, **2** (4), 304–17.

Krings, T. (2009), 'A race to the bottom? Trade unions, EU enlargement and the free movement of labour', *European Journal of Industrial Relations*, **15** (1), 49–69.

Kröger, S. (2009), 'The open method of coordination: underconceptualisation, overdetermination, depoliticisation and beyond', in S. Kröger (ed.), *What We Have Learnt: Advances, Pitfalls and Remaining Questions in OMC Research*, European Integration online Papers (EIoP), **13** (5), pp. 1–16, available at: http://eiop.or.at/eiop/texte/2009-005a.htm (accessed 15 March 2010).

Ksiezopolski, M. (2004), 'Co dalejz polityka spoleczna w Polsce? Od socjalistycznych gwarancji do paternalistyczno-rynkowej hybrydy', in M. Rymsza (ed.), *Reformy Spoleczne Bilans Dekady*, Warsaw: Instytut Spraw Publicznych.

Kvist, J. and L. Pedersen (2007), 'Danish labour market activation policies', *National Institute Economic Review*, **202** (1), 99–112.

Lagares Perez, A.M. (2000), 'The process of pension reform in Spain', in E. Reynaud (ed.), *Social Dialogue and Pension Reform: United Kingdom, United States, Germany, Japan, Sweden, Italy, Spain*, Geneva: International Labour Office, pp. 97–107.

Lash, S. and J. Urry (1987), *The End of Organised Capitalism*, Madison: University of Wisconsin Press.

Lawson, C. and J. Nemec (2003), 'The political economy of Slovak and Czech health policy: 1989–2000', *International Political Science Review*, **24** (2), 219–35.

Leeuw, F.L. and S. van Thiel (1999), 'Quangocratization in the Netherlands', in M. Flinders and M.J. Smith (eds), *Quangos, Accountability and Reform: The Politics of Quasi-government*, London: Macmillan.

Lewis, D. (2005), *The Essential Guide to British Quangos*, London: Centre for Policy Studies.

Lian, O. (2008), 'Global challenges, global solutions? A cross-national comparison of primary health care in Britain, Norway and the Czech Republic', *Health Sociology Review*, **17** (1), 27–40.

Liebfried, S. (1992), 'Towards a European welfare state? On integrating poverty regimes into the European Community', in Z. Ferge and J.E. Kolberg (eds), *Social Policy in a Changing Europe*, Frankfurt Am Main: Campus Verlag, pp. 245–79.

Lindsay, C. and M. Mailand (2009), 'Delivering employability in a vanguard "active" welfare state: the case of Greater Copenhagen in Denmark', *Environment and Planning C: Government and Policy*, **27**, 1040–54.

Lindsay, C. and R.W. McQuaid (2008), 'Inter-agency co-operation in activation: comparing experiences in three vanguard "active" welfare states', *Social Policy and Society*, **7** (3), 353–65.

Lindsay, C. and R.W. McQuaid (2009), 'New governance and the case of activation policies: comparing experiences in Denmark and the Netherlands', *Social Policy & Administration*, **43** (5), 445–63.

Lødemel, I. (2001), 'Discussion: workfare in the welfare state', in I. Lødemel and H. Trickey (eds), *'An Offer you Can't Refuse': Workfare in International Perspective*, Bristol: Policy Press, pp. 295–343.

Lødemel, I. and H. Trickey (2001), *'An Offer You Can't Refuse': Workfare in International Perspective*, Bristol: Policy Press.

Lönnroth, J. (2002), 'The European social model of the future', speech at the EU Conference organized by the Ecumenical EU – Office of Sweden (Nov.), Brussels.

López-Santana, M. (2009), 'Having a say and acting: assessing the effectiveness of the European Employment Strategy as an intra-governmental coordinative instrument', in S. Kröger (ed.), *What We Have Learnt: Advances, Pitfalls and Remaining Questions in OMC Research*, European Integration OnlinePapers (EIoP), **13** (15), 1–17, available at http://eiop.or.at/eiop/texte/2009-015a.htm (accessed 15 March 2010).

Lundahl, L. (2002), 'From centralisation to decentralisation: governance of education in Sweden', *European Educational Research Journal*, **1** (4), 625–36.

Lyon-Callo, V. and S. Hyatt (2003), 'The neoliberal state and the depoliticization of poverty: activist anthropology and "ethnography from below"', *Urban Anthropology: Studies of Cultural Systems and World Economic Development*, **30** (2), 105–20.

Lyons, K. and C. Cheyne (2011), 'Social insurance mechanisms in the European Union', RECON Online Working Paper 2011/26, available at http://www.reconproject.eu/main.php/RECON_wp_1126.pdf?fileitem= 5456373 (accessed May 2013).

McDermott, K. (1999), *Controlling Public Education: Localism Versus Equity*, Lawrence: University Press of Kansas.

McDowell, L. (2004), 'Work, workfare, work/life balance and an ethic of care', *Progress in Human Geography*, **28** (2), 145–63.

McKinstry, L. (2011), 'Shameless quangocrats who jump from one state-funded gravy train on to another', *Mail Online*, available at http://www.dailymail.co.uk/ debate/article-2027694/Shameless-quango crats-jump-state-funded-gravy-train-another.html (accessed May 2013).

MacLeavy, J. and O. Gay (2005), 'The quango debate', *House of Commons Library Research Paper*, available at http://www.parliament. uk/briefing-papers/RP05-30 (accessed August 2011).

McMenamin, I. and V. Timonen (2002), 'Poland's health reform: politics, markets and informal payments', *Journal of Social Policy*, **31** (1), 103–18.

Maarse, H. (2006), 'The privatization of health care in Europe: an eight-country analysis', *Journal of Health Politics, Policy and Law*, **31**(5), 981–1014.

Mabli, J., R. Cohen, F. Potter and Z. Zhao (2010), 'Hunger in America 2010', National report prepared for Feeding America by Mathematica Policy Research, Inc.

Madsen, P.K. (2002), 'The Danish model of "flexicurity": a paradise with some snakes', presentation for conference *Interactions between Labour*

Market and Social Protection, Brussels, European Foundation for the Improvement of Living and Working Conditions.

Madsen, P.K. (2008), 'Flexicurity in Denmark: a model for labor market reforms in the EU?', in W. Bienkowski, J.C. Brada and M. Radlo (eds), *Growth versus Security: Old and New EU Members Quest for a New Economic and Social Model*, Basingstoke: Macmillan, pp. 33–53.

Maggetti, M. (2010), 'Legitimacy and accountability of independent regulatory agencies: a critical review', *Living Reviews in Democracy*, **2**, 1–9.

Main Association of Austrian Social Security Institutions (n.d.), 'The organisation of the Austrian social insurance', available at http://www.sozialversicherung.at/mediaDB/MMDB73466_Austrian%20Social%20Insurance.pdf (accessed 27 April 2010).

Majone, G. (2011), 'Political and normative limits to regional integration: rethinking the European project after the crisis of the monetary union', paper at RECON final conference, *What is Left of European Democracy*, Oslo, 2–26 November.

Mansbridge, J. (1999), 'Everyday talk in the deliberative system', in S. Macedo (ed.), *Deliberative Politics: Essays on Democracy and Disagreement*, Cary, NC, USA: Oxford University Press, pp. 211–39.

Mansuri, G. and V. Rao (2004), 'Community-based and -driven development: a critical review', *World Bank Observer*, **19** (1), 1–39.

Martin, C.J. (2004), 'Reinventing welfare regimes: employers and the implementation of active social policy', *World Politics*, **57** (1), 39–69.

Mathie, A. and G. Cunningham (2003), 'From clients to citizens: asset-based community development as a strategy for community-driven development', *Development in Practice*, **13** (5), 474–86.

Maurer, A. and W. Wessels (eds) (2001), *National Parliaments on their Ways to Europe: Losers or Latecomers?*, Baden Baden: Nomos.

Mayes, D.G. and M. Thomson (2013), *The Costs of Children: Parenting and Democracy in Contemporary Europe*, Cheltenham, UK and Northampton, MA, USA: Edward Elgar.

Mayes, D.G. and M. Viren (2002), 'Macroeconomic factors, policies and the development of social exclusion', in R.J.A. Muffels, P. Tsakloglou and D.G. Mayes (eds), *Social Exclusion in European Welfare States*, Cheltenham, UK and Northampton, MA, USA: Edward Elgar, pp. 21–50.

Mayston, D. (1999), 'The private finance initiative in the National Health Service: an unhealthy development in new public management?', *Financial Accountability and Management*, **15** (3), 249–74.

Meyer, B. and D. Rosenbaum (1999), 'Welfare, the earned income tax credit, and the labor supply of single mothers', National Bureau of Economic Research Working Paper Series.

Michalski, A. (2004), *The Lisbon Process: Lack of Commitment, Hard Choices and the Search for Political Will*, Study, **23**, The Clingendael Institute, The Hague.

Michalski, A. (2012), 'Social welfare and the levels of democratic government in the EU', *Journal of European Integration*, **34** (4), 397–418.

Michalski, A. (2013), 'Europa 2020: EU:s samhällsekonomiska ramverk på gott och ont', in A. Bakardjieva Engelbrekt, L. Oxelheim, T. Persson (eds), *Ett konkurrenskraftigt EU till rätt pris*, Europaperspektiv, Stockholm: Santérus förlag, pp. 27–59.

Midgley, J. (1999), 'Growth, redistribution, and welfare: toward social investment', *Social Science Review*, **73** (1), 1–12.

Mitchell, D. and L.A. Staeheli (2006), 'Clean and safe? Property redevelopment, public space, and homelessness in downtown San Diego', in S. Low and N. Smith (eds), *The Politics of Public Space*, New York: Routledge, pp. 143–75.

Mitchell, J. (2001), 'Business improvement districts and the "new" revitalization of downtown', *Economic Development Quarterly*, **15** (2), 115–123.

Mitchell, J. (2008), *Business Improvement Districts and the Shape of American Cities*, New York: State University of New York Press.

Moene, K.O. and M. Wallerstein (2008), 'Social democracy as a development strategy', in D. Austen-Smith, J.A. Frieden, M.A. Golden, K.O. Moene and A. Przeworski (eds), *Selected Works of Micheal Wallerstein: The Political Economy of Inequality, Unions, and Social Democracy*, Cambridge: Cambridge University Press, pp. 443–63.

Mohan, B. (2012), 'Editorial', *Journal of Comparative Social Welfare*, **28** (2), 91–2.

Monbiot, G. (2006), 'An Easter egg hunt', available at http://www.monbiot.com/archives/2006/05/09/an-easter-egg-hunt/ (accessed 10 February 2010).

Morçöl, G. and U. Zimmermann (2008), 'Metropolitan governance and business improvement districts', in G. Morçöl, L. Hoyt, J. Meek and U. Zimmermann (eds), *Business Improvement Districts: Research, Theories, and Controversies*, Florida: CRC Press, pp. 27–51.

Morçöl, G., L. Hoyt, J. Meek and U. Zimmermann (2008), 'Business improvement districts: research, theories, and controversies', in G. Morçöl, L. Hoyt, J. Meek and U. Zimmermann (eds), *Business Improvement Districts: Research, Theories, and Controversies*, Florida: CRC Press, pp. 1–26.

Morel, N., B. Palier and J. Palme (eds) (2012), *Towards a Social Investment Welfare State? Ideas, Policies and Challenges*, Bristol: The Policy Press.

Morrison, A. (1996), 'The Employment Contracts Act and its economic impact', *Parliamentary Library Background Paper*, Wellington.

Mörth, U. (2008), *European Public-private Collaboration: A Choice between Efficiency and Democratic Accountability*, Cheltenham, UK and Northampton, MA, USA: Edward Elgar.

Moser, C. and A. Dani (2008), 'Asset-based social policy and public action in a polycentric world', in C. Moser and A. Dani (eds), *Assets, Livelihoods, and Social Policy*, Washington, DC: The World Bank, pp. 3–42.

Muffels, R.J.A. and D.J.A.G. Fouarge (2002), 'Do European welfare regimes matter in explaining social exclusion?', in R.J.A. Muffels, P. Tsakloglou and D.G. Mayes (eds), *Social Exclusion in European Welfare States*, Cheltenham, UK and Northampton, MA, USA: Edward Elgar, pp. 202–32.

Muffels, R.J.A. and P. Tsakloglou (2002), 'Introduction: empirical approaches to analysing social exclusion in European welfare states', in R.J.A. Muffels, P. Tsakloglou and D.G. Mayes (eds), *Social Exclusion in European Welfare States*, Cheltenham, UK and North-ampton, MA, USA: Edward Elgar, pp. 1–18.

Muffels, R.J.A., P. Tsakloglou and D.G. Mayes (eds) (2002), *Social Exclusion in European Welfare States*, Cheltenham, UK and North-ampton, MA, USA: Edward Elgar.

Musick, M. and J. Wilson (2008), *Volunteers: A Social Profile*, Bloom-ington, IN: Indiana University Press.

National Audit Office (NAO) (2005), *The Refinancing of the Norfolk and Norwich PFI Hospital: How the Deal can be Viewed in the Light of the Refinancing*, London: House of Commons National Audit Office, pp. 1–25.

Neuhold, H. (2010), 'Common security: the litmus test of international solidarity', in R. Wolfrum and C. Kojima (eds), *Solidarity: A Struc-tural Principle of International Law*, London and New York: Springer Heidelberg Dordrecht, pp. 193–224.

Neunreither, K. (2005), 'The European Parliament and national parlia-ments: conflict or cooperation?', *The Journal of Legislative Studies*, **11** (3/4), 466–89.

Nice, K., J. Davidson and R. Sainsbury (2009), 'Provider–led Pathways: experiences and views of early implementation', *Research Report No. 595*, London: Department for Work and Pensions Research.

O'Connor, J.S. (2005), 'Policy coordination, social indicators and the social-policy agenda in the European Union', *Journal of European Social Policy*, **15** (4), 345–61.

O'Connor, J. S. and V. Bankauskaite (2008), 'Public health development in the Baltic countries (1992–2005): from problems to policy', *European Journal of Public Health*, **18** (6), 586–92.

O'Dowd, A. (2010), 'Government halves the number of NHS quangos to save £180m', *British Medical Journal*, **341** (July 27), C4074.

Oates, W.E. (1973), 'The effects of property taxes and local public spending on property values: a reply and yet further results', *Journal of Political Economy*, **81** (4), 1004–8.

OECD (2009), 'Forum partnerships 2009: country fact-sheets', *LEED Forum on Partnerships and Local Governance*, Paris: OECD.

OECD (2009a), 'Private pensions outlook 2008', OECD, available at: www.oecd.org/daf/pensions/outlook

OECD (2011), 'OECD Perspectives: Spain: Policies for a sustainable recovery', available at http://www.oecd.org/dataoecd/45/46/44686629.pdf

OECD Development Assistance Committee (1995), *Participatory Development and Good Governance*, Paris: OECD.

Offe, C. (1985), *Disorganised Capitalism: Contemporary Transformations of Work and Politics*, Cambridge: Polity Press.

Offe, C. (2008), 'Governance – "empty signifier" oder sozialwissenschaftliches forschungsprogramm?', *Politische Vierteljahresschrift*, Sonderheft, **41**, 61–76.

Olson, M. (1971), *The Logic of Collective Action: Good and the Theory of Groups*, Harvard University Press.

Orenstein, M.A. (2008), 'Poverty, inequality, and democracy: postcommunist welfare states', *Journal of Democracy*, **19** (4), 80–94.

Oswald, S.L. (2000), 'Economic transition in the Czech Republic: attempts to privatize the health system', *Administration & Society*, **32** (3), 227–54.

Parkinson, J. (2003), 'Legitimacy problems in deliberative democracy', *Political Studies*, **51** (1), 180–96.

Paterson, L. and C. Iannelli (2007), 'Social class and educational attainment: a comparative study of England, Wales and Scotland', *Sociology of Education*, **80** (4), 330–58.

Peck, J. (2001), *Workfare States*, New York: The Guilford Press.

Peel, D. and M.G. Lloyd (2005), 'A case for business improvement districts in Scotland: policy transfer in practice?', *Planning Practice and Research*, **20** (1), 89–95.

Perroni, C. and K.A. Scharf (2001), 'Tiebout with politics: capital tax competition and constitutional choices', *Review of Economic Studies*, **68**, 133–54.

Peterman, W. (2000), *Neighborhood Planning and Community-based Development: The Potential and Limits of Grassroots Action*, London: Sage.

Pfister, T. (2009), 'Governing the knowledge society: studying Lisbon as epistemic setting', in S. Kröger (ed.), *What We Have Learnt: Advances, Pitfalls and Remaining Questions in OMC Research*, European Integration online Papers (EIoP), **13** (6), pp. 1–14, available at http://eiop.or.at/eiop/texte/2009-006a.htm (accessed 15 March 2010).

Pincetl, S. (2003), 'Nonprofits and park provision in Los Angeles: an exploration of the rise of governance approaches to the provision of local services', *Social Science Quarterly*, **84** (4), 979–1001.

Plank, D.N. and W.L. Boyd (1994), 'Antipolitics, education, and institutional choice: the flight from democracy', *American Educational Research Journal*, **31** (2), 263–81.

Pollit, C., S. van Thiel and V. Homburg (eds) (2007), *New Public Management in Europe: Adaptation and Alternatives*, Basingstoke and New York: Palgrave Macmillan.

Polluste, K., G. Mannik and R. Axelsson (2005), 'Public health reforms in Estonia: impact on the health of the population', *British Medical Journal*, **331** (7510), 210–13.

Pontusson, J. (2005), *Inequality and Prosperity: Social Europe vs. Liberal America*, Ithaca, NY: Cornell University Press.

Poole, L. (2007), 'Working in the non-profit welfare sector: contract culture, partnership, compacts and the "shadow state"', in G. Mooney and A. Law (eds), *New Labour/Hard Labour? Restructuring and Resistance inside the Welfare Industry*, Bristol: Policy Press, pp. 233–63.

Potůček, M. (2004), 'Accession and social policy: the case of the Czech Republic', *Journal of European Social Policy*, **14** (3), 253–66.

Potůček, M. (2009), 'The Czech national model of the welfare state. Tradition and changes', in S. Golinowska, P. Hengstenberg and M. Żukowski (eds), *Diversity and Commonality in European Social Policies: The Forging of a European Social Model*, Warsaw: Fredrich Ebert Stiftung and Wydawnictwo Naukowe Scholar, pp. 33–69.

Power, S., D. Halpin and G. Whitty (1997), 'Managing the state and the market: "new" education management in five countries', *British Journal of Educational Studies*, **45** (4), 342–62.

Pratchett, L. (2004), 'Local autonomy, local democracy and the "new localism"', *Political Studies*, **52** (2), 358–75.

Preece, D.V. (2009), *Dismantling Social Europe: The Political Economy of Social Policy in the European Union*, London and Colorado: First Forum Press.

Prud'homme, R. (1995), 'The dangers of decentralization', *The World Bank Research Observer*, **10** (2), 201.

Public Administration Select Committee (2010–11), *Smaller Government: Shrinking the Quango State*, 2010–11, available at http://www.publications.parliament.uk/ pa/ cm 201011/cmselect/cmpubadm/537/537.pdf (accessed May 2013).

Purcell, M. (2006), 'Urban democracy and the local trap', *Urban Studies*, **43** (11), 1921–41.

Putnam, R. (2000), *Bowling Alone: The Collapse and Revival of American Community*, New York: Simon and Schuster.

Radaelli, C.M. (2003), *The Open Method of Coordination: A New Governance Architecture for the European Union*, The Swedish Institute for European Policy Studies, Stockholm.

Radulova, E. (2007), 'The OMC: an opaque method of consideration or deliberative governance in action?', *Journal of European Integration*, **29** (3), 363–80.

Ramia, G. (2002), 'The "new contractualism", social protection and the Yeatman thesis', *Journal of Sociology*, **38** (1), 49–68.

Ramia, G. and N. Wailes (2006), 'Putting wage-earners into wage-earners welfare states: the relationship between social policy and industrial relations in Australia and New Zealand', *Australian Journal of Social Issues*, **14** (1), 49–68.

Rasmussen, E. and F. Lamm (2005), 'From collectivism to individualism in New Zealand employment relations', *AIRAANZ*, 479–86.

Raunio, T. (2007), 'National parliament and OMC: destined to remain apart?', paper presented at the conference *Fifty Years of Interparliamentary Cooperation: Progressing towards Effective Cross-Level Parliamentarism*, Bundestag, Berlin.

Raveaud, G. (2007), 'The European employment strategy: towards more and better jobs?', *Journal of Common Market Studies*, **45** (2), 411–34.

Rees, A. (2000), 'Citizenship and work obligation in Britain and France', in J. Edwards and J.P. Révauger (eds), *Employment and Citizenship in Britain and France*, Aldershot: Ashgate, pp. 200–26.

Regulski, J. (1999), 'Building democracy in Poland: the state reform of 1998', Discussion Papers No. 9, Budapest: Local Government and Public Service Reform Initiative, Open Society Institute.

Republic of Estonia Stability Programme 2011 (2011), available at http://ec.europa.eu/economy_finance/economic_governance/sgp/pdf/20_scps/2011/01_programme/ee_2011-04-28_sp_en.pdf (accessed May 2013).

Rhodes, M. (1996), 'Southern European welfare states: identity, problems and prospects for reform', *South European Society and Politics*, **1** (3), 1–22.

Rivelt, G. (2011), *National Health Service History*, available at www.nhshistory.net/chater%207.htm#0 (accessed 22 April 2013).

Rodríguez-Pose, A. and N. Gill (2003), 'The global trend towards devolution and its implications', *Environment and Planning*, **21** (3), 333–52.

Rokosová, M. and P. Háva (2005), *Health Care Systems in Transitions: Czech Republic 2005*, Copenhagen: WHO Regional Office for Europe on behalf of the European Observatory on Health Systems and Policies.

Rose, N. (1996), 'Governing "advanced" liberal democracies', in A. Barry, T. Osborne and N. Rose (eds), *Foucault and Political Reason: Liberalism, Neoliberalism and the Rationalities of Government*, London: UCL Press.

Ross, B.H. and M.A. Levine (2006), *Urban Politics: Power in Metropolitan America*, Belmont, CA: Thomson Wadsworth.

Sabel, F. and J. Zeitlin (2007), 'Learning from difference: the new architecture of experimentalist governance in the European Union', Working Paper, **020**, 1–92, Wisconsin-Madison: La Follette School, available at http://www.lafollette.wisc.edu/publications/workingpapers/zeitlin2007-020.pdf (accessed 15 March 2010).

Sainsbury, D. (2006), 'Immigrants' social rights in comparative perspective: welfare regimes, forms in immigration and immigration policy regimes', *Journal of European Social Policy*, **16** (3), 229–44.

Salais, R. (2003), 'Work and welfare: toward a capability approach', in J. Zeitlin and D.M. Trubek (eds), *Governing Work and Welfare in a New Economy: European and American Experiments*, Oxford: Oxford University Press, pp. 317–44.

Salais, R. and R. Villeneuve (2004), 'Introduction: Europe and the politics of capabilities', in R. Salais and R. Villeneuve (eds), *Europe and the Politics of Capabilities*, Cambridge: Cambridge University Press, pp. 1–18.

Salamon, L.M. (1999), 'The nonprofit sector at a crossroads: the case of America', *Voluntas: International Journal of Voluntary and Nonprofit Organizations*, **10** (1), 5–23.

Salognon, M. (2007), 'Reorienting companies' hiring behaviour: an innovative "back-to-work" method in France', *Work, Employment & Society*, **21** (4), 713–30.

Saltman, R., J. Figueras and C. Sakellarides (eds) (1998), *Critical Challenges for Health Care Reform in Europe*, Philadelphia: Open University Press.

Santiso, C. (2001), 'Good governance and aid effectiveness: the World Bank and conditionality', *The Georgetown Public Policy Review*, **7** (1), 1–22.

Sapir, A. (2006), 'Globalization and the reform of European social models', *Journal of Common Market Studies*, **44** (2), 369–90.

Schäfer, A. (2004), 'Beyond the Community Method: Why the Open Method of Coordination was introduced to EU Policy-Making', European Integration online Papers (EIoP), **8** (13), 1–19, available at http://eiop.or.at/eiop/texte/2004-013a.htm (accessed 15 March 2010).

Schäfer, A. and S. Leiber (2009), 'The double voluntarism in EU social dialogue and employment policy', in S. Kröger (ed.), *What We Have Learnt: Advances, Pitfalls and Remaining Questions in OMC Research*, European Integration Online Papers (EIoP), **13** (9), 1–19, available at http://eiop.or.at/eiop/index.php/eiop/article/view/2009_009a/116 (accessed 15 March 2010).

Scharpf, F.W. (1997), 'Economic integration, democracy and the welfare state', *Journal of European Public Policy*, **4** (1), 18–36.

Scharpf, F.W. (1999), *Governing in Europe: Effective and Democratic?*, Oxford: Oxford University Press.

Scharpf, F.W. (2002), 'The European Social Model: coping with the challenges of diversity', *Journal of Common Market Studies*, **40** (4), 645–70.

Scharpf, F.W. (2009), 'The double asymmetry of European integration: or: why the EU cannot be a social market economy', MPIfG Working Paper **12**, 1–37, Cologne: Max Planck Institute for the Study of Societies.

Scharpf, F.W and V.A. Schmidt (eds) (2000), *Welfare and Work in the Open Economy*, 2 vols, Oxford: Oxford University Press.

Schelkle, W. (2008), 'Can there be a European social model?', in E.O. Eriksen, F. Rödl and C. Joerges (eds), *Law, Democracy and Solidarity in a Post-national Union: The Unsettled Political Order of Europe*, London: Routledge, pp. 233–57.

Schick, A. (1998), 'Why most developing countries should not try New Zealand's reforms', *World Bank Research Observer*, **13** (1), 123–31.

Schmid, G. (2009), 'Transitional labour markets and flexicurity: managing social risks over the lifecourse', CES Working Paper, **75**, 1–26.

Scott, E., A. London and K. Edin (2000), 'Looking to the future: welfare-reliant women talk about their job aspirations in the context of welfare reform', *Journal of Social Issues*, **56** (4), 727–46.

Scruton, R. (1982), *A Dictionary of Political Thought*, London: Macmillan.

Scully, T. (2007), 'Polish health system adjusts to challenges of democracy', *Irish Medical Times*, 20 July, 20.

Seifert, H. and A. Tangian (2006), 'Globalization and deregulation: does flexicurity protect atypically employed?', *International Labour Process Conference (ILPC)*, University of London and Royal Holloway.

Sellers, J.M. (1999), 'Public goods and the politics of segregation: an analysis and cross-national comparison', *Journal of Urban Affairs*, **21** (2), 237–62.

Sen, A. (1997), 'Inequality, unemployment and contemporary Europe', *International Labour Review*, **136** (2), 155–72.

Sen, A. (1999), *Development as Freedom*, Oxford: Oxford University Press.

Sen, A. (2003), 'Democracy and its global roots', *The New Republic*, **229** (4), 28–35.

Shankar, R. and A. Shah (2009), *Lessons from European Union Policies for Regional Development, World Bank Policy Research Working Paper No. 4977*, World Bank.

Shaoul, J., A. Stafford and P. Stapleton (2008), 'The cost of using private finance to build, finance and operate hospitals', *Public Money and Management*, **28** (2), April, 101–8.

Shore, C. (2000), *Building Europe: The Cultural Politics of European Integration*, London, New York: Routledge.

Shore, C. (2011), '"Governance" or "Governmentality"? The Europpean Commission and the future of democratic government', *European Law Journal*, **17** (3), 287–302.

Shutes, I. (2010), 'Welfare-to-work and the responsiveness of employment providers to the needs of refugees', *Journal of Social Policy*, **40** (3), 1–18.

Sissenich, B. (2007), *Building States Without Society: European Union Enlargement and the Transfer of EU Social Policy to Poland and Hungary*, Plymouth: Lexington Books.

Skelcher, C., S. Weir and L. Wilson (2000), *Advance of the Quango State*, London: Local Government Information Unit.

Slovak Republic Ministry of Finance (2011), 'Stability programme of the Slovak Republic for 2011–2014', available at http://ec.europa.eu/europe2020/pdf/nrp/sp_slovakia_en.pdf (accessed May 2013).

Snower, D.J., A.J.G. Brown and C. Merkl (2009), 'Globalization and the welfare state: a review of Hans-Werner Sinn's *Can Germany be Saved?*', *Journal of Economic Literature*, **47** (1), 136–58.

Social Security Administration and International Social Security Association (2010), *Social Security Programs Throughout the World: Europe, 2010*, Washington: US Government Printing Office.

Spackman, M. (2002), 'Public–private partnerships: lessons from the British approach', *Economic Systems*, **26**, 283–301.

Spiegel, P. and K. Hope (2012), 'Greek fury at plan for EU budget control', *Financial Times*, 29 January, available at http://www.ft.com/intl/cms/s/0/c54ff27c-4a99-11e1-a11e-00144feabdc0.html?ftcamp=rss#axzz1ku5Y2LI5

Staehr, K. (2009), 'Employment and welfare effects of a flat income tax', in D. Mayes (ed.) *Microfoundations of Economic Success: Lessons from Estonia*, Cheltenham, UK and Northampton, MA, USA: Edward Elgar, pp. 242–90.

Stein, J.G. (2001), *The Cult of Efficiency*, Toronto: House of Anansi Press Limited.

Stiglitz, J. (2002), 'Employment, social justice and societal well-being', *International Labour Review*, **141** (1–2), 9–29.

Stott, T. (2000), 'Quangos: are they unloved and misunderstood?', in L. Robins and B. Jones (eds), *Debates in British Politics Today*, Manchester: Manchester University Press, pp. 89–103.

Struyven, L. and G. Steurs (2005), 'Design and redesign of a quasi-market for the reintegration of jobseekers: empirical evidence from Australia and the Netherlands', *Journal of European Social Policy*, **15** (3), 211–29.

Symes, M. and M. Steel (2003), 'Lessons from America: the role of business improvement districts as an agent of urban regeneration', *Town Planning Review*, **74** (3), 301–13.

Talbot, C. (2001), 'UK public services and management (1979–2000): evolution or revolution?', *The International Journal of Public Sector Management*, **14** (4), pp. 281–303.

Teelken, C. (1999), 'Market mechanisms in education: school choice in the Netherlands, England and Scotland in a comparative perspective', *Comparative Education*, **35** (3), 283–302.

Threlfall, M. (2007), 'The social dimension of the European Union', *Global Social Policy*, **7**, 271–93.

Tibaijuka, A.K. (2003), 'ABCD and the enabling approach: complimentary strategies for developing countries', address given at St George's House, Windsor Castle, for the Building and Social Housing Foundation.

Tiebout, C.M. (1956), 'A pure theory of local expenditures', *Journal of Political Economy*, **64** (5), 416–24.

Toens, K. (2007), 'The dilemma of regress', *European Journal of Political Theory*, **6** (2), 160–79.

Trades Union Congress (2009), 'Exploding privatisation myths', available at www.tuc.org.uk/extras/speakupprivatisation.pdf (accessed 17 March 2010).

Trickey, H. (2001), 'Comparing workfare programmes – features and implications', in I. Lødemel and H. Trickey (eds), *'An Offer You Can't Refuse'*: *Workfare in International Perspective*, Bristol: The Policy Press, pp. 249–95.

Tsakatika, M. (2007), 'A parliamentary dimension for EU soft governance', *European Integration*, **29** (5), 549–64.

Tyszko, P., W.M. Wierzba, K. Kanecki and A. Ziółkowska (2007), 'Transformation of the ownership structure in Polish healthcare and its effects', *Central European Journal of Medicine*, **2** (4), 528–38.

Vail, M.I. (2008), 'From "welfare without work" to "buttressed liberalization": the shifting dynamics of labour market adjustment in France and Germany', *European Journal of Political Research*, **47** (3), 334–58.

van Berkel, R. and M. Roche (2002), 'Activation policies as reflexive social policies', in R. van Berkel and I.H. Møller (eds), *Active Social Policies in the EU: Inclusion through Participation?*, Bristol: The Policy Press, pp. 197–224.

van Berkel, R. and B. Valkenburg (eds) (2007), *Making It Personal: Individualising Activation Services in the EU*, Bristol: Policy Press.

van Berkel, R. and P. van der Aa (2005), 'The marketization of activation services: a modern panacea? Some lessons from the Dutch experience', *Journal of European Social Policy*, **15** (4), 329–43.

van Berkel, R., W. de Graaf and T. Sirovàtka (2011), *The Governance of Active Welfare States in Europe*, Basingstoke: Palgrave Macmillan.

van der Meer, T.W.G. and E.J. van Ingen (2009), 'Schools of democracy? Disentangling the relationship between civic participation and political action in 17 European countries', *European Journal of Political Research*, **48** (2), 281–308.

van Gestel, N. and Herbillon, J.M. (2007), 'Changing modes of governance in activation policies in France and The Netherlands: common path or countermodel?', *International Journal of Sociology and Social Policy*, **27** (7/8), 324–33.

van Gestel, R.A.J., P. Eijlander and J.A.F. Peters (2007), 'The regulatory powers of quangos in the Netherlands: are Trojan horses invading our democracy?', *Electronic Journal of Comparative Law*, **11** (1), available at http://www.ejcl.org/111/art111-9.pdf (accessed May 2013).

van Langen, A. and H. Dekkers (2001), 'Decentralisation and combating educational exclusion', *Comparative Education*, **37** (3), 367–84.

van Oorschot, W. and W. Uunk (2007), 'Multilevel determinants of the public's informal solidarity towards immigrants in European welfare states', in S. Mau and B. Veghte (eds), *Social Justice, Legitimacy and the Welfare State*, Aldershot: Ashgate, pp. 217–38.

van Thiel, S. (2001), *Quangos: Trends, Causes and Consequences*, Aldershot: Ashgate.

van Thiel, S. (2004a), 'Quangos in Dutch government', in C. Pollit and C. Talbot (eds), *Unbundled Government: A Critical Analysis to the Global Trend to Agencies, Quangos and Contractualisation*, London: Routledge, pp. 167–83.

van Thiel, S. (2004b), 'Why politicians prefer quasi-autonomous organization', *Journal of Theoretical Politics*, **16** (2), 175–201.

Vandenbroucke, F., A. Hemerijck and B. Palier (2011), 'The EU needs a social investment pact', available at http://www.ose.be/files/Opinion Paper5_Vandenbroucke-Hemerijk-Palier_2011.pdf (accessed May 2013).

Vaughan-Whitehead, D.C. (2003), *EU Enlargement Versus Social Europe? The Uncertain Future of the European Social Model*, Cheltenham, UK and Northampton, MA, USA: Edward Elgar.

Vepřek, J., Z. Papeš and P. Vepřek (1995), 'Czech health care in economic transformation', *Eastern European Economics*, **33** (3), 44–79.

Vibert, F. (2007), *The Rise of the Unelected: Democracy and the New Separation of Powers*, Cambridge: Cambridge University Press.

Vilks, A. (2011), 'Convergence programme of the Republic of Latvia: 2011–2014' available at http://ec.europa.eu/economy_finance/economic_governance/sgp/pdf/20_scps/2011/01_programme/lv_2011-04-29_cp_en.pdf (accessed May 2013).

Vis, B. (2007), 'States of welfare or states of workfare? Welfare state restructuring in 16 capitalist democracies, 1985–2002', *Policy & Politics*, **35** (1), 105–22.

Vis, B., K. van Kersbergen and T. Hylands (2011), 'To what extent did the financial crisis intensify the pressure to reform the welfare state', *Social Policy & Administration*, **45** (4), 338–53.

Visser, J. (2005), 'The OMC as a selective amplifier for national strategies of reform', in J. Zeitlin, P. Pochet and L. Magnusson (eds), *The Open Method of Coordination in Action: The European Employment and Social Inclusion Strategies*, Brussels: Peter Lang, pp. 173–215.

Výborna, O. (1995), 'The reform of the Czech health-care system', *Eastern European Economics*, **33** (3), 80–95.

Waldegrave, T., D. Anderson and K. Wong (2003), *Evaluation of the Short-term Impacts of the Employment Relations Act 2000*, Report for the Department of Labour, Wellington, New Zealand Government.

Walker, B. and S. Sankey (2008), 'International review of effective governance arrangements for employment-related initiatives', *Research Report No. 543*, London: Department for Work and Pensions.

Wall, K., S. Aboim, V. Cunha and P. Vasconcelos (2001), 'Families and informal support networks in Portugal: the reproduction of inequality', *Journal of European Social Policy*, **11** (3), 213–33.

Wallis, J. and B. Dollery (2001), 'Government failure, social capital and the appropriateness of the New Zealand model for public sector reform in developing countries', *World Development*, **29** (2), 245–63.

Ward, K. (2006), 'Policies in motion, urban management and state restructuring: the trans-local expansion of business improvement districts', *International Journal of Urban and Regional Research*, **30** (1), 54.

Watts, R. (2007), 'Boom in quangos costs Britain £170bn a year', *The Telegraph*, available at http://www.telegraph.co.uk/news/uknews/1560697/Boom-in-quangos-costs-Britain-170bn-a-year.html (accessed May 2013).

Weir, S. and W. Hall (1994), *EGO trip: Extra-governmental Organisations in the United Kingdom and their Accountability*, London: Charter 88.

Weishaupt, T. (2009), 'Money, votes or "good" ideas? Partisan politics and the effectiveness of the European employment strategy in Austria and Ireland', in S. Kröger (ed.), *What We Have Learnt: Advances, Pitfalls and Remaining Questions in OMC Research*, European Integration online Papers (EIoP), **13** (14), pp. 1–18, available at http://eiop.or.at/eiop/texte/2009–014a.htm (accessed 10 March 2010).

Weiss, T.G. (2000), 'Governance, good governance and global governance: conceptual and actual challenges', *Third World Quarterly*, **21** (5), 795–814.

Whitty, G., S. Power and D. Halpin (1998), *Devolution and Choice in Education: the School, the State and the Market*, Buckingham: Open University Press.

Wiktorow, A. (2007), 'Pension reform in Poland', *The Geneva Papers on Risk and Insurance – Issues and Practice*, **32** (4), 483–93.

Wilding, P. (1997), 'Globalisation, regionalisation and social policy', *Social Policy and Administration*, **31** (4), 410–28.

Wilthagen, T. (2008), 'Mapping out flexicurity pathways in the European Union', *Tilburg University Flexicurity Working Paper 14*, available at http://www.tilburguniversity.nl/faculties/law/research/reflect/publications/papers/fxp2008-14mappingoutpathwayseu.pdf (accessed 22 April 2013).

Wilthagen, T. and F. Tros (2004), 'The concept of "flexicurity": a new approach to regulating employment and labour markets', *Transfer, European Review of Labour and Research*, **10** (2), 166–86.

Wolch, J. (1990), *The Shadow State: Government and Voluntary Sector in Transition*, New York: Foundation Center.

Wong, N. (1990), 'A comparison of the performance of private, mixed and state-owned enterprises in New Zealand', M.Com Dissertation, University of Auckland.

Woolfson, C. (2007), 'Labour standards and migration in the new Europe: post-communist legacies and perspectives', *European Journal of Industrial Relations*, **13** (2), 199–218.

Woolfson, C. and J. Sommers (2006), 'Labour mobility in construction: European implications of the Laval un Partneri dispute with Swedish labour', *European Journal of Industrial Relations*, **12** (1), 49–68.

World Bank (1989), *Sub-Saharan Africa: from Crisis to Sustainable Development*, Washington: World Bank.

World Bank (1994), *Governance: The World Bank's Experience*, Washington: World Bank.

Yeatman, A. (1995), 'Interpreting contemporary contractualism', in J. Boston (ed.), *The State under Contract*, Wellington: Bridget Williams Books, pp. 124–39.

Young, I.M. (2000), *Inclusion and Democracy*, Oxford and New York: Oxford University Press.

Zajac, M. (2004), 'Free movement of health professionals: the Polish experience', in M. McKee, L. MacLehose and E. Nolte (eds) *Health Policy and European Union Enlargement*, Berkshire, England: Open University Press, pp. 109–29.

Zajda, J. (2006), *Decentralisation and Privatisation in Education: The Role of the State*, Dordrecht: Springer.

Zeitlin, J. (2005), 'Social Europe and experimental governance: towards a new constitutional compromise?', Working Paper, **1**, 1–34, Wisconsin-Madison: La Follette School, available at http://www.lafollette. wisc.edu/publications/workingpapers/zeitlin2005-001.pdf (accessed 15 March 2010).

Zeitlin, J. (2007), 'Strengthening the social dimension of the Lisbon Strategy', Working Paper, **22**, 1–10, La Follette School: Wisconsin-Madison, available at http://www.lafollette.wisc.edu/publications/ workingpapers/zeitlin2007-022.pdf (accessed 15 March 2010).

Zucker, R. (2001), *Democratic Distributive Justice*, Cambridge: Cambridge University Press.

Żukowski, M. (2009), 'Social policy regimes in the European countries', in S. Golinowska, M. Hengstenberg and M. Żukowski (eds), *Diversity and Commonality in European Social Policies: The Forging of a European Social Model*, Warsaw: Friedrich Ebert Stiftung and Wydawnictwo Naukowe Scholar, pp. 23–32.

Zurich Municipal (2009), 'Public sector supply chain: risks, myths and opportunities', available at www.zurich.co.uk/.../36148_Horizon_ Precis_2pp_DC_AW_lr.pdf (accessed 17 March 2010).

Index